6NPOD

13.95

Daniel Mc⟨signature⟩

F

□

WILLIAM FEZLER, Ph.D.

A FIRESIDE BOOK
Published by
Simon & Schuster Inc.
New York London
Toronto Sydney Tokyo

CREATIVE IMAGERY

□

How to
Visualize
□ in All
Five □
□ Senses

Fireside
Simon & Schuster Building
Rockefeller Center
1230 Avenue of the Americas
New York, New York 10020

FIRESIDE and colophon are registered trademarks
of Simon & Schuster Inc.

Designed by Marysarah Quinn
Manufactured in the United States of America

10   9   8   7   6   5   4   3   2   1

Library of Congress Cataloging in Publication Data

Fezler, William D.
    Creative imagery : how to visualize in all five senses / William
Fezler.
        p.   cm.
    "A Fireside book."
    Includes index.
    ISBN 0-671-68238-5
    1. Imagery (Psychology)—Therapeutic use. 2. Psychotherapy.
I. Title.
RC489.F35F49   1989
616.89'14—dc20   89-10182
                                                           CIP

I am, as Protagoras says, the judge of the existence of the things that are to me and of the non-existence of those that are not to me . . . knowledge is nothing else than perception . . . man is the measure of all things.

—SOCRATES

For apprehension by the senses supplies after all, directly or indirectly, the material of all human knowledge, or at least the stimulus necessary to develop every inborn faculty of the mind.

—HELMHOLTZ

The senses never delude and never indicate correctly. We actually know nothing except that the senses act differently under different circumstances.

—MACH

The knower and the known are one. Simple people imagine that they should see God, as if He stood there and they here. This is not so. God and I, we are one in knowledge.

—MEISTER ECKHART

CONTENTS

Introduction

Images—what you imagine—possess not only the power to heal, but to take you to higher realms of knowledge and experience than you've ever visited. How can I truly convey to you an incredible experience I've had with imagery unless I actually *give* you that experience? I want you to get such an experience out of this book, to *feel* a greater awareness of life and love. I want learning to be an adventure for you, a surging, overpowering force moving you ever forward. I want you to be able to eliminate your phobias, headaches, and depression; heal your asthma, skin disorders, and overweight problems; and get a handle on any addictions that might be troubling you, such as smoking, alcoholism, or drug abuse. Most of all, it is my greatest desire that you experience paradise. This is a higher level of consciousness, your original and natural state of happiness, a condition of innocence free of the negative influence of your past experience. Here you are more sensitive to all positive stimuli and impervious to negativity. Your glimpse of paradise may be only for a moment, but however momentary, once you have been there you will never stop trying to return.

You may already be asking yourself, "How can I do all this? How can I glimpse paradise?" Let me put it to you this way: I want you to experience something *better*—to have a positive experience greater than any you've ever known, to soar higher than you've ever flown. I'm prepared to tell you how to do this because I've been there. It was an experience of my own such as this that became the impetus for writing this book. Your way has been mapped exactly and precisely.

You may have been taught that you must die to experience paradise. This is not so. The levels above you are infinite, as are the levels below, and the only thing stopping your ascension is not knowing how to get there. This book is your beginning.

Not long ago, I would have considered myself crazy for speaking of such things as experiencing paradise or infinite realities. But something happened to me a few years back, events so profound and covering such an extended period of time, that I have not been able to dismiss them, though at times I have surely tried. This incredible chain of events that changed the course of my life is what I want to share with you. The experience was too powerful, too joyous, not to be passed on. In the course of my experience I received messages from a source higher than any I had ever accessed, messages that made me realize that what we do here on earth is important and influences totally where we go from here. We can't just wait around to die and expect it to be paradise. We have to work, continue to pursue higher knowledge for as long as we live, if we are to ascend. Where we go, what we become, after death, depends upon what we do in life. Life is sacred.

There *is* a paradise, a higher dimension of being. You can get there yourself by learning *how*. You learn how by accessing higher knowledge that lies within you. You can access this knowledge through using the progression of images I'm going to give you in this book. For you see, the amazing thing is there is a *recipe*, a set of ingredients that will give you a similarly moving and wondrous experience. Your results may not be exactly the same as mine, but I trust they will be as sweet. We are all different, but we are all also very much alike, with commonalities of experience and mutual hurdles in spiritual growth that never cease to amaze me.

My initiation began with my patients, who were to be my point of entry into a dimension of reality greater than any I had ever known or even dreamed of. It was through them and the feedback from their experiences that I was able to chart a way, a course to mastery of the five physical senses and exploration of what lies beyond.

The vehicles I used for them—and that you too can use—are *sensory images*, mental pictures vivid in all five senses, that will be discussed in later chapters. Through the use of these images you will learn to find your own truth, the greater reality that lies outside your present sensory world. The remarkable thing about images is that properly used, they can provide a totally new *experience*. A group of 250 words or so composing one image can be used to create a new experience which, when paired with *one new word*, will trigger the same experience it previously took 250 to conjure. These "higher order" words can then be combined to produce ever more advanced positive states of consciousness.

Creative Imagery is thus a blueprint to your spiritual growth (as well as your physical, mental, and emotional health) and a call for understanding the source of all power, your self. In it I give you a definite method of change. This vehicle for transformation is a *progression* of images of ascending power and complexity, not just *one* specific image for one particular problem, as prior less advanced works have done. I introduce to you here a sequence of over 30 images, a progression of lessons to take you further than you've ever been before through self-healing, self-induction of positive feelings, and mapping new psychic geography.

You begin by learning how to use imagery for treating a broad range of diagnostic categories including anxiety, pain, drug abuse, smoking, obesity, phobias, sexual dysfunction, skin disorders, speech problems, insomnia, asthma, anorexia, enuresis, gastrointestinal troubles, alcoholism, headaches, and depression. I'll show you how to use imagery to create the phenomena of profound relaxation, glove anesthesia, time expansion and concentration, dissociation, sexual energy, age regression, and negative hallucinations to eliminate these problems.

Imagery further maximizes your potential by helping you to develop greater energy, concentration, memory, confidence, work efficiency, athletic ability, and intuition. Finally, the images teach you to access a higher reality of consciousness, independent of the illusion of your five-sensory world, an interface between this dimension and the one above where lies greater knowledge, truth, and happiness—your paradise.

These images average a page in length or five minutes on tape if you choose to read them into a recorder for practice rather than recall them from memory. They have been standardized on over three thousand patients in the last 16 years and finely honed on the basis of feedback given by psychiatrists, psychologists, and physicians in more than two hundred seminars I have conducted personally.

The premise of working with imagery is that by mastering your inner reality, you conquer your external one as well. The thrust is on learning to create inner realities so powerful they effect a change in your outer. Your images are sequential, each one more advanced than the one that came before. Step by step, image by image, using basic psychophysical principles that govern your modes of perception, you are taken ever further into higher realms of understanding and self-control. Feeling better and better is a natural result.

Unlike many of the dogmatic approaches of the past that give answers pre-packaged, the message here is, "The answers, the truths, already lie within you. You have only to find them." It is the goal of *Creative Imagery* to help you gain access to this information, for only by discovering it yourself can you thoroughly appreciate its truth. This is the natural jumping-off point for a new age, childhood's end when answers no longer come from external empowered authorities, but from inside your own being. Rather than having to wait until the last chapter to find out how to gain this heightened awareness and surging power, I give you the methods for clearing your mind and planting ever-expanding images within each chapter so that by the time you finish the book, you will, if you have done your exercises, be well on your way to feeling greater love, greater health, and a sense of motion ever upward.

To provide you with as much opportunity for growth as possible, I present each chapter in the warm, inviting format of a counseling session. I discuss possible questions you might have based on notes I have accumulated from hundreds of my own patients concerning reactions they have had in their pilgrimage through the imagery progression. I invite you to follow them as they soar upward spiraling through increasing personal knowledge. Their cases sharply illustrate the drama and impact the imagery material produces. While there is a cosmic commonality of experience among us all in our evolution there are also many differences, so I show you cases not for your comparison, but your motivation. Other people's experiences have been a continual inspiration to me and I trust they will serve equally well to stimulate you, a future voyager, in the quest for new and better dimensions of consciousness.

I've tried to encourage your growth by starting you out in areas you're comfortable and familiar with before extending your levels of reality further. You begin in the comfortable waters of relaxation and imagery techniques used for mind clearing, positive thinking, and stress reduction before you move into the well documented, but not as well known, mental phenomena of glove anesthesia, time distortion, heat transfers, and dissociation. These latter phenomena are widely used in medical hypnosis for pain control, drug abuse, smoking, weight control, phobias, sexual dysfunction, and a broad range of other diagnostic categories. I refer you to my first book, *Hypnosis and Behavior Modification: Imagery Conditioning*, coauthored with William S. Kroger, M.D., published by the medical division of Lippincott in 1976, where we list over 90 pages of bibliography covering the research for this documentation.

While many self-help books have mentioned imagery and visualization, sometimes giving you simple exercises to do, they may have left you saying, "Yeah, that sounds good, but *how* do I visualize strongly enough to make a difference in reality? Here, *Creative Imagery* is a major breakthrough. I'll show you not only *what* to visualize, but *how*, employing research from the field of sensation and perception never described before. This imagery program is an uncomplicated, straightforward approach to achieving a state in which you are free to choose your present-moment emotional feelings, liberating yourself from the need to live your life as others tell you to or give up control in order to flee responsibility.

I've devoted the final part of the book to taking you beyond the achievement of positive emotional states and healing into levels of knowledge and awareness you have never experienced before, levels you might find mentioned in certain esoteric works, but which many people would deny existed.

While I appreciate the seriousness of the material, I do not support the notion that the attainment of happiness or paradise must be a humorless enterprise, filled with threats of doom and destruction to those who fall along the way. I will therefore avoid moralistic preachings, largely because I believe attaining paradise is an upbeat affair. There is no room for hell in this cosmology. The worst thing that can happen to you is that nothing will happen.

It takes time for you to love, to heal, and to ascend. This is especially true if you look to others to tell you the way, rather than turning inward to find your own truth. Parents have much opportunity to encourage such self-discovery in their children; thus this is a book for parents. Wives, husbands, friends, and lovers have further occasions to encourage independent thinking within their relationships; thus this is a book for any concerned person in your life. Ultimately, the responsibility for positive change lies with you. That's why the book will most benefit anyone willing to exert the energy necessary to follow its blueprint. You have my love, my caring, my positive thoughts, every step of your way.

ONE

The
Beginning

In the spring of 1972, during the last few months of my internship as a clinical psychologist at the Los Angeles County–University of Southern California Medical Center, I started looking for a job. I set aside three hours every Friday to make calls to the professional mental health facilities in the greater Los Angeles area, hoping they would have need of my services. After nearly six weeks of rejections, I got a wrong number. I thought I was speaking to a secretary in a major medical clinic, but after I'd finished giving her my qualifications, the woman replied, "I think one of the doctors on our service may be able to use you." I then realized I'd mistakenly reached an answering service rather than the clinic I was after. This was a fortunate error because the number then given me by the woman turned out to be that of psychiatrist William S. Kroger, M.D., the leading practitioner of medical hypnosis in the world. This was to be not only the beginning of a wonderful, loving partnership between Dr. Kroger and myself, but also my start on a fantastic journey into psychic lands called hypnosis.

My first exposure to hypnosis had come from Dr. Milton Erikson while I was a graduate student at Arizona State University in Tempe. Although my college training had taught me the history of this age-old healing art, as well as how to induce a hypnotic state, I doubt that I would ever have actually used hypnosis in my practice if I hadn't been literally forced to. My alliance with Dr. Kroger made it necessary for me to perfect and use this technique every day since almost every client we saw came to us for hypnosis, due to Kroger's reputation in the field. I had been trained primarily in the psychological orientation called behavior modification and regarded hypnosis purely as a good way to produce relaxation. Behavior mod concerned itself with learning principles, conditioning—what makes you learn and unlearn the behaviors that constitute your life. Its primary focus was on outwardly *observable* pieces of behavior, behavioral units that could be calibrated and quantified by as many external observers as possible. Something as outwardly unobservable as an altered state of consciousness such as hypnosis was not something my basic training had equipped me to value or consider, and I justified the introduction of hypnosis into my bag of therapeutic tools by calling it relaxation training.

As the first few months of my practice with Dr. Kroger progressed, however, I came to see that hypnosis was much more than relaxation, and that the relaxation it did produce was more profound than any of the garden variety forms of relaxation I'd encountered before. As a behavior modifier I'd been taught a method for inducing relaxation called "Jacobson's Progressive Relaxation." This technique involves your progressively tensing and relaxing approximately fourteen different muscle groups. Since a muscle relaxes more after you tense it, you can greatly relax your whole body by first tightening your muscle groups, as any physical exercise will prove. However, the hypnotic relaxation I was witnessing in my patients far surpassed the results I'd ever seen using physical methods alone. The hypnotic state produced a relaxation so profound that it was difficult for many patients to even move until a few seconds after dehypnotization. Along with this incredible relaxation came beautiful positive feelings and a desire to stay in this state always. I marveled at these reports and knew that I was on to something. Anything that felt that good had to be therapeutic and healing. I knew that anxiety was at the core of all problems, whether they concerned drug addiction, excess weight, or depression, and I could see that no anxiety existed in this sublime state of hypnotic relaxation. The state itself had to be beneficial.

What really convinced me of the value of hypnosis, more than my having to use it because of Dr. Kroger and more than the positive results I saw in my patients, was my experiencing the state myself. Strangely enough, although I'd been shown how to hypnotize others and had embarked on a practice specializing in hypnosis, I'd never really been hypnotized. In fact, many of my colleagues have confessed to me that while they are masters at hypnotizing others, they themselves have never experienced hypnosis. After a few weeks of instructing my patients in the method for inducing hypnosis, I found I was following my own instructions and I experienced a beatific sense of relaxation at the end of each hypnotic session. Rather than feeling tired or drained as I often did after an hour of therapy, I felt charged, clear-headed, and motivated by an inexplicable desire to do even more. This refreshing relaxation, clarity of thought, and rising energy were to be only the beginning of the many new phenomena I was to experience with hypnosis. This is why I'm eager to teach and share the state with you.

HYPNOSIS

You begin your ascent into paradise by learning to clear your mind and remove all negativity. Hypnosis, which is defined as a *state of increased concentration*, helps you to do exactly that. It enables you to focus with pinpoint specificity while eliminating all competing negative stimuli or "noise" from your consciousness.

Surprisingly, although we can define hypnosis as increased concentration, nobody knows exactly what this state *is*. Scientists have long failed to determine the physiological correlates of this state, to answer, "What is going on in my body when I am hypnotized?" You see, the thing is you can use concentration to produce any feeling imaginable—sleep, alertness, sexual arousal, sadness, happiness. These feelings may register on our psychophysical instrumentation in various peaks of alpha, delta, beta, and theta waves, but the concentration itself takes no particular form. In other words, I might be able to use an instrument to tell you what you are feeling in hypnosis, but I still wouldn't be able to tell if you were actually in such a state by looking at your brain waves. Scientists have similarly failed to find physiological correlates to the yogic states and other Eastern mental disciplines. To date, these states, including hypnosis, stand as the ultimate outwardly unobservables. An observer may look for certain *signs* that you are indeed hypnotized, such as a trembling or flutter of your eyelids; slow, deep, regular breathing; a masklike quality to your features. However, these signs only indicate you are experiencing the hypnotic state. The signs do not cause or explain what the state is.

QUESTIONS OFTEN ASKED

Very often, when I first ask a patient if he has any questions about hypnosis, the answer is, "How can I ask a question if I don't know anything about it?" I take this to mean he wants to experience this state first. Some people, on the other hand, voice a normal fear of the unknown and feel better getting information beforehand. For the benefit of this group, I'll give you the commonly asked questions before you experience hypnosis rather than after. In all cases the state feels wonderful. It is a positive, exciting adventure into new and wondrous inner spaces.

1. What is hypnosis?

As I explained above, hypnosis is defined as a state of increased concentration, but as to what is actually going on in your body to produce this state, nobody knows.

2. What is the difference between clinical hypnosis, stage hypnosis, and self-hypnosis?

All hypnosis is really self-hypnosis. I only serve as your instructor or director, telling you what to do to access this state of mind. Once you learn the technique, you can do it on your own.

3. Who can be hypnotized?

Anyone and everyone can be hypnotized unless he is retarded or psychotic to the point of not being able to concentrate at all. This state of mind exists and you definitely can learn to get there. As with all learning, some people may learn faster than others, but all will accomplish it eventually. Especially don't be alarmed if you are slow to start. Late bloomers often surpass those who are quick in the beginning. Hypnosis is an infinite state and you are never so deep you can't go deeper. As you grow, you will experience ever-new phenomena.

4. How do I know if I'm hypnotized?

When you first start practicing self-hypnosis you probably won't know that you are hypnotized. I've seen stage hypnotists have their subjects perform incredible feats such as going rigid between two chairs while someone stands on their stomach, but invariably when the subject is asked afterward whether or not he thinks he was hypnotized, he replies, "No way," even though to the entire audience it was obvious that he was. Often my patients also swear the first time I hypnotize them that they don't feel any different. But I can tell they went under by the signs I mentioned earlier such as a rapid eye movement, deep breathing, or expressionless face. You, however, will not be able to look at yourself for such indications.

In the beginning be content for simply feeling more relaxed. You'll be unaware of your lids fluttering or breathing deepening. As you practice you may notice a numbness or tingling in your arms and legs. Some dissociation may appear where your legs feel crossed when they're not or you think your hands are on your chest when they're really at your sides. There may be a distortion of your time sense where it seems more or less time has passed than actually has or your sense of time may be obliterated completely, your having lost all track of it. Please don't concern yourself with whether you are or aren't hypnotized. If you practice the technique as I give it to you, you'll clear your mind and achieve the desired results. That is really the only important thing.

5. Will I know what's going on around me while I'm hypnotized?

Yes. You'll be *more* aware of your surroundings when you're in a hypnotic state. Many people equate hypnosis with sleep and think they will be "out of it" when hypnotized. Just the opposite is true. Your sensory thresholds will lower. You will be more sensitive in all five sensory modalities. The grass will be greener, the sky will be bluer. Sounds will be louder. The touch of your body against your chair or couch will be heightened. Tastes and smells will be accentuated. Reality is intensified as concentration increases.

6. Will I remember the hypnotic session?

Approximately 90 percent of the time you'll remember your practice sessions and recall them more vividly than you would ordinarily. The remaining 10 percent of the time you do self-hypnosis you may spontaneously experience amnesia. By amnesia I mean that you will not remember parts or all of your practice session. Amnesia is a natural hypnotic phenomenon and occurs without your intending or giving a suggestion for it. It is a sign of a very deep hypnotic state. Be grateful if you get it.

7. Am I in control when I'm hypnotized?

Yes. The object of hypnosis is to give you *more* self-control. You can do anything while you are in a hypnotic state and actually do it better because your mind is free from distraction. You can take an exam, have sex, walk a tightrope, or perform a play in a hypnotic state and be the best you've ever been because of your exquisite concentration. No one will ever know you're in an altered state. You'll appear perfectly normal.

8. Is there ever any trouble coming out of hypnosis?

No. There'll never be a time when you can't open your eyes, sit up, or leave the room if you want. Since the hypnotic state requires concentration, the moment your concentration lapses, your hypnosis ends. If you fall asleep during self-hypnosis, your hypnotic state will merge into safe, restful sleep, more refreshing to you than it would be if you hadn't preceded it with hypnosis.

9. Will I ever do something I don't want to do?

No. You can use hypnosis to remove your inhibitions, eliminate blocks and fears that keep you from your desired actions. It can also help you to get in touch with your feelings, goals, and aspirations. But it will never make you go against yourself. It can't. It *is* a higher aspect of yourself.

10. Why are positive affirmations and images more powerful if I give them to myself in a hypnotic state?

The hypnotic state is one of profound clarity and pinpoint

specificity. There is nothing in mind except what you *choose* to focus on. In psychology we say that hypnosis is a state that bypasses criticalness. That means that what you tell yourself or what you imagine in this state goes straight to your subconscious without being screened by your conscious mind. In the state you are going to create, you can envision yourself healed, filled with love and joy, and believe it because the judging conscious mind is not there to say it isn't so. If you believe you have no pain, then you have none. If you believe you are in ecstasy, you most definitely are.

Now that I've given you some of the answers to questions you might have concerning the nature of hypnosis, it's time for you to see for yourself. Once you experience this state, the answers to your questions will come to you. The mental state we call hypnosis is no longer going to be a mystery to you.

PUTTING YOURSELF INTO A HYPNOTIC STATE

Following is the complete set of words I use to induce hypnosis in my patients. I'm giving it to you in its entirety so that you too can use it to clear your mind and make it ready for the images that will come after. While this procedure is called self-hypnosis, it is simply a method for producing deep relaxation and clearing your head.

You can memorize the clearing procedure or you can read it into a cassette recorder and play it back for practice. I advise my patients that if they choose to practice from tapes, they do so only every other time. There are advantages to your using a tape as well as your doing it from memory. With a tape you don't have to worry about remembering all the words of the induction, although the exact words aren't necessary anyway as long as you get the general idea of it. You can thus devote your total concentration to following the taped hypnotic procedure without forgetting part of it or worrying about remembering it.

On the other hand, practicing self-hypnosis from memory lets you proceed at your own rate. As you will see, the hypnotic induction asks you to do certain things such as recall what it felt like when your legs fell asleep. This recall is an active process and you may be just beginning to feel a numbness in your legs, when the tape goes on and asks you to focus on your arms. If you were practicing from memory in this case, you could linger as long as you desired, concentrating on the recall of numbness in your legs until they were truly wooden.

Also, sometimes practicing from memory forces you to concentrate more. It's often more tempting, when using a tape, to just lie back and listen. I can't emphasize enough that in practicing self-hypnosis and imagery you do more than just listen. Really try to get the feelings and sensations that are being suggested to you. Since tape offers you the advantage of your not wasting energy recalling the procedure and memory gives you the bonus of being able to go at your own rate, I recommend you alternate between tape and memory when you practice. That way you will reap the best of two possible worlds.

TECHNIQUE FOR SELF-HYPNOSIS

"It has been stated that one picture is worth a thousand words. For instance, if you say, 'I will be confident,' the words must be implemented by a picture of yourself as the confident person you want to be. If you keep fortifying this image with appropriate suggestions, eventually these mental impressions will give rise to the confident feelings that you seek.

"I know that this technique seems simple, but if you keep implanting positive images into your mind, they will become a part of your personality. Do not expect immediate results when you begin to use self-hypnosis and don't ask, 'What's wrong?' All you have to do to attain self-hypnosis is to use what we call sensory or visual-imagery conditioning. This is an old technique that has been the basis for many different types of prayer.

"Anyone can learn and practice self-hypnosis, but to achieve the best results you must carefully consider what you wish to accomplish. Through self-exploration you can establish reasonable goals for improvement. Don't think that you have to be 'out of this world' to be in self-hypnosis. This idea has been produced by novels, comic strips, and motion pictures. Actually, you will only be in a very deep state of relaxation and concentration. You may develop a feeling of detachment or you may experience a very pleasant sinking feeling, or you may get a feeling of peace and serenity. At times you may not even feel a definite change; it may just seem as if you had your eyes closed and heard everything at all times. However, if you aim for a deeply relaxed state, you will reach it.

"After you are satisfied that you have achieved self-hypnosis you may give yourself further suggestions to deepen it if you wish. Also, remember that it is not too important to reach a deep state on your initial attempts. Just realize that you are trying to establish a conditioned response which will cause you to react instantly to any cue you wish to use. Through frequent repetition, the cue will bring on the self-hypnosis.

"During every attempt to achieve self-hypnosis, visualize yourself going *deeper* and *deeper*. At first you may experience some difficulty, but as you stick to it you will be able to picture yourself deeply relaxed. Always use the visual imagery techniques whether or not you think you are under hypnosis. The images will become clear as you constantly repeat the appropriate suggestions. As you continue working with yourself, you will develop confidence in giving yourself suggestions. To be effective, they cannot be given in a hesitant manner but with enthusiasm and anticipation. If you follow these instructions, you will see results of your suggestions and efforts.

"When you practice this on your own at home, begin by

selecting a quiet place and arrange to spend an uninterrupted ten minutes three times a day practicing there. Seat yourself in a comfortable chair with your hands resting in your lap and your feet on the floor, or recline with your hands at your sides. Fix your eyes on a spot on the ceiling above eye level.

"Then begin counting to yourself slowly from 1 to 10. Direct your attention to your eyelids and, between numbers, tell yourself repeatedly that your eyelids are getting *very, very heavy*, and that your eyes are getting *very, very tired*. Again and again say: 'My lids are getting *heavier* and *heavier*. I feel my lids getting so *heavy*, and the *heavier* they get, the *deeper relaxed* I will become, and the better able I will be to follow all suggestions I give myself. My lids are getting *very heavy*. It will feel so good to close my eyes.'

"By the time you count to 2, think of enough suggestions like the ones just mentioned so that you actually feel the heaviness of your eyelids. When you are sure that your lids are indeed heavy, count to 3 and let your eyes roll up into the back of your head for a few seconds. Then say, 'My lids are now locked so tight that I doubt very much that I can open them. My lids shut tighter and tighter, and as my lids lock tight, I begin to feel a nice, calm, soothing, relaxed feeling beginning in my toes, moving into my legs and into my thighs as I keep counting. It's the same feeling that I have in my jaws when the dentist injects Novocaine into them; the same feeling that I have when I fall asleep on my arm; the same feeling that I have when I sit too long in one position; the identical feeling that I would have in my legs if I sat cross-legged on them for very long. A numb, wooden feeling starting in my toes is beginning to move up, up, up from my toes into my legs.'

"Next, count to 4 and say, 'By the time I have counted to 5, my legs from my toes to my thighs will be just as heavy as lead. I can feel my legs relaxing from my toes to my thighs. I can feel them getting *heavier* and *heavier* and *heavier* . . . 5. They are so *heavy* now that I don't think I can move them.' Then double back for repetition. 'My eyelids are locked *tight*, so *tight* that I don't believe I can open them. My legs from my toes to my thighs are completely *relaxed*.' Each time you retrace these suggestions, you stamp in the learned response pattern.

"You continue in this way, 'By the time I have counted to 6 and 7, my fingers, hands, and arms will be very, very *heavy*. I am beginning to feel that same numbness moving up from my fingers to my shoulders. A *heavy*, detached feeling is moving up from my fingers to my hand, to my wrist, past my elbows, up to my arm, to my shoulders. Both my arms, from my hands to my shoulders, are getting very numb—a heavy woodenlike numbness. When I have counted to 7, my arms will be just as *heavy* and relaxed as my eyelids, and as numb as my legs are now, as if I have been sleeping on them.'

"Don't worry if you forget the exact words. The exact words are far less important than the effect that you are trying to achieve: a feeling of numbness all the way from the fingertips to the wrist, to the elbow, to the shoulder, to the neck. In practice, this may be a bit more difficult to accomplish in the first few sessions at home, but the feeling will come faster in subsequent attempts. It is most important that you never become discouraged and that you not tire yourself by spending more than 30 minutes a day in practice.

"When you finally reach the point where, by the count of 7, your limbs are sufficiently relaxed, you repeat again all the suggestions you have given yourself going back to your eyelids: 'My eyes are locked so tight that I doubt that I can open them. My legs are so *heavy* that I don't believe I can move them. My arms are so *heavy* that I cannot lift them.' Then add: 'And, by the time I have counted from 7 to 8, my trunk will be *relaxed*.'

"Now go back to the lids, legs, and arms. Then say, 'By the time I count from 8 to 9, my chest will have relaxed, too. With every breath I take, I can just feel myself going *deeper* and *deeper* into a *relaxed* state. My back and abdomen are getting very, very *numb*. I can feel the muscles in my chest completely *relaxed*. I can't open my eyes. I can't move my legs. I can't move my arms. I feel my whole body *relaxed*, thoroughly and deeply. It is so refreshing to remain in this deep, quiet state.

" 'I will now relax my neck and head, so that, at the count of 10, I will be completely relaxed from my head to my toes. I can feel that with every breath I take I am becoming calmer and *deeper relaxed* . . . *deeper* and *deeper relaxed* . . . into a calm, soothing, *refreshing* state. Everything is just getting more and more *relaxed*. I feel as if I am floating away . . . falling *deeper* and *deeper* . . . not asleep, but just thoroughly relaxed . . . 10. I am completely relaxed. My eyes and limbs are as heavy as lead. My entire body feels numb, heavy, woodenlike, as I go *deeper* and *deeper*.

" 'I am now going to count to 3. At the count of 3, I will open my eyes. I will be completely *relaxed*, totally *refreshed*. . . . 1 . . . 2 . . . 3.' "

After you have practiced the above technique for a week you are ready to begin the imagery sequence described in this book. I suggest practicing no more than three times a day, ten minutes each time, and spacing these practice sessions as evenly over the day as possible. People often find that before breakfast, the hour they get home from work, and right before bed are good times to do self-hypnosis. Three spot commercials evenly placed throughout your day are more effective at influencing your subconscious than a lump you've run together. Three times a day is Utopia, the ideal stratagem for practice, and please don't worry if you do less than this. I'm sure you have a busy schedule and if you practice at all you're to be congratulated. Once a day or even once a week will get you there in time. Be good to yourself. Don't get on your case for not practicing. Sooner or later you'll reach your desired state.

POINTS TO REMEMBER

You may wish to shorten the self-hypnosis technique after you become proficient with it. It can be abbreviated to the point where the mere blinking and closing of your eyes will trigger hypnosis. The important thing for you to remember when shortening the technique is to keep the basic structure intact. There are certain crucial elements operating in this induction. The rest is filler. Beginners often throw out the skeleton and keep the filler. If you hold to the following basic outline you can't go wrong:

1. Look at a spot above the level of your eyes. There should be a little bit of eyestrain, not a lot, but a little. Keep looking at that spot. Don't for a second, not for an instant, take your attention off that spot. That one spot is the only thing in the world that matters to you at this point in time.

2. While you are looking at the spot really say to yourself, "My lids are getting very, very *heavy*; very, very *tired*. It would feel so good to close my eyes." This is the first suggestion or affirmation you give yourself and it's important that it come true. You tell yourself that your lids are getting heavy not because they are, but because you want them to *become* heavy. It is a *suggestion*, not a statement of fact. You are in the process of building a belief system.

If you keep staring, without blinking, long enough at one area, your lids will tire on their own accord and they will truly feel heavy. Presto! Your first suggestion has come true and nothing succeeds like success. Your expectation that your next affirmation will also come true is thus heightened. Simple as it may seem, give yourself the affirmation for lid heaviness *every* time you use the self-hypnosis technique. It's amazing how many people forget to do this.

3. When it would feel more comfortable for you to close your eyes than leave them open, close them. Sometimes your eyes will shut on

their own, but in most cases you close them *voluntarily*. It's helpful to remember that the technique induces hypnosis; hypnosis does not induce the technique. People often think their lids will *grow* heavy automatically without their having to stare and their lids will close in like fashion as if an external force were acting upon them. This is not so. By *deliberately* following this method you will access an altered state of consciousness. Please don't think the altered state will take you through the technique before you've even created it!

4. The moment you close your eyes, roll your eyeballs up into the back of your head for 30 seconds and say to yourself, "My lids are now locked so tight I doubt that I can open them." This is your second affirmation and it's important that it also come true in order to continue compounding your positive belief system that what you tell yourself will come to be.

Again, physiologically, your affirmation *has* to come true because when your eyes are rolled back it really *feels* as though you can't open your eyes. Of course you can if you want to, but what you really want is to increase you feeling of lid closure and make your second suggestion manifest. This increases the probability that your next affirmation will also come true so that by the time you affirm something such as, "My system is healthy and well," or "I resist cigarettes effortlessly," there is a good chance of your manifesting this suggestion.

If you have difficulty keeping your eyes closed while you roll your eyeballs back, I'll tell you an exercise I show my patients to make this easier for them. In your normal, nonhypnotic state, hold your thumb before you at eye level. Rivet your attention on its tip and, without tilting your chin up, gradually raise your thumb straight up, all the time keeping your eyes fixed upon it. When you can no longer see the end of your thumb you'll notice an intense muscle tension through your eyeballs and around your eyebrows. Focus on the tension, holding your eyeballs in place. Take a beat to realize you are now about to let your eyelids drop. Then close your lids slowly, taking care to keep your eyeballs rolled back, maintaining the tension. Once you have experienced your lids closed with your eyeballs still rolled back, let your eyes relax.

You'll feel a wonderful rush of relaxation starting at the base of your neck and spreading out through the usually tense trapezius and shoulder muscles. Incidentally, gurus of the East used this eyeball-induced relaxation rush for centuries for creating their meditative states. This relaxation rush can be so strong as to make you giddy and induce a hypnotic state by itself. It order to write this explanation for you I just did the eyeball roll myself and find my arms so relaxed from the rush starting at the base of my neck that I need to pause before being able to hold my pen. It feels marvelous.

The eyeball roll has a purpose other than ensuring that your second affirmation comes true and producing a rush of relaxation throughout your body. It serves to provide you with a basis for comparison for monitoring the anxiety or muscle-tension level throughout your body. Your body may be in such a constant or chronic state of anxiety that you aren't able to discriminate it. Stress and muscle tension may now be normal to you. However, when you profoundly relax a muscle group, as you did with the muscles around your eyes with the eyeball roll, by first tensing, then relaxing, you are able to spot tension in your other muscle groups by *comparison*. Compared to your eye muscles, tissues in the rest of your body may now feel like taut steel strings. Your goal is to *match* the relaxation of your eye muscles with the rest of your body in the remainder of your self-hypnosis exercise.

5. Right before letting your eyeballs drop and relaxing your eye muscles, say to yourself, "My lids shut *tighter* and *tighter*, and as my lids lock *tight* . . ." Now let your eyeballs relax and finish your third affirmation with, "I begin to feel a rhythmic wave of relaxation washing through my legs . . . arms . . . chest . . . stomach . . . neck . . . around my jaws . . . eyes . . . forehead . . . scalp . . . till

from head to toe, every muscle, every fiber in my body is totally, completely relaxed."

If you follow this five-step outline you will find it easy to induce a profound state of relaxation and good hypnotic level. Use as much of the rest of the technique as works for you and feel free to embellish it with methods of your own. After they get the hang of it some people like to induce hypnosis rapidly and go immediately into their images and affirmations. Personally I prefer a long induction, and even though I have been doing the self-hypnosis technique described on pages 9-13 nearly verbatim for over seventeen years now, if I have the time, I continue to use it as a preface, a clearing for what is to come. My mind is never so pure that I can't use a few minutes of clearing. I also find that practicing long inductions (10-15 minutes) serves as booster shots or reinforcements that make it easier for me to go into hypnosis rapidly if there is a situation where I need to.

There is a final point which I have already mentioned in brief but want to stress again because it is so important and easily neglected. *Every* time you practice your self-hypnosis technique really try to *recall* the sensations you are attempting to produce. Work at remembering times when you felt relaxation, numbness, wooden-like, heaviness, floating, detached, Novocaine, loss of circulation in your arms or legs. The key here and to the images that follow is *sensory recall. By remembering sensations you can produce them.* This is an active process. Really attempt to conjure up these feelings from your memory banks.

Every sensation you've ever experienced is recorded forever. You have the ability to recall it as vividly as the first time you experienced it. Recalling a sensation is the same process as remembering a date or the answer to a question. You must think, not passively listen. When the results of my own self-hypnosis practice cease to impress me I usually find it's because I have stopped actively trying to recall the sensations I want to produce. This kind of concentration never becomes automatic. But if you maintain your awareness of your need for it you will continue to grow. Growth takes energy and concentration *is* energy.

REACTIONS AND USES

The most common initial reaction that you can expect from practicing self-hypnosis is a profound sense of relaxation. Janice, a 32-year-old court reporter suffering from nervous exhaustion, sighed after her first self-hypnosis session, "That's the first time I've relaxed in four weeks. I feel like a new person." "I feel more relaxed than I ever have before," said Jack, a 30-year-old sound engineer. "My legs felt so heavy I didn't think I could move them." Profound relaxation such as you will achieve from self-hypnosis often produces heaviness in your extremities. You're so relaxed you don't want to move a muscle. "I don't want to come back," purred Sylvia, 26, a systems manager for a major bank. "I can't move my arms." It feels so good you just want to lie there!

Other phenomena are often combined with relaxation. Stan, 64, a high-pressure interior designer for many Hollywood celebrities, said, "The muscles in my shoulders relaxed and there's a tingling in my stomach." Tingling sensations are common after practicing self-hypnosis. Your recall of numbness and woodenness throughout your body causes your blood to redistribute. Your recalling numbness in a particular part of your body results in blood actually leaving that physical region. Conversely, if you recall heat in a given portion of your body, as you will learn to do later, blood will congest in that region. Experiencing a tingling, such as occurs when your foot or arm has been asleep and starts to wake up, shows that you are already on the road to gaining mastery of your circulatory system.

Your self-hypnosis technique contains many affirmations for numbness and you will most likely come to experience numb, wooden-like feelings throughout your body along with tingling deep relaxation. "My hands are numb," said Claudia, a 24-year-old dental technician. "It feels like I can't move them." This resulting combination of new feelings often leads patients to describe their first experience with self-hypnosis as "weird." In fact, this is probably an accurate report. The new wonderful sensations you are in the process of experiencing are weird to you because they're unlike anything you've been through before. Another common reaction to the initial experience of self-hypnosis is one of surprise. "Strange," breathed Sam, a 42-year-old plumber with ulcers, "I didn't think I could do any of that." "I'm surprised," confessed Nicole, a 31-year-old bookkeeper complaining of chronic low back pain. "I did feel something. Those dots blurred. I felt something with my arm. Felt pretty good." *Any* change at all shows you are capable of creating a positive move for the better and you should be encouraged by it. Even if your reaction is similar to that of Sheila, a 54-year-old housewife and mother of four grown children, who reported, "I'm so relaxed, but I'm not sure I was hypnotized," take heart, you're doing better than you realize. The ability to self-induce relaxation is a major step in the right direction.

If you've been running around on nervous energy, this hypnotic relaxation can give you a tremendous emotional as well as physical release. "I feel a little tired," said Maria, 44, struggling through an identity as well as a financial crisis in the face of a divorce, as she began coming out of her self-induced hypnotic state. "Like I want to cry." Suddenly her hands made a fist. "I haven't cried in a long time," she sobbed, finally releasing the painful emotions that had been welling up inside for months. Hypnotic relaxation allows you to let go, to release the junk from the past and get on with creating a new, bright future. The world is beautiful when you are this relaxed.

Along with a great sense of release and clearing away of negativity often comes a healthy clarity of thought. Linda, 37, a schoolteacher, wife, and mother of two teenage girls, had such excessive worry over what people thought of her and needed to please them so badly that she developed severe colitis. After the clearing procedure of self-hypnosis she smiled. "That clearing was great. You know what I realized once I got all the junk out of my head for a while? That I've been indulging myself in the worst kind of vanity there is. Self-deprecation. Vanity is thinking too ·much about yourself, right? Well, thinking too much about yourself in a negative light is the worst kind of vanity there is! All the guilt I have about not being a good enough person, not being approved of enough by other people, is just plain vanity. Once I realized I should stop thinking so much about myself, period, I immediately felt better."

"I have the greatest fear in the world today," said Audrey, 42, a writer of children's books and short stories, living with her husband, Bill, 46, an attorney, and their eight-year-old daughter, Tracey, "the fear of public speaking." Audrey's publisher wanted her to go on a lecture tour promoting her latest work and she was terrified. "I have this image of a shy, stuttering little girl that I just can't shake," she explained to me. "Maybe it's because my mother never let me grow up. She never let me think for myself. She was the total *Portnoy's Complaint* mother; Jewish, overprotective. Smothering. Too much love. She didn't let me separate from her or her insecurities. Actually she's a bulldozer. Strong. I can't stand to be with her more than 24 hours. After one day I feel total anxiety, depression. She's a very negative person."

Just as Audrey was still empowering her mother, being the dependent little girl, she was also empowering her audience and experiencing the same fearful intimidation. Since fear and relaxation are incompatible, you cannot be afraid *and* relaxed at the same time. I knew it was time to teach Audrey how to relax in front of her audience.

After I took Audrey through the self-hypnosis technique she exclaimed, "I don't believe this! The noise of cars outside on the street and the doctor next door on the phone bothered me, but I still couldn't lift my arm. It felt like a hundred pounds pushing it down.

Felt as if my body was hollow. I never felt anything like this before in my life. It was like I didn't have a body. I was so relaxed I wasn't even aware of my body. I've taken yoga and been relaxed, but never like this. But my arm . . . I couldn't lift my arm up. If felt like lead. My body was relaxed. And the only images coming into my mind were the ones you told me." Audrey was later able to induce this same state of hypnotic relaxation when she was before an audience. With her mind cleared, no distracting images of a dependent little girl were able to enter her consciousness and she succeeded in keeping her attention focused on her talk and the relaxation she associated with it.

Audrey's description that it felt as if she wasn't aware of or didn't have a body is a phenomenon that you too may experience at any point in your progression through the exercises in this book. The phenomenon is termed "dissociation" and refers to a feeling of your mind separated from your body. You may report that you simply feel "detached." It's a very positive state and usually associated with a good depth of concentration. The extreme form of dissociation is what is called the "out of body" experience where it feels as if your mind leaves your body and travels to collect data which can later be verified. There is much debate as to whether it is actually possible to do such a thing or whether it merely *feels* as if you have.

What we are concerned with here is the *feeling* of a separateness of mind and body. This feeling produces an incredible state of relaxation and can be used in many ways for healing and transcendence, as you will see in later chapters. Also, it is not necessary that you feel completely disembodied before you can lay claim to having experienced this phenomenon. Any feeling of distortion of your body boundary qualifies to be called dissociation. Your legs may feel as if they are crossed when they aren't; your hand may feel straight when in reality it is slightly bent; your body may feel that it's subtly arching when it's really flat. Any distortion of your sense of your body in space is a dissociative phenomenon and should be welcomed with open arms. It's a natural hypnotic phenomenon and shows that your concentration and self-control are growing. The more positive altered feeling states you are capable of inducing, the more power you have and the greater range you possess for effecting positive change.

AFFIRMATIONS

You can see from the various reactions to self-hypnosis described in the above section that the hypnotic state itself feels positive and healing. The effects of hypnosis alone, such as relaxation, time distortion, anesthesia, and dissociation can be used in many wonderful ways to change your life. When most people think of hypnosis, however, the word *suggestion* immediately comes to mind. One is supposed to be hypnotized and then told or given a suggestion that one will be able to do some desired thing. As I have already mentioned, the probability of a suggestion coming true is greater if you give it to yourself while you are hypnotized because hypnosis is a state that bypasses criticalness. What you tell yourself in this state goes straight to your subconscious without your conscious mind there to screen or filter it. You can, for example, tell your hypnotized self, "I feel totally at ease on an airplane," and believe it because your conscious mind is not there to negate it by saying, "I'm terrified of flying." If you believe you can fly without fear, you can.

These suggestions that are so much associated with the hypnosis movement are now making their way into many of the new books and programs for self-help and are being called "affirmations." An affirmation is something positive you tell yourself, whether or not you are hypnotized. Again, an affirmation you give yourself in a hypnotic state is more powerful because it bypasses criticalness. In Audrey's case I had her affirm, "I speak effortlessly and am relaxed before any audience and they love me," whenever she did self-hypnosis.

Your brain works like a computer and giving yourself an affirmation is similar to reprogramming it. Just as the material you feed into a computer determines its program, so does the material injected into your consciousness determine your life. It is therefore important that you program yourself with the right data, i.e., your affirmations should be worded properly in order to produce the desired effect. That is why I like to spend some time with my patients before I give them specific suggestions or affirmations. I want to know as much about them as possible in order to construct the affirmations I give them. This is why years of training to be a therapist are so critical when using hypnosis as a clinician. Anyone can learn to hypnotize someone in a relatively short period. It's what you do with that state once you've created it that is crucial.

I want to help you to be able to create your own affirmations to achieve maximum effectiveness. The best place to give them is at the end of your self-hypnosis technique, just before you count to 3 to bring yourself out. If you're using a tape you may want to tape your affirmations on your self-hypnosis tape or simply put a long pause between your induction and 3-count for dehypnotization so that you can insert different affirmations to give yourself each time you play the tape.

There are definite principles governing how to construct a positive affirmation. Your results can only be as good as your programming. Following are seven rules you can use to program yourself to manifest your goals, whether they be related to health, emotions, or material success.

SEVEN KEYS TO MAKING YOUR OWN AFFIRMATIONS

1. THE GREAT "I AM"—Always say "I" when giving yourself an affirmation. If one of your goals is to smile more, tell yourself, "I smile a great deal." A generality such as "Smiling wins friends"

sounds good but it doesn't *connect* with yourself. Your subconscious will believe it, but won't take it personally.

2. POSITIVE—State what you wish to be, not what you want to avoid. If your goal is to be more friendly, tell yourself, "I am friendly and outgoing to all." This is much better than saying, "I will never be impolite to anyone." The word *impolite* conjures up a negative feeling. The purpose of your affirmation is to take you up, toward the positive.

3. STAY IN THE PRESENT—Make reference only to what is, not what was or is going to be. If you would like to have an even temper, say, "I *am* calm and even-tempered." If you say, "I have better control of my temper than I used to," that brings up a negative image of your losing your temper in the past. On the other hand, if you say, "I *am going to* control my temper," you put this trait off to the future of free-floating possibilities. Not only does your subconscious not take such "promises" seriously, the wording hints that perhaps you now have a temper and this again brings up a negative image.

4. DEFINITE—Leave no room for misunderstanding or misinterpretation. If your goal is to be more complimentary, tell yourself, "I give compliments freely." This is a definite statement. It can only mean one thing. "I am trying to be more complimentary," or "Sometimes I give a lot of compliments," is vague. It makes you ask yourself how hard is the trying? How often is sometimes? What about the other times? (This last question could bring up a negative image.) Your subconscious will be confused and respond inappropriately.

5. FINISHED—Word your affirmation as if your desired goal were an accomplished fact. If your goal is to be someone who never raises his voice, say, "I speak softly," not, "I am toning down my vocal volume."

6. NONCOMPETITIVE—Think in terms of absolutes, not comparisons. Avoid words like *best*, *least*, *most*. If, for example, your aim is better budgeting of your time, tell yourself, "I arrange my daily schedule efficiently." Statements like "I budget my time better than anyone in the office," or "I am the best budgeter of time there is," are not only indefinite (how good are the others?), they can create hostile competitive feelings. You are trying to achieve a definite objective.

7. EMBELLISH—"Soup up" your statements once in a while to make them more interesting. Rather than just affirming, "I always take time when someone needs my attention," blow your horn a little with "It's fantastic that I give people attention whenever they need it," or "It's wonderful that I make myself available to help people whenever they want it."

THE TWO UNIVERSAL KEYS TO MANIFESTATION

Images and affirmations are the two keys to getting what you want. Put another way, combining both your cerebral hemispheres, right-brain imagery with left-brain self-talk (affirmations), leads to the manifestation of your goals. The foundation to manifesting anything, whether it be speaking freely in public, anesthetizing your hand, or making a million dollars, is to imagine you are in your desired condition and tell yourself (affirm) that you are. The hypnotic state will help you to make your image and affirmation powerful enough to produce your manifestation.

This book is devoted primarily to the first universal key to manifestation, namely, imagery. Traditionally hypnosis concerned itself only with affirmations. The procedure is simple. You clear your mind using the hypnotic induction technique. Then in the fertile field of a clear mind you plant the seed of a suggestion. There are no weeds or competing stimuli to choke out this seed in such a prepared hotbed and it germinates to fruition; or, as explained in the last section, the suggestion bypasses criticalness and manifests itself in reality.

Only recently, in about the last ten years, have hypnotists asked their clients to also *imagine* the results of their affirmations. Combining right-brain images with left-brain affirmations will give you dynamically powerful results. Once you have achieved the results you desire they are usually permanent and you no longer need to practice your imagery and affirmations to maintain them. If your problem ever does resurface, a few more sessions of hypnotic affirmations and imagery should nip it in the bud early. The remainder of this book will show you how to create images so vivid they will make a positive difference in your reality.

TWO

Images of Power: Steps to a Better Reality

☐Over eighteen years ago, when I first started practicing hypnosis with Dr. Kroger, the treatment I observed him do was fairly orthodox. He would clear his patients' minds and produce profound relaxation using the self-hypnosis technique you learned in Chapter One. Then, with the client in this state of heightened suggestibility and concentration, where what you tell yourself goes straight to your subconscious mind without your conscious mind negating it, he would give his clients positive affirmations or suggestions. Using the rules for effective affirmation construction outlined in the last chapter, he would positively program people to believe they had achieved their goals. If a patient desired to lose weight, one of the suggestions Dr. Kroger would give him was, "You eat only as much as you decide to eat." If the client wanted to stop smoking, he would affirm, "You are a non-smoker." This was the then traditional approach to hypnotic therapy, relying heavily on hypnotic inductions and positive suggestions. There was little use of imagery.

However, Dr. Kroger used one particular hypnotic suggestion with his clients that made such an impression on me it changed the course of the way I did therapy forever. He did a considerable amount of work with patients experiencing pain from one source or another, including using hypnosis to induce anesthesia during surgery. Traditionally, if you wanted to induce anesthesia in your hand, for example, you'd suggest something like this to yourself: "My hand is numb."

I noticed in this case, however, that one of Dr. Kroger's suggestions for anesthesia contained an image within it. He would suggest to his patient, "Imagine thrusting your hand into a bucket of ice." He knew that recalling cold in a particular area of your body would cause blood to leave that area and produce numbness. He also knew it was more effective to *imagine* cold than to simply affirm, "My hand is cold." What surprised me most at that time was that hypnosis potentiated not only affirmations, but images as well. Both positive affirmations and images you give yourself in a hypnotic state are more powerful than if you experience them in your normal state of consciousness. Nearly a hundred years ago the great Russian physiological psychologist, Pavlov, had demonstrated that hypnosis improves conditionability or learning. It should not have come as such a revelation to me that if hypnosis increases left-brain learning it will also maximize right-brain learning, i.e., imagery.

My graduate training in behavior modification had already given me a good exposure to imagery techniques. There, the focus was primarily on desensitization, counterconditioning phobias by pairing what you were afraid of, such as snakes or heights, with a deep state of relaxation, induced by progressively tensing and relaxing the muscles of your body. I suddenly realized that all the behavior modification techniques I'd been taught that required progressive relaxation would work even better if I used hypnosis to induce the relaxation. Hypnosis was a godsend. I could use it to enhance every treatment strategy I had ever learned.

As I began using Dr. Kroger's suggestion to imagine ice for inducing anesthesia, I found it quite successful, but there were times I wished the results would be better. Often I heard my patients say, "I felt it a little," or "I think I was beginning to get numb," or "I'm not sure if I got it or not." There had to be a way to intensify the feeling we were after, to magnify the sense of numbness. Then it hit me. Why not make the image longer? It didn't seem to me that one sentence gave anyone much of a chance to create a very vivid image. It was remarkable the results were as good as they were.

I therefore set out to construct an image about a page long, approximately 250 words, to induce the anesthesia I had previously used only a sentence to conjure. The results were greatly gratifying. More patients were able to control their pain using this embellished form of hypnotic imagery and they were able to do it more quickly and intensely. I could see that imagery is not only more effective for healing and manifesting your goals if you do it in a hypnotic state, but it also gives better results if it is elaborated, given over a longer period, so that you can get involved in it.

My initial success using hypnotic imagery to induce anesthesia for pain control opened vistas to limitless horizons. I saw therapeutic possibilities for hypnotic imagery virtually everywhere. I set out to construct images to induce all the other hypnotic phenomena I had heretofore used left-brain affirmations to produce: profound relaxation, time distortion, dissociation, and age regression. Some patients complained they had difficulty making their images real, so I next created images to strengthen your powers of imagining, to make it easier for you to imagine. At this juncture I learned another valuable lesson: The most powerful images are those you experience in all five senses. In later pages I'll show you how to use this *sensory recall* to your full advantage in creating a better reality.

Finally, and even more exciting to me than all my previous discoveries, I began building images to expand my own positive experience, to take me into realms of mind and consciousness I'd never experienced before. The feedback of my patients' imagery experiences provided me a blueprint to mapping new psychic geography, previously uncharted dimensions of being I felt compelled to explore, till at this point there exist over five hundred images of ascending complexity that evolve like piano lessons to take you ever higher into understanding the music and harmony of the universe that is you.

I didn't one day just say to myself, "I think I'll sit down and make up a series of five hundred images for exploring my psychic cosmos." The images evolved *one* at a time. My initial intent was a single image to produce anesthesia, but every time I created an image, it seemed that it would then provide information for the creation of its successor. The feedback that patients gave me from experiencing the image made me think of new imagery to extend the phenomena. With this seemingly self-perpetuating sequence of images came new and wondrous knowledge and experience, and truly a glimpse of paradise. I'm eager to share all this with you as you learn to create your own like experiences. To help you do this, let's look at the nuts and bolts of imagery.

THREE KINDS OF IMAGERY

You'll be working with three types of images in the course of reading this book. The first type is what most people think of when imagery is mentioned. It is what I call "a specific image for a specific problem." It embodies the first key to manifestation wherein you imagine whatever it is you wish to have happen. If, for example, you have bad acne, you imagine your lesions drying and your skin clearing. If you are a guitarist who is having trouble fingering the chords, you see yourself nimbly making your desired digital maneuvers. If you lack concentration in your studies, you envision sitting relaxed and focused, effortlessly absorbing the information in your textbooks. Specific images for specific problems are the ones you find most commonly referred to in literature pertaining to imagery.

The second kind of imagery you'll be learning to do is imagery to produce a specific phenomenon. This is the type of image such as Dr. Kroger and I created where you imagine cold in order to induce anesthesia. This type of imagery is seldom, if ever mentioned in popular reading material. Its time is yet to come, but you'll be using it now to create all sorts of wonderful phenomena such as anesthesia, time expansion and concentration, out-of-body floating sensations, and time travel. Once you learn to create these phenomena, I'll tell you exactly how to use them to benefit your everyday living.

The third type of imagery, to my knowledge, will be found nowhere else but in these pages. This is imagery to strengthen imagery. These images ask you to work on recalling sensations and sensory combinations that you've never practiced creating before. The first three images that I'll give you in Chapters Three and Four—*Beach*, *Mountain Cabin*, and *Garden* scenes—are good for helping you develop your powers of imagery because they teach you to recall nearly every sensory component that comprises your reality. The images beginning in Chapter Nine will strengthen these developing powers to help you produce an even more vivid image. By practicing these images you increase your powers for making the first two types of imagery more vivid. The more intense your specific image for a specific problem is, the sooner it will generalize to reality, i.e., become real. The stronger your image to induce a specific phenomenon is, the more powerful that phenomenon will be and the more quickly you will be able to produce it.

In actuality, you will discover that not only does this third type of imagery enhance the power of your other imagery, it serves as a vehicle to higher levels of experience. This third kind of imagery gains you access to a new dimension in consciousness, a far better reality than you now know. To better understand how this is so, let's first examine the nature of reality and imagery.

REALITY AND IMAGERY

I define reality, for practical purposes, as *what you feel*, what comes to you through the five senses of sight, sound, touch, taste, and smell. An image is a mental representation of your five-sensory reality. The point I wish to stress so that you can benefit from this information is that images, if "real" enough, can produce the same feelings as the actual objects you imagine.

Before you begin the exercises that will make your imagery so vivid you'll be able to attain the object of your vision, I want you to reexamine your belief system about imagery. How much power do you believe an image has? What do you think it can do?

There is a talk I give at the beginning of my lectures on imagery. Its purpose is to stretch the belief system of my audience. It helps them to expand their horizons, to realize they are limited only by the scope of their imagination. I repeat that same talk now to broaden your belief system and heighten your expectations. It involves a continuum of activities and phenomena that people have claimed imagery to be capable of producing down through the ages. I will start you at the most "far-fetched" extreme end of the continuum and then take you back to the beginning where I'm sure you'll be comfortable. Then we can move slowly forward again.

A guru sits with his disciples in a cavern in the majestic Himalayas. They've fasted many days and it's time to eat, but there are no provisions. The master imagines a palace and it appears, along with a banquet hall and royal feast. The group dines and satisfies itself. In the morning the guru relaxes his concentration and the palace is gone.

In Galilee a man called Christ imagines a few fish and loaves of bread are many and feeds a multitude. His faith, his belief, becomes reality.

At a hospital in Los Angeles a young woman with cancer imagines her white blood cells are knights in shining armor vanquishing cancer cells which she pictures as rotten hamburger. Much to the staff's amazement the cancer disappears.

I hope the last three paragraphs didn't make you want to close your book in total disbelief. You may have considered this material as too "far out" for you to pursue further. Obviously a little backtracking is in order. I'll digress to the level of the severest critic, the one who thinks gurus are fairy tales, Christ is an imposter, and those so-called cancer cures are flukes due to uncontrolled variables.

What *do* you believe? Right now, today, at this point in time? How much power do you believe an image has? By an image I again mean "a mental representation of an object." What effects, what "real" events, can your mental representations produce?

YOUR EMOTIONAL RESPONSES

No one would argue with the idea that an image has the power to evoke a strong emotional response. If you recall a past unhappy scene such as the death of someone you loved you can produce sorrow and tears. Your image may not be "real," but the tears that result from it certainly are. On the other hand, if you remember a past positive event, you can evoke joy and laughter.

The famous school of Method acting relies on the power of images to elicit emotions. Method actors use "sensory recall" to really feel their parts. An actor who wishes to cry imagines an unhappy scene. If, on the other hand, he desires to laugh, he imagines a funny scene.

Emotions of disgust and revulsion are frequently used by

therapists who practice behavior modification with aversive conditioning. Here, you are asked to create an unpleasant image involving a revolting stimulus such as vomit. Your negative image, if strong enough, will actually cause you to be nauseated. You can then pair your image-induced nausea with an image of something you want to discourage the use of, like drugs, alcohol, cigarettes, or fattening foods.

Emotional responses of laughter, tears, and nausea are all under the control of your imagination. In fact, you can elicit any emotional response including joy, fear, hate, jealousy, love, passion, greed, envy, desire, lust, or relaxation and tranquillity by using the right image.

YOUR PHYSIOLOGICAL RESPONSES

Let's take your chain of belief further. Images can produce not only your emotional states but your physiological responses as well. An imagined lemon can produce as much salivation as a real lemon, *if* your image is vivid. Your stimulus may be imaginary but your response definitely isn't; the imagined and the real lemon give you the same result. You could even argue that the image and the object are equally real. They certainly can be equally powerful. They both materialize the same reality!

Salivation is only one example of a physical process under your mental control. The great lesson you are to learn in life is that *all* your physical processes are under your mental control.

A physical manifestation more dramatic than your salivation is controlling your vasoconstriction or blood flow. Few people realize they have mental control over their circulation. I've seen filmed demonstrations of Eastern cultures where people stick swords through one cheek and out the other and do not bleed. Their control over this phenomenon is truly remarkable.

I used to do seminars with a man who would stick a safety pin through his palm, in and out, making a stitch. Then he'd ask the audience to choose the opening from which they would like him to bleed. The medical implications of that demonstration are incredible. With voluntary control over your circulation, you would never need to experience high or low blood pressure.

Control over circulation as described in the above two examples can be achieved through imagery. If you can imagine a certain area of your body being warm, blood will flow into it. If you imagine an area is cold, blood will leave. There's no doubt about it; this type of vasocontrol has been documented.

You can transcend your pain threshold using an image of numbness. In this case, your blood actually leaves the area to be operated on. Surgeons find that muscles cut like butter and there is very little bleeding when their patients use images of numbness to aid their surgery.

While your imagining cold or numbness can cause blood to leave an area of your body, imagining warmth can result in getting your blood to congest in the region you are concentrating on. There have been reports of people being able to raise a fever blister by concentrating on an image of heat long and hard enough to cause an eruption in their area of focus.

On the negative side of the coin, an unpleasant image can bore a hole in your intestinal wall. Ulcers are the prime example of what can happen to people who overindulge in aversive images. It's not one event that gives you an ulcer. It's not those few seconds when the boss says, "You're fired!" that causes your ulcer. It's the days, weeks, or even years that you live in fear of the dreaded event—your anticipation, and the months or years after, that you spend recalling it. Dread and recall are forms of imagery. Only the actual five seconds of the event's occurrence are reality.

The problems we label "psychosomatic" are all negative physiological responses you produce by indulging in unpleasant imagery. You can eliminate asthma, allergies, acne, neurodermatitis, even warts, by imagining positively.

DRIVES

"All right," you may say, "an image has the power to produce my emotional responses such as laughter and tears and physiological reactions including salivation, channeling my circulation, and psychosomatic disorders. What more can it do?"

Beyond your emotions and physical reactions, it has been demonstrated that images have the power to control your drives. Drives are what motivate you. They are your source of energy. The desire to achieve your goal is a drive. You can whip up a white heat of desire by *imagining* that you desperately want something.

Your three basic drives are hunger, thirst, and sex. Your desire for these is built in. You have this in common with all humanity.

Just as an image precedes your emotions and physical reactions, it also precedes your drives. Your thought of a juicy steak or other delectable food precedes your hunger, your thought of cool, clear water comes before your thirst, your image of a naked man or woman is the beginning of your sexual desire. You can, therefore, *create* your drive by imagining your goal *and* your desire for it. Imagining a delicious steak will make you hungry; imagining an ice-cold glass of lemonade will make you thirsty; imagining a beautiful man or woman will arouse you sexually. Imagining your goal creates energy. It makes you want the thing you imagine if you envision it positively.

Your image, if strong enough, can actually cause you to have an orgasm. Several people at the seminars we give were able to produce intense erotic images to the point where they climaxed without physically being touched. This isn't really so unusual if you consider the common nocturnal emission or "wet dream" that men often experience. Here a dream, or night image, is powerful enough to make the dreamer climax.

YOUR DISEASES

Nowhere has the power of imagery been more controversially documented than in the field of our most dreaded disease, cancer. Working at their Cancer Counseling and Research Center in Fort Worth, Texas, Carl and Stephanie Simonton have reported cancer cures with the effective use of imagery. Basically, their method involves having their patients imagine their cancer attacked by beneficial agents which destroy it. The cancer is given a negative form such as a black rat or rotten hamburger and the destroying agent is seen in a positive metaphor such as a white knight or angel armed with a bow.

Their research has shaken a lot of belief systems and created a virtual hotbed of debate. Most modern physicians and psychologists grant that the mind plays a significant role in many diseases, including our number one killer, heart disease. We've already seen how imagery can control circulation. That your mind can directly influence cancer, however, is something many health professionals are grappling with.

Recently, however, there has been more support for the Simontons' research. It was found that positive imagery produces a rise in T killer lymphocytes, prime components of the immune system and destroying agents of cancer cells. Other images have been shown to trigger the body's release of endorphins, the opiate receptors so crucial to mood elevation and pain management.

YOUR MIND TO THE MIND OF ANOTHER

Let's return to your belief system, for it's what you do and do not believe that gives you your reality. If I've lost you at this point, if you absolutely believe that imagery cannot cure cancer, that's fine. Many people share your belief. I'm not sure myself where I get off in this progression. But please read the remainder of this section if for nothing more than interest, just to learn what powers have been attributed to imagery down through the ages.

So far we've discussed the amazing effects your imagery can have on your body. What we need to ask next is, "Can imagery exert any influence *outside* of your body?" Can you influence another mind by what you imagine? Can you send your image to the mind of another? Radio and TV waves can be transmitted and received through the air. Can brain waves be similarly transmitted? Sending an image from one mind to another is called telepathy. Although there has been laboratory research to support this phenomenon, most scholars still consider the data inconclusive. However, an estimated 70 percent of the population has reported "telepathic" experiences.

There's one incident involving this phenomenon I think you'll find especially interesting. A recent major innovation in the fields of medicine and psychology has been the use of biofeedback for lowering blood pressure and stress reduction. Essentially, the biofeedback method entails monitoring various physical systems such as blood pressure, muscle tension, brain spikings, and galvanic skin response using different instruments.

The instruments give you feedback as to how your systems are doing, and on the basis of this feedback you are able to control them. One particular research project required its subjects to have their brain waves spiking in synchronicity. Although they weren't looking for it, these researchers found that when subjects' brain waves were similar, they reported having the same images. It was as though they were "in tune" with each other's minds when their brain waves were alike!

YOUR MIND INFLUENCES MATTER

We've discussed the possibility of an image in your mind being transmitted to, or influencing, the mind of someone else. Our next question is, "What influence could your image have on external, non-living matter?" The phenomenon of an image influencing matter is call psychokinesis. Again, psychics have reportedly demonstrated this phenomenon under controlled laboratory conditions but the conclusions are debatable to say the least. Few scholars believe in the validity of this phenomenon.

I would, however, like to take the time now to tell you a little story, a personal experience I had, related to this phenomenon. A friend of mine, a Hollywood screenwriter, was commissioned by Paramount Studios to write a screenplay on the life story of the reputed psychic Uri Geller.

Paramount had several cans of film footage on Uri's stage performances. For his finale, Uri Geller would often ask people to bring clocks and watches that weren't working and heap them up on the stage. It didn't matter what was wrong with a timepiece, as long as it had all its parts.

Next, the audience was to yell, "Start!" along with Uri in conjunction with *imagining* the clock hands moving. Invariably a good percentage of the clocks would begin ticking. This feat has often been attributed to body heat if the watch is held during the demonstration. However, in this particular case, there was no physical contact with the timepieces.

What the studio wanted to determine was whether the image of Uri Geller, Uri on screen, could produce the same effect as Uri on stage. If this was the case, they had a terrific advertising gimmick.

They asked twenty of us to bring watches that didn't work to the screening room at Paramount. We piled them up under the screen and the projector was turned on. When Uri on film yelled, "Start," the screening room audience also yelled, "Start," simultaneously *imagining* the hands of the watches commencing to move. Eight of the twenty watches started.

There are certainly many possible explanations for the event I just described. Scientists are still trying to explain such demonstrations. What I find particularly interesting, however, is the technique that Geller used. He combined the image (the right side of your brain) of the hand moving with the command or affirmation (the left side of your brain) to move. Using the whole brain simultaneously was the basis for producing this phenomenon.

Even Geller's spoon-bending demonstrations, for which he is famous, make use of both sides of the brain. He imagines the spoon bending in conjunction with a command to bend.

How much do I believe in psychokinesis now that I've "seen" it? I honestly don't know. I've never produced psychokinesis on my own and many respected authorities have debunked those who claim to be capable of producing this phenomenon. One bookstore refused to stock a book I wrote that included my account of this last incident, so incensed were they by even the idea of it. I do think, however, that it's always best to keep a clear and open mind, to at least entertain all possibilities. If faith can move mountains, it certainly should be able to move the hand on a wristwatch.

YOUR MIND TRANSFORMS MATTER

From the influence of matter by mind, psychokinesis, we move to the transformation of matter by mind. Through the centuries this has been called magic. The ancient alchemists claimed the power to transform lead into gold. Witches, magicians, wizards, and medicine men have been said to be capable of turning people into frogs, and bat wings into hurricanes, and all sorts of other fantastic transformations, simply by *conjuring*, or *imagining* them. Conjure means to imagine.

By now, you're probably heaving a sigh of relief. You've finally reached a stage in this progression of your belief system where you are absolutely certain of where you stand. You unequivocally draw the line on magic.

But isn't conjuring a blister by imagining heat in your right hand transforming mind (your imaginal blister) into matter (your physical blister)? We're all magicians; we all have the power to conjure.

Why haven't most of us produced more remarkable feats? The answer is simple. We never *believed* we had the power.

YOUR MIND CREATES MATTER

You are now at the final step in your belief system. A power greater than moving or transforming matter is creating it. Do you believe you have the power of creation? This brings us full circle to the guru and Christ who imagine food and gain nourishment from it.

Many say we're entering a new age, the dawn of a new era, evolving into beings whose brain waves produce their own reality. Or are we already there? Is reality at this moment your own creation? If so, strengthen the positive and eliminate the negative. Free your mind from failure and *belief* in its existence. The time has come for you to conjure a better reality.

THREE

Creating
an Image

☐ What I intend to help you discover in this chapter is that "magic" is the natural, normal functioning of mind and brain. It is using *all* the mental resources available to you rather than just a small fraction of them. You are now going to learn to create imagery so powerful it can change "real" things in your life.

THE BEACH SCENE

Your first image puts you on the beach. I have given it to over three thousand of my patients as their first exercise in imagery. Relaxing at the beach seems to be a universal experience, one nearly everyone has been through. The scene is wonderfully pleasant and positive. *However*, its purpose is more than to relax you and make you feel good. Your first image is a tool for learning to create new and powerful imagery, imagery so vivid that it will produce results in your reality.

It will probably take you between five and ten minutes to create your image, although some people report spending as long as half an hour getting the effects called for. Take as long as you like, lingering to vivify each new sensation. Always use the self-hypnosis technique to clear your mind before giving yourself an image. The hypnotic state will greatly potentiate your imagery.

Make your image as real as possible, *working* to remember what the sensations called for really feel like. The more energy you expend, the better your results will be. Also, try to *be there*. Practice the image as if you are actually in it. At first, you may sometimes experience your image as if you are watching yourself on a screen. Don't worry if this happens. Just continue striving to conjure it as if you are in the scene, not merely observing it.

Your imagery will become more vivid with practice. Don't worry if at first some elements aren't as real as you'd like them to be. Getting them vivid is only a matter of time. The sensory data you desire is there, on record in your cortex. Practice will inevitably lead to its retrieval.

As you did with self-hypnosis alone, it's best to not practice hypnotic imagery more than three times a day. After four days to a week of practice you will be ready to go on to your next image. Don't worry if you don't get it perfect before moving on. You needn't master the recall of every sensation asked for. If you are working on the *Beach Scene* to remedy a specific problem or to create a particular phenomenon such as relaxation, stick with the image until you have your desired effect. You may want to refer to the Glossary listing the images you can use to treat certain clinical problems or to achieve a particular result. Otherwise, if your chief concern is to strengthen your powers of imagining, progress to the next image after a few days of practice.

BEACH SCENE:

"Every sensation you've ever experienced is recorded forever. You have the ability to relive those sensations as vividly as the first time they were experienced. You are now going to take a sensory voyage. You are going to construct a scene in your mind's eye so vivid it will be as if you are actually there.

"You are walking along the beach. It's mid-July; very, very *hot*; five o'clock in the afternoon. The sun is getting low on the horizon although it has not yet begun to set. The sky is a brilliant *blue*, the sun a blazing *yellow*. Feel the *heat* from the sun against your face; feel the *warmth* of its rays against your skin.

"You are barefoot. Feel the *hot*, *dry* sand beneath your feet. Walk closer to the water. Feel the *wet*, *cold*, firmly packed sand beneath your feet.

"Hear the beating of the waves, the rhythmic crashing, back and forth, to and fro, of the water against the sand. Hear the *loud*, *high* cries of the gulls circling overhead. You continue walking.

"Suddenly you come to a sand dune, a mound of *white* sand covered with deep *pink* moss roses, bright *yellow* buttercups. You sit down on that mound of sand. You look out to sea. The sea is like a mirror of *silver* reflecting the sun's rays, a mass of pure, *white* light.

"You are gazing fixedly into that light. As you continue to stare at the sun's reflection off the water, you begin to see dots of *purple*, darting flecks of violet. There's a violet line along the horizon, a *purple* halo around the flowers; everywhere *purple* and *silver*.

"Now the sun is beginning to set. With each motion, with each movement of the sun into the sea, you go deeper and deeper relaxed . . . and when the sun has sunk into the ocean, you will be in a profound state of relaxation.

"The sky is turning *red*, *crimson*, *scarlet*, *gold*, *amber*, as the sun sets. You are engulfed in a deep *purple* twilight, a velvety *blue* haze. You look up at the night sky. It's clear, filled with stars . . . a brilliant starry night . . . the *soft*, *low* roar of the waves, the taste and smell of the *salt*, the sea, the sky, and you. . . . And you feel yourself carried upward and outward into space, one with the universe."

You then bring yourself out of your imagery state the same way you end any hypnotic state, by telling yourself, "I am now going to count to 3. At the count of 3, I will open my eyes. I will be completely relaxed, totally refreshed. . . . 1 . . . 2 . . . 3 . . ."

REACTIONS AND USES

As when you practice self-hypnosis, one of the first positive effects you will achieve from the *Beach Scene* is a profound sense of relaxation. Examples of common reactions to this image are: "My arms and legs are so relaxed," "It felt like I took a nap," "It's difficult to come back. . . . Just let me lie there a couple of days," "I'm not fatigued like I usually am after a nap," "I really like that . . . so relaxing . . . I've often had a dream of a house at the beach."

Relaxation is tremendously therapeutic. Your ability to self-induce it puts you well on the road to healing and experiencing a better reality. In a state of deep relaxation you feel good, there are no negative thoughts bringing you down; your body heals, and your immune system strengthens. Relaxation enables you to transcend your problems, come from a different, more positive space entirely.

I have always espoused an "anxiety model" of therapy, the premise of which is that the removal of anxiety or negativity from your mind helps you alleviate any problem. It has been my experience that no matter what my patients' presenting problems were, whether they were seeing me for smoking, weight control, depression, or whatever, when I was able to teach them to relax, they were much improved.

In many cases just learning to relax alone eliminated their problem. Without anxiety, alcoholics lost their drive to drink, addicts no longer craved drugs, phobics were not afraid.

Anxiety and relaxation are incompatible. You cannot be anxious and relaxed at the same time. Practicing the *Beach Scene* will induce the relaxation you need to eliminate the anxiety in your life, along with the maladaptive forms of behavior it is manifesting.

PHOBIAS

The axiom that you cannot be relaxed and fearful at the same time worked well to help Audrey get over her fear of public speaking. After I gave her the *Beach Scene* she responded, "I feel great! I was worried at first I wouldn't go into it. Why didn't you give me suggestions for anxiety and worry? I felt I was falling into the hollow shape of a mummy. That image of a mummy was a big help. Wow!" She stopped momentarily, rearranging her jaw. "I can't even talk, I'm so relaxed."

I told Audrey to practice the *Beach Scene* three times a day for a week. Then, just before she was about to give a speech, to flash upon this image, i.e., bring the thought of that image to mind, thereby automatically triggering the sensory material. In getting its essence, she triggered the whole relaxation response she had set up through her practice sessions. You see from this case that the *Beach Scene* can be used in two ways to overcome phobias: You can practice it away from your feared situation to reduce your general anxiety level and feel more comfortable all around; or, once you have a good handle on the image, you can flash on a part of it or its essence during the event you fear, whether it be a speech, airflight, or encounter with your boss.

It's also noteworthy in Audrey's reaction to the *Beach Scene* that she asked me why I hadn't given her a suggestion for anxiety or worry in front of an audience. I had. I suggested, as I mentioned in the section of affirmations, "You feel totally relaxed before an audience and they love you," but Audrey was *amnesic* for this affirmation. Amnesia, the phenomenon where you forget what is told to you, or even what you tell yourself, is a natural hypnotic occurrence. It shows that your state is deepening. But don't worry if you don't get amnesia. Its presence means you are concentrating deeply. Its absence means nothing. You may remember your deepest states with pinpoint clarity and precision.

PAIN

You can use the relaxation you create from the *Beach Scene* not only to reduce your stress and countercondition your fears and phobias, but also to manage any problems you may be having with pain. While we will be dealing with pain management in greater detail in Chapter Four, I want to underscore here the important role relaxation plays in treating pain. The ruling axiom is: Relaxation raises your pain threshold. That means that relaxation makes you *less* sensitive to pain. Psychophysically speaking, your pain threshold is the intensity a stimulus must reach before you experience it as pain. The more relaxed you are, the stronger the painful stimulus must be before you can feel it as negative.

Conversely: Anxiety lowers your pain threshold. Anxiety makes you more sensitive to pain. When you are in an anxious state you may perceive even a mildly negative stimulus as painful. The chances of the world looking grim are much higher if you start out viewing it from an anxious state, rather than one of profound relaxation. Reality is very much a function of the perceiving organism. You color the world by the state of mind in which you receive it. I think you can see from what I'm saying just how important it is for you to clear negativity from your mind and experience positive relaxation if you are to heal yourself and reach paradise.

Michael, a 28-year-old court reporter, complained of a "severe, burning, aching feeling" in his legs and the outside of his left foot.

He'd seen several doctors in varied specialties including a neurologist and an orthopedist. None of them had reached a diagnosis for the cause of his polyneuropathy. Neurological tests revealed no disorder. Michael confessed from the beginning to being a negative person. From childhood he had always expected the worst and equated a pessimistic outlook with survival. "There's something wrong with feeling good," he said. "I feel vulnerable when I feel good. Pain, feeling bad, puts me on the alert."

Michael had to agree to give up his pain before I could help him. "Relaxation allows you to process your external world," I explained to him. "Pain competes with the outside world for your attention. In point of fact, you are much more vulnerable in the pain state because it blocks your awareness of what is going on around you."

Using the *Beach Scene*, Michael worked to create a new experience for himself, relaxation. As his anxiety and negativity subsided, the burning, stinging sensations stopped. While you should always consult a doctor first to rule out a physical base for your pain, its origin is often psychosomatic—too much anxiety, not enough relaxation in your life.

SKIN

Another physical problem you may have had that often has psychosomatic roots, the product of your negative feelings, is a skin disorder. Your skin is extremely sensitive to your emotional state, erupting when you are tense and thriving when you are relaxed. Paul, 17, a high-school senior, suffered bouts of acne that played havoc with his social life. "I'm really happy when my face is clear," he told me. "But I have too many platonic relationships. I think the acne scares the girls off." Paul's parents were in the midst of divorce and he was experiencing a strong conflict of allegiances. This, combined with the pressure of his senior year and a mother he described as "overcritical, always telling me how spoiled I am," was giving him considerable stress. "I just want away from L.A.," he explained. "I want to start over with new people."

It wasn't Los Angeles, but his emotional state that Paul needed to escape from. He responded beautifully to his first encounter with the *Beach Scene*: "Weird," he sighed. "I could almost feel it. It was neat. I concentrated on my eyeballs and my whole body beneath me vanished." I asked Paul to recall this scene three times a day and give himself the affirmation, "My skin is clear, smooth, soothed, healthy," after his hypnotic clearing procedure and before beginning the image. After two weeks of practicing this image Paul's face began to clear. The last time I saw him he had plans to take a girl to his prom in a rented, white Rolls-Royce. L.A. was looking better to him all the time.

STUTTERING

Another problem the *Beach Scene* can help alleviate is stuttering, or what is commonly called "pressured speech." People with speech problems are almost always free of symptoms when their ears are plugged, when they are reading from a prepared text, when they are speaking in unison with someone, or when alone. Pressure comes from a fear you will not be able to pronounce a word if someone is listening and you are on your own. This is somewhat similar to what is called the "intention tremor" in multiple sclerosis. In this case a patient is easily able to reach for a glass or make a like movement if he does it automatically, without thinking about it first. If, however, he first considers his move or intention, there is often a tremor. His thinking abut the intended movement causes tension and fear of failure, resulting in his meeting his negative expectations. Likewise, your fear that you will botch the first letter of a word generates fear and produces the response you dread.

There is a technique used in hypnosis called "loose contact" that takes advantage of your intention to fail in your speech. Most stutterers block on only the first letter or two of any word. You can reverse this emphasis by affirming to yourself, "I worry only about the last syllables." If, for example, you have trouble saying the word *elephant*, and you find yourself saying, "el-, el-, el-," become more interested in the "e-phant" portion. You'll slide easily over the first two or three letters.

If you stutter, it also helps to pair your speaking each syllable of a word with other physical phenomena such as your breathing, the swinging of your hand, or the beat of a metronome. This is termed "rhythmic" or "syllable-timed" speech. It gets you to stay in the moment, to not rush ahead, to not anticipate. As with the intention tremor of multiple sclerosis, it's only when you look ahead that your speech is impaired. Images such as the *Beach Scene* that pair breathing and relaxation with other physical phenomena are particularly effective in training yourself to pace or pair proper breathing and relaxation with speaking.

Luke, a 52-year-old business manager, found that he had a bothersome stutter when he met new clients. "Sometimes I don't even think about it," he reported. "Other times it's downright embarrassing. People must think I'm an idiot. I try to avoid certain words I have trouble with, but sometimes I just can't. It's really a drag if I can't say the client's name." I asked Luke to really concentrate on the suggestion in the *Beach Scene*, "As the sun goes lower and lower, you go deeper and deeper relaxed." After he had practiced the image for a week, I told him, "Before meeting a client I want you to tell yourself, 'Every syllable I speak, I go deeper and deeper relaxed.'" Pairing relaxation with the physical phenomenon of the sun going down in the *Beach Scene* now prepared Luke to pair relaxation with the physical phenomenon of speech.

SEXUAL PERFORMANCE

The *Beach Scene* is also excellent for enhancing your sex life. Since relaxation renders you less sensitive to pain and more sensitive to pleasure, it is the ultimate aphrodisiac; it makes you sensual. It allows you to feel free from the competing stimuli of tension and anxiety. This is probably why relaxants such as Quaaludes were claimed to produce such heightened sex, not because the drug was a stimulant, but because it allowed the user to feel his own sexual feelings, unblocked by negative tension. Relaxation, however, is not the only sexual bonus you will gain from this image.

The suggestion at the end of the *Beach Scene*, "And you feel yourself carried upward and outward into space, one with the universe," often produces a sense of dissociation. You feel detached, drifting, floating, euphoric. You can use this feeling of detachment derived from dissociation to create a feeling of uninhibited sexuality, where you have no thought of past failures or fear of future ones. You dissociate yourself from your apprehension and inhibition and live only for the present sexual experience.

Magrite, 30, a free-lance designer, hated sex and could not bear to be touched by a man since her brother, Arnold, molested her between the ages of eight and fourteen. "I didn't even know why I hated it so much until a couple of years ago," she explained. "In therapy I was able to remember those times with Arnie. We didn't even have intercourse. He just rubbed his penis on my vagina. I felt betrayed. Like no one cared. I was a nonentity. My feelings didn't count and I didn't count. My father drank all the time. Mother was always sick. They wouldn't have believed me if I'd told them. Arnie was their darling. I felt it was my fault to hate this person everyone loved. I felt I never had the right to say no. My parents should have prevented this. I thought they felt it was okay to sacrifice me for him.

"I was a devout Catholic and was sure I'd burn in hell for what was happening. Finally I told Arnie, 'If you touch me again, I'll kill you.' He never came after me again. But I see his face every time I have sex. Although I've never enjoyed sex I used to get by thinking of neutral things during it, like a fashion pattern or something. Now that doesn't work. Lately I've cried during sex and when I explain my situation, the guys never see me again. I guess somewhere I believe if I enjoy sex, Arnie has won."

Magrite was unable to be in the moment sexually. Her present pleasant sexual reality was blocked by a negative memory, an event that happened to her over 22 year ago. This negative memory was so traumatic it raised her threshold to sexual pleasure to the point where she could feel nothing but the terror of her memory.

Magrite's case illustrates the crucial difference between the psychophysical terms of *sensation* and *perception*. In the field of psychophysics which studies the way our bodies act to receive the real world of light, sound, heat, pressure, and other energy forms, sensation is defined as pure experience. Perception, on the other hand, is sensation colored by past experience or memory. An infant, seeing a flame for the first time, has the pure visual experience of orange light. Then, perhaps, he ventures toward the flame and notices it has warmth. The next time he sees fire, his visual experience is no longer pure sensation. It's influenced by his knowledge that this orange light also has warmth. It is now a perception. Years of experience make you more and more perceptual, less and less sensational. Your world becomes more a function of your memories than the reality of the stimuli impinging upon you at the moment.

In Magrite's case, sex was *nothing* but memory, *bad* memory—all perception and no sensation, in the psychophysical sense. I taught her to induce relaxation by practicing the *Beach Scene*. This made her more sensitive to positive sensation. She started to feel again during sex. The dissociation she produced by using this image enabled her to detach herself from her memory of Arnold so much that it lost its impact for her. Magrite's was a severe case and I used several more images on her before she was finally able to enjoy sex and put Arnold out of her head for good. You'll see what these images are in future chapters, especially Chapter Ten that focuses on imagery primarily to create sexual arousal. The *Beach Scene*, however, is a good place for you to begin on your road to heightened sensuality.

Men and women benefit equally well from using the *Beach Scene* to free their sexual feelings. Mark, a 46-year-old insurance adjuster, had been impotent since the death of his wife, Mona, four years ago. "I get an erection during foreplay," he confided, "and I'm okay with oral sex, but it disappears the moment I penetrate. Sometimes I feel old, like I should be sitting in front of a fire. Dating is a bore." Mark had functioned quite well the first six months after his wife died. Then he lost his job and went into a depression. He had too much time to think and found himself feeling guilty desiring other women. "I tell myself that Mona wouldn't want me to be alone, that she'd want me to be happy, but part of me just doesn't believe it, I guess."

I knew Mark's sex life would improve if he learned to lower his positive sensory thresholds with relaxation and detach himself from his guilt using dissociation. I gave him the *Beach Scene* and he responded, "I felt I was sleeping. I dream. I can't explain it. I feel you are off in the background. I could smell the salt, hear waves crashing . . . but little dreams kept coming through. Yet I felt relaxed. I've never been able to relax. My hand feels one place and looks another. The same time I'm doing this I felt it was bull, but things still happened." I told Mark to masturbate at home immediately after practicing the *Beach Scene*, while he was still feeling its effects and he was in a sensual mode. After a week, he reported his erections were lasting longer during masturbation and sometimes after he penetrated a woman, he could last a few seconds longer before his erection went down. In time, using further images I'll describe in future chapters, he returned to full sexual vigor.

DRUGS

In addition to using the dissociation produced by the *Beach Scene* to heighten your sexuality, you can incorporate it to alleviate a drug problem. Many of the effects you can produce using imagery are similar to those created by drug states and you can substitute them for the reinforcing sensations of the drug state once you've mastered them. The floating "out of body" feeling associated with dissociation is a common component of the marijuana experience and you can use it to substitute for grass, a much healthier alternative.

Susan, 29, a concert promoter for major rock groups, was concerned over her dependence on hash and marijuana. "I've used pot off and on for over ten years," she said. "It gives me a buzz. Makes it easier for me to work. I mellow out. This is a tough business, music. You're alone on the road with these guys for weeks, lousy food, little sleep . . . and all that craziness . . . you know, the groupies, the fans. Most of all it's just plain boring. With grass I can just cut off and go somewhere else. But I'm doing it every day now and I notice my concentration is shot. I drift off in conversations and I can't remember things. I know it's time to stop. I'm getting dysfunctional. It's scary."

After the *Beach Scene* Susan said, "It's like something I did when I was stoned." I told her to do the image whenever she craved the effects of marijuana. She didn't stop cold turkey, right off the bat, but in six months she was off grass. Imagery proved a far better substitute. You can use imagery, as Susan did, to produce any sensation you're capable of experiencing. Let's take a closer look now at how this works.

IMAGES ARE MADE OF SENSORY "BITS" STORED IN YOUR CORTEX

You possess the power of imagination. It's only a matter of developing this power. Many people complain to me that they have "lousy" imaginations. The fact is they haven't learned to use their brain's right side properly.

You don't have to know the intricate workings of brain chemistry in order to think, but it does help to know a little about the runnings of the great computer called the brain in order to maximize its efficiency. First of all, every sensation you've ever experienced is recorded forever. You have the ability to relive those sensations as vividly as the first time they were experienced.

In computer terminology a bit is the smallest unit of information. It is defined as "a unit of computer memory corresponding to the ability to store the result of a choice between two alternatives."

You perceive "reality" in much the same way you do a picture on a television screen. The TV picture is composed of thousands of tiny "bits," or dots, which combined give you the total image. Sounds, tastes, smells, and tactile feelings are also the result of a combination of thousands of "bits" involving wave frequencies, chemical configurations, and electromagnetic patterns.

You can recall the bits in the same design and order that you received them or you can replay them in new combinations. When sensory bits stored in your brain's cortex are replayed the way you received them, you experience the memory of a once-lived situation. When you rearrange the bits, the result is a dream or image of something that never actually "happened." The bits happened, but their particular combination is a new experience for you.

The power of your imagination and imagery is a function of your ability to retrieve those recorded sensory bits. All imagery involves your recall of sensory bits once recorded in your cortex. The more bits you are able to recall the more vivid your image will be. The same principle applies in a television image. The more dots on the screen per square inch, the clearer the picture.

BEGIN BY RECALLING SENSORY COMPONENTS

You are learning how to imagine so clearly that your image will effect changes in your reality. While it is true that images consist of sensory bits, these units of information are too tiny to retrieve individually. Restructuring an image dot by dot is unnecessarily tedious.

The next largest unit of information constituting an image is the sensory component. This is where you begin. Sensory components taken together equal sensations. Sensations combined equal images.

Let's review, this time starting with the whole, the image. Imagining refers to recalling an effect in all five senses. Your five senses are sight, hearing, touch, smell, and taste. Each of these five basic senses is composed of sensory components. Many, many sensory bits combine to form a sensory component, just as a small area of red on a TV screen is composed of tens of tinier red units.

Now, let's examine the sensory components. Sight has two basic components: *hue* and *saturation*. Hue refers to the particular color of objects you see in your world. Saturation is the intensity, or lightness and darkness of these colors.

Hearing also has two components: *pitch* and *volume*. Pitch relates to the frequency of the sounds you hear, how high or low they seem to you. Volume is the loudness of these sounds.

Touch has three components: *temperature, pressure,* and *liquidity*. Temperature relates to degrees of hot and cold you experience. Pressure entails gradations of lightness and heaviness you can sense. Liquidity is a term devised to denote increments of wetness and dryness.

Taste and smell have four common components: *salt, sour, sweet,* and *bitter*. These components in various combinations constitute all tastes and smells you've ever experienced.

Master the retrieval of these sensory components and you have mastered your reality. Learn to create an image vivid as reality and it will become reality!

As you will come to see, retrieving sensory components is purely a matter of concentration. You recall a sensory component the same way you remember a date, or where you hid a piece of jewelry. You simply *try* to remember what a certain color looked like, how food smelled and tasted, how a touch felt, what was distinctive about a sound.

COMPONENTS OF THE BEACH SCENE

Your *Beach Scene* is specifically designed to give you practice in recalling a wide range of sensory components. All three primary hues of red, yellow, and blue along with secondary hues of white, pink, silver, purple, gold, crimson, and scarlet are included. Saturation of the sky varies from brilliant blue to deep purple. Saturation of the sunset also varies as it goes from blazing gold, amber, red, scarlet, and crimson to darker intensities and finally purple. The saturation of the entire seascape changes, passing from dazzling sunlit brilliance to starlight.

All possible audio components are also present. The waves are loud and low, becoming soft and low as you leave the shore and mount the mound. The cry of gulls is loud and high, varying in volume as they circle overhead.

Two of the three tactile components are represented, temperature and liquidity. The sand is hot and dry, becoming cold and wet as you approach the water's edge. The sun is hot, the twilight cool. The beach is dry, the water wet.

One of the four components for taste and smell is included in the *Beach Scene*. The air tastes and smells of salt which is also deposited upon your lips.

This is therefore how you create an image: by individually recalling separate sensory components and putting them altogether to form a whole. You will learn to use more of the available sensory components in the next chapter.

FOUR

Developing Sensory Recall

☐Making your images vivid enough to produce the positive changes you desire in reality is dependent on your facility for sensory recall, your ability to remember your past sensory experiences. In Chapter Four you'll learn to recall the remaining sensory components available to you for creating vivid imagery. Once you have developed these you'll be the master of the entire gamut of sensations comprising your standard five-sensory world.

MOUNTAIN CABIN SCENE

After you have practiced your *Beach Scene* for a week, it's time to go on to the next image. It builds upon the imagery skills you've gained from rehearsing your first image. Try to work three times a day for a week on this one also.

MOUNTAIN CABIN SCENE:

"You are in a cabin in the mountains. It's midnight, the dead of winter. Hear the *soft*, *high* howling of the wind outside. You are sitting in front of a fire, gazing fixedly into the flames.

"Feel the *heat* from the flames, the *warmth* from the fire. There is a prickling, almost itching sensation in your thighs, the *heat* on the front of your body is so intense.

"Smell the *sweet* smoke from the burning pine logs. Hear the *loud*, *high* crackling of the logs as the sap hits the fire. See the flickering shadows on the wall. The only source of light comes from the *orange* fire. The rest of the cabin is in *purple* darkness.

"Now you get up. Walk over to the window. The panes are covered with a lace-like pattern of frost. Put your *warm* fingertips to the *cold*, hard glass of the windowpane. Feel their *warmth* melt the ice.

"Look outside. The night is clear, the sky filled with stars. There are tall ever*green* trees casting deep *purple* shadows across the snowy *whiteness*. Everything has a *bluish* tinge to it. Even the snow looks *blue*.

"You are going to open the window. Feel it give way against the *pressure* of your hand. It opens! Take a big, deep breath of *cool*, clean, crisp, pure, fresh, mountain air. Your entire rib cage collapses in total, utter relaxation. It feels so good to breathe. Smell the sharp, *bitter* scent of the pine. Reach out and pick a pine needle. Chew it. Your mouth puckers at the pungent, *bitter* flavor.

"Walk back over to the fire. Lie down beside the flames on a bearskin rug. The *sweet* smell of the smoke, the *loud*, *high* crackling of the logs, the *soft*, *high* howling of the wind, the flickering *orange* of the fire . . . all those sights and sounds and smells getting very, very far away as you drift and float and dream in that cabin that winter's night."

REACTIONS AND USES

One of the first benefits you'll notice from practicing imagery is that you'll be sleeping better. Your sleep will be deep, restful, and undisturbed, and you'll awaken refreshed. The *Mountain Cabin Scene* is particularly effective at improving your sleep because it ends with the suggestion, "You drift and float and dream," as you doze off by the fireplace.

Mat, 62, a screenwriter, complained of chronic insomnia starting from when he was age 7, and his mother, a night duty nurse, would wake him up at midnight to give him his supper. "Lately I've been mixing my sleep medication with vodka," he said, "to get a stronger effect. I know this is bad. You should never mix a drug with alcohol, but it's the only way I can get even three hours of sleep a night. I feel rotten in the morning, but it's better than no sleep at all." Mat taped the *Mountain Cabin Scene* and played it every night after he got into bed. In two weeks he was drifting off without the vodka. In a month he began reducing the medication he took to sleep. On occasion he still takes a sleeping pill, but the frequency is decreasing. He no longer uses alcohol and he awakens rested.

Not only your sleep, but your breathing will improve from your practicing the *Mountain Cabin Scene*. Deep, regular breathing ensures a sufficient oxygen supply to your brain and tissues and is the foundation to good health. Your continued recall of deeply breathing "cool, clean, fresh, crisp, pure" air with the resulting overwhelming relaxation of your rib cage conditions you to breathe properly in reality.

Maurine, 39, a manager for a city department of parks and recreation, had been asthmatic for as long as she could recall. "I remember missing a lot of school in the spring, during hayfever season in New York." she said. "Mother once told me she didn't think I'd live out my childhood. I was always being hospitalized with asthma attacks. I hated that feeling of not being able to breathe. Just the thought of it would bring on another attack. They went away for a while when I was a teenager. And when I moved to California I thought I was out of the woods for good. Lately, though, I'm having trouble breathing again. Maybe it's all that pollen from my hikes with the Sierra Club. I hate to give that up. I love the outdoors."

Practicing the *Mountain Cabin Scene* helped Maurine to *conceive* of taking deep, easy breaths. She was so sensitized from childhood on to expect to have trouble breathing that, as she explained, just the thought of an attack brought one on. If her thinking of faulty breathing could produce that effect, so could her thought of deep, healthy breathing produce that result. To this day Maurine recalls the *Mountain Cabin Scene* to relax her breathing whenever she feels a shortness of breath, the signal she may be heading for an asthma attack.

YOUR IMAGERY PRODUCES REAL PHYSIOLOGICAL EFFECTS

What you imagine directly influences the systems of your body. You can exercise control over your circulatory system using the *Mountain Cabin Scene*. If you imagine cold in an area, blood leaves that region of your body. If you recall heat, blood congests in the part of your body you are focusing on. People often react to this image with statements such as, "My nose went numb when I sniffed that cold air," or "I got prickly feelings in my thighs sitting in front of the fire."

When I went over and felt the nose of one man who said it had gone numb, it actually felt cold! The blood was *really* gone. His imagery had produced a real physiological effect. When I examined the legs of patients who reported prickly sensations I could see a real redness. They had managed to get their blood to concentrate there simply by imagining heat in that part of their body. You can use the suggestion for heat recall that comes from imagining sitting in front of the cabin fire for several things. One of them is to keep your skin free from blemishes. Your recall of heat in your skin and the resulting congesting of blood there brings nutrients to the skin and dries up eruptions.

Sandy, a 38-year-old buyer for the women's wear department of a major store, had an embarrassing outbreak of psoriasis a month before her scheduled wedding to Stan, 42, an electrical contractor. She'd dated Stan over seven years, always intending to marry him, but feeling pressured whenever he tried to set the date. She wanted children and finally the pressure of her own biological time clock led her to agree on a time. "I love him. I want to marry him," she told me. "I really do. I don't know what all the fuss is about. Why can't I just go through with it without breaking into a rash?" Sandy had thought out her marriage to Stan carefully and made an intelligent decision to get married. There really wasn't any need for her to endure the psoriasis. I had her practice the *Mountain Cabin Scene* focusing on her recall of heat all over her body as she sat in front of the fire. By the time of her wedding, her skin had cleared.

You can also use your ability to recall heat to intensify your sexual arousal and improve your love life. The male erection and female arousal are both products of a congestion of blood in the genital area. You can therefore create sexual feelings by recalling heat in the area of your genitals. The suggestion, "There is a prickling, almost itching sensation in your thighs, the heat on the front of your body is so intense," is especially effective in increasing your sex drive and sexual prowess.

After Mark used relaxation and dissociation from the *Beach Scene* to heighten his sensuality and detach himself from guilt over having sex since his wife died, I taught him to use the *Mountain Cabin Scene* to directly induce sexual arousal. He was to practice this image for a week, increasing his ability to recall heat in his genital area. Then, when he was making love to a woman, I suggested he concentrate on recalling heat when he attempted penetration. This exercise not only helped maintain his erection by directing blood there, it gave him something to take his mind off his expectation of failure, a big factor in all cases of male impotence. After working with this technique for a month, Mark was able to maintain an erection after penetration on an average of 30 seconds, real progress from his original complaint of losing potency immediately on penetration.

If you have problems in your own sex life, I suggest you try using these methods as they are presented. You may want to look at the glossary in the back for a compendium of all images to be used for sexual enhancement. Experiment. Some exercises work better for some people than others. One method might be sufficient, or you may want to try more. I would bet, however, that your problem will be corrected before you've tried all the imagery techniques available to treat it.

Magrite also benefited from recalling heat in her treatment to regain positive sexual feelings. She had successfully used relaxation and dissociation from the *Beach Scene* to start feeling sexy again and detach herself from the horrible memory of her brother molesting her. Now I asked her to hone her powers of heat recall by practicing the *Mountain Cabin Scene* for a week. Then, the next time she made love, I suggested she concentrate on recalling the sensation of heat in her vaginal area. It's not necessary to do the whole image during sex, only the pertinent part, remembering heat from the fire.

Fortunately, Magrite was currently dating Jim, a sensitive man, who unlike most of the other men she'd seen, was understanding and would go only as far sexually as she was comfortable with. "He's so gorgeous, women come after him," she said. "He's secure. He doesn't take it as an insult if I'm not able to make love to him. Other guys just don't get it. Even when I tell them my problem they see it as a challenge. They think they can make it all better for me by being great lovers and that only makes it worse." As in Mark's case, Magrite's focus on heat recall during sex helped her not only because it directed blood to her genital area, thus arousing her, it also took her mind off any thoughts of her brother that might still be blocking her feeling good about sex. After working on this technique a couple of weeks, she reported, "There are times when it actually feels good." She smiled. "That's when my concentration is the best, when my recall of heat is most vivid." Let's take a close look at what goes into making your imagery vivid enough to produce sexual arousal and the other effects you'll be using it for.

PSYCHOPHYSICAL PRINCIPLES USED TO MAKE YOUR IMAGE VIVID

I've designed your images to help you make use of certain basic psychophysical principles. As I mentioned, psychophysics is the branch of psychology that studies the effects of physical processes on your mental state, how energy forms such as light and sound affect your senses.

A basic psychophysical principle is that complementary colors placed next to each other serve to intensify each other's brilliance. Great artists such as Constable, Van Gogh, and Seurat made use of this principle to enhance their paintings, to make them more vibrant and lifelike.

Common complementary colors are red/green, blue/orange, and yellow/purple. If you put these colors next to each other you will make them more vivid. If you study the works of master artists you will often find these colors in combination.

Your *Mountain Cabin Scene* shows you how to use the principle of complementary colors to intensify the visual component of your image. The inside of the cabin is fiery orange, while the outside is cool blue. Both the orange and the blue are thus enhanced by your imagining them next to each other. It is important to keep this principle in mind when you begin to imagine your goals. You may choose to incorporate complementary colors to make your image more visually intense.

You also use contrast of saturation in your image to make it more vivid. You imagine brilliant fire next to dark shadow. You imagine deep shadows cast on brilliant white snow. Contrast makes your image clearer. Think of the contrast button on your TV set. You always get a better picture with high contrast.

In keeping with our television analogy, a good picture involves not only sharp contrast but clarity. Outlines of objects are crisp and clean. In your image of the mountain cabin, the night is clear. Strive for contrast and clarity in all your imagery.

COMPONENTS OF YOUR MOUNTAIN CABIN SCENE

It always helps if you give attention to detail when you use imagery. The lace-like pattern of frost on the windowpane is a good example of an element included in your image to strengthen your ability for creating details. Achieve contrast, clarity, and detail and the visual part of your imagery will be superb.

Two colors not used in your *Beach Scene*, orange and green, are a part of this image to increase the range of hues you are able to retrieve. Image by image you'll add new skills to make your imagining vivid.

New sounds with the same audio components included in your *Beach Scene* are introduced in the *Mountain Cabin Scene*. They are the high-pitched wind and loud, high-pitched crackling logs.

Your tactile sensation of temperature is heightened by having you recall it in its extremes. From the warm sunshine and cold water of your *Beach Scene* you progress to the blazing, prickling heat of fire and the icy cold of frost in your *Mountain Cabin Scene*. Pressure, one of the three components of touch, is introduced to you for the first time when you imagine pressing your hand against the window to open it.

The *Mountain Cabin Scene* also introduces you to two new gustatory and olfactory sensations: bitter, as you experience in your taste and smell of the pine needles, and sweet, as you sense in your smell of the smoke.

GARDEN SCENE: BEEFING UP YOUR RECALL OF TASTE AND SMELL

Taste and smell are usually the weakest sensations in people's imagery. Sight is often the easiest to recall. This is probably due to our visual preoccupation with reading, television, and movies. Hearing runs a close second. Again we may have the movie, TV, and record industries to thank for this.

I designed the following *Garden Scene* to help make your recall of taste and smell more vivid. What you imagine should be experienced equally in all five senses. This scene will help you build up the senses that are hardest for you to recall so that you can form a totally potent image.

GARDEN SCENE:

"You are standing, gazing intently at a brilliant red sun hovering near the horizon. Now you close your eyes.

"Begin to see leaves of brilliant *green*, shimmering in the moonlight. You are suddenly in the middle of a vast garden, a garden that stretches for miles and miles. It is midnight. It is midsummer. The moon is full and *silver*, the sky, clear, filled with stars. The air is *warm* and balmy. Hear the *low, soft* rustle of a breeze through the leaves.

"You are walking down a path on either side of which are tall orange trees laden with oranges. They glow phosphorescent in the moonlight, brilliant *orange* against deep *green* foliage. The oranges are ripe. They hang heavy from their branches. There are oranges on the ground. The *sweet* scent of oranges permeates the air.

"Reach up. Pick an orange. Feel the coarse outer surface of the peel. Now you peel the fruit. Feel the soft, moist inner surface. Bite into the orange. The *sweet* orange juice squirts into your mouth.

"You continue walking. Suddenly you come to an intersection, where two paths cross. You turn right, going down a path on either side of which are lemon trees. Pick a lemon. Peel it. Smell the *sour*, lemony fragrance of the rind. Bite into the lemon. The *sour* lemon juice spurts into your mouth. Your cheeks pucker, the saliva flows, as you suck the *sour* lemon juice.

"And you continue walking. Next, you come to a long, descending *white* marble staircase, glistening in the moonlight. You begin to descend the stairs. Each step downward you go deeper and deeper relaxed. When you reach the base of the stairs you will be in a profound state of relaxation.

"You are now standing at the base of the stairs. Before you is a massive marble pool. All around the pool are *red*, and *white*, and *yellow* roses, velvety soft in the moonlight, covered with dew. The *sweet* smell of roses is heavy in the air.

"Remove your clothes. Glide into the *cool* liquid of the pool. The water is filled with millions of rose petals. Float, buoyant on your back in the rose water, gazing up at the stars.

"Now you get out of the water. The *cool* night air touches your *wet* skin, sends chills down your back. Gooseflesh appears.

"You smell *sweet* smoke. Turn in the direction from which the smoke is coming. See a forested area at the far side of the pool. Walk toward it. Pass through the trees.

"There before you is a blazing bonfire of burning leaves. It smells like autumn. It smells like fall. You lie down in a bed of *dry*, *warm* leaves . . . the sweet scent of earth beneath you, the night sky above you. You drift, you float, you dream . . . that midsummer's night."

REACTIONS AND USES

Developing your facility for the recall of taste and smell as the *Garden Scene* teaches you to do is very important in helping you to create vivid imagery. The more real your imagery is to you in all five senses, the more power it has; the more you can use it to improve your reality. It's amazing how intense the sensations you create by recalling them from memory can become. I remember, for example, that two days after I'd first given Audrey the *Beach Scene* she called me saying she had a strong taste of salt on her tongue ever since her session. She was about to call the bottled water people to complain about how salty the water tasted when she realized this perception of salt was a figment of her imagination, the residual effect of recalling salt on her lips in the *Beach Scene*.

WEIGHT CONTROL

You can use your heightened facility for recalling taste and smell that the *Garden Scene* helps you to develop by applying it to the behavior modification technique of covert sensitization. This is a treatment method whereby you turn yourself off to something by imagining a distaste for it. There are many things you might wish to turn off or sensitize yourself to: fattening foods, alcohol, drugs, cigarettes, even a lover who has been bad for you and you're having trouble getting out of your mind. The key to using the sensitization technique effectively is to imagine you're having a negative reaction to whatever you now crave and want to get out of your system. Good recall of taste and smell play a primary role in making your aversive image strong enough to turn you off to the object of your desire in reality.

Sonia, 49, with two sons in their early twenties, started putting weight on when she was 40 and went through a trying divorce. "I married my mother when I married Georgio," she said. "He made me think I couldn't make it without him. Both he and my mother knew every trick in the book to make me feel inadequate. So, even though I finally got wise, I still carried a lot of the beliefs I couldn't make it on my own when I left. I got a job as a travel agent and worked my tail off. I was glad to be on my own, but I overdid it. I got mono. I couldn't exercise, I couldn't work; all I did was eat. Now I'm back to work, but I'm still eating. I'm under so much stress. I think eating relaxes me." Sonia wanted to drop twenty pounds and we immediately set out to accomplish this.

First, I told her she could go on any diet she wished, but I would appreciate it if she restricted cane sugar and bread. I've come across many diets in my practice and I think eliminating bread and sweets is one of the best ways to loss weight safely. Of course everyone's metabolism is different and if you have a diet you prefer, more power to you. As long as it's healthy and you lose weight I won't quibble. Almost everyone is willing to give up sugar, but some like to keep a piece or two of bread. That's okay if it works. My chief concern here is to help you eat the foods you *decide* to eat, to stay on a healthy eating regimen.

Second, I asked Sonia to chart: to take a small pocket notebook and make a record of everything she ate. Along with the food, she was to record the time, place, and activity associated with it when she ate: the time of day; where she was, such as the kitchen, garden, car; and what she was doing in conjunction with her eating. Was she talking to friends, watching television, on the phone, what? I also asked her to write down the food *before* she ate it. This helps break the chain of behaviors leading to eating and gives you a full awareness of what you are doing. People with weight problems often go on automatic pilot when they fall off their diets so they won't have to think about their transgressing. Above all, the charting gives you an accounting of your behavior, so that you know *exactly* what foods need working on in imagery. You can give yourself a general affirmation for weight control such as, "I resist food easily," but you cannot give yourself a general image. It's impossible to simply imagine "food." You must know what kind of food, down to the last detail, before you can construct an image of it.

Third, when Sonia brought her first charting in I examined it carefully and saw that her one sin had been three chocolate chip cookies she'd eaten the night before her session. I created an image for her in which she was to imagine eating a chocolate chip cookie, vividly recalling its taste and smell, and then feeling nauseated for having eaten it. She then imagined avoiding the cookie, leaving the room, and feeling great. She thus rewarded herself for the behavior she desired, resisting eating chocolate chip cookies. This is an example of a specific image for a specific problem. By practicing the *Garden Scene*, a lesson in sensory recall, you help make these kinds of images stronger.

To illustrate how you can create your own sensitization image to turn you off to a special food, a specific image for a specific problem, let's pretend you have a problem with chocolate. You like it much too much, but it doesn't like you. You're gaining weight and are peppered with blemishes. The following is a scenario you can make up just as I did for Sonia:

"You are sitting in your living room. It's 8 P.M. Really be there. What are you wearing? How do you feel? What is the room temperature? Notice the arrangement of the furniture, the colors in the room. Before you, on a table, is a white plate. On the plate is a square of chocolate fudge. Sniff the fudge. Smell the chocolate. Pick up the square. Feel it between your fingers. Bite into it. Feel it give way between your teeth. Taste the chocolaty flavor. Swallow. Take another bite. And another.

"Every bite you take you notice a growing distension in your stomach, a feeling of nausea. You have the urge to vomit. You throw up all over the table. Gobs of slimy vomit everywhere. Notice the sour, rancid taste and smell of puke, the sweet taste of chocolate. Swish the vomit and chocolate around in your mouth. Swallow. You have another urge to retch.

"Stand up. Leave the room. The moment you are out of taste and smell of the chocolate, you feel fine. Take a big, deep breath of fresh air. Feel wonderful. Experience the clean taste of mint in your mouth. From this point forth, whenever you taste chocolate, you will experience the same revolting sensations and desire to escape chocolate that you just did."

You needn't pair vomit with the thing you wish to turn off to when creating your own sensitization image. Anything that already turns you off will do. Patients have pictured everything from rotting flesh to smelly socks. This technique works equally well with drugs, cigarettes, and alcohol. Just remember to be specific. What drugs, what brand of cigarettes, what kind of liquor?

You can also use negative imagery to turn yourself off to a lover you need to get out of your mind. If he's treated you badly or left you for someone else, aversive imagery can be especially effective. Work at recalling all the negative sensory experiences associated with your lover: the taste of his/her mouth in the morning; smell of the feet after a hard day; snoring, belching, coughing; touch of his/her body when sticky and perspiring; how he/she looks in the early morning when sick or hung over. Bring these images to mind whenever you find yourself yearning for his/her return. (For more detailed methods using imagery to get over a lover, you might try reading my book, *Breaking Free: 90 Ways to Leave Your Lover & Survive*.)

If the use of aversive imagery bothers you, apply only the last part of the technique described to turn yourself off to chocolate. Imagine sitting in your living room before the fudge. Sniff it, but don't eat it. Walk out of the room, take a deep breath, and feel fantastic! Imagine that you feel marvelous for *not eating* the fudge. But please remember to make that fudge you resist as real as you can in your mind. Sonia never touched chocolate again after practicing sensitizing imagery for three days. She also learned to use the relaxation produced by the first three images I've given you to substitute for the momentary stress reduction she was getting from eating. Naturally, the temporary release and relaxation she initially experienced from giving in to her hunger drive were too high a price to pay for the feelings of self-recrimination and low self-worth that settled in later. With imagery to relax her she no longer needed to gorge herself.

ANOREXIA

Sometimes you may need just the opposite effect. You don't wish to turn off to something, but on. Your life would be better if you liked something *more*. This is especially true if you have a phobic response. You'd be much happier, for example, if you could feel more comfortable when flying, standing in elevators, shopping in crowded supermarkets, or driving on an expressway. Maybe you'd like to turn on more to sex and get more enjoyment out of that. Most people can't imagine wanting to turn on more to food, but if you have trouble gaining weight, as I have all my life, have a poor appetite, or are anorexic, the *Garden Scene* can help you turn on as well as off to food. Turning on to something you've grown to dislike is called "desensitization," and I'll show you how to do it.

Marnie, 17, a junior in high school, weighed 84 pounds and was still losing weight. She'd been hospitalized twice for anorexia and her doctors wanted her to go in again, but she hated the hospital and was fighting them. Fear of another hospitalization was what prompted her to see me. "They won't let me exercise, not even swim, until I get my weight up to 90 pounds," she complained. "I hate my parents. They're so demanding and rigid: 'Wash the car. . . . Clean your room.' All they do is give orders. Now they're threatening to take me to the hospital if I don't eat what they say."

Marnie was filled with anger and as I talked with her I came to see she felt she gave up control when she was angry. She hated giving up control. Not eating made her feel she had control. It was a way of getting back what she felt she lost from her anger. Not all her anger was directed at her parents. She felt both academic pressure and pressure to be popular. A seven-week bike trip in England the previous summer made things worse and precipitated anorexia. "I felt so left out," she said. "I didn't get along with the group, especially two of the guys. I was cut off, alienated, and unconnected. I was so miserable. I felt worthless."

"Eating gives you more control, not less," I told Marnie. "I want you to be able to picture yourself hungry, eating, and feeling in control." I asked her to practice the *Garden Scene*, imagining herself enjoying eating the delicious oranges and feeling self-control for doing so. The same technique will work to turn you on to eating.

The key is to imagine not only that you are hungry and eating foods you wish to like, but also that you enjoy eating them and feel good about yourself for doing so. Marnie used the relaxation she gained from practicing the *Beach* and *Mountain Cabin* scenes to counter her anger. She could not be angry and profoundly relaxed at the same time. And she used the *Garden Scene* to help her conceive of eating and feeling good about herself in the process.

ENHANCING SEX

Food is not the only thing you can turn yourself on to using the *Garden Scene*. Your sex life can also be greatly improved using this image. Its focus on your recall of taste, smell, and touch intensifies your sensitivity in these senses. Evolutionarily, these three senses have been the primary elicitors of sexual arousal. Faulty conditioning has caused many people to inhibit these senses and feel that tastes and smells associated with the sex act are "dirty." All five senses are capable of arousing you and therefore you should use and develop all five to attain a strong and balanced sexual response. Both Magrite and Mark were able to build and intensify positive sexual feelings using the *Garden Scene* to strengthen their gustatory and olfactory sensuality. Focusing attention on taste and smell in imagery heightens their potency in reality. It's a five-sensory world. Make use of it!

RESTFUL SLEEP

The *Garden Scene* is, in effect, a midsummer night's dream and is particularly effective for giving you a deep, restful sleep. I taught Mat to combine its effects with the *Mountain Cabin Scene* to cure his insomnia. The ending, "You drift, you float, you dream . . . that midsummer's night," makes it especially easy for you to go directly from your image into sleep, and you can induce it at bedtime.

*   *   *

While all images progressively serve to help you develop your concentration, deepen relaxation, and gain greater control over your basic physiological processes, some are outstanding for treatment of certain problems and I will continue to highlight them for you in the appropriate chapters that follow. Now let's look at how the *Garden Scene* is constructed to give you its power.

YOUR VISUALIZING A RED SUN MAKES YOUR GREEN MORE VIVID

The *Garden Scene* begins by your imagining staring intently into a brilliant red sun. You next imagine closing your eyes in the scene, although in reality your eyes are already closed.

It is important for you to know that all the psychophysical principles that apply in your reality also apply in your imagery. If in reality you stare at a brilliant red sun and then close your eyes, you will see an afterimage, an area of intense color in the complementary color of the object you were looking at. Gazing at a bright red object and then closing your eyes will produce the complementary after-image of dazzling green.

Now, if you *imagine* concentrating on a red sun and then *imagine* closing your eyes in the image, the complementary color, green, will appear to you just as if you had gone through the procedure in reality. Most importantly the green will be of a far more vivid intensity than you could ever imagine without your *first* imagining gazing into the red. The afterimage color is always of heightened intensity.

The *Garden Scene* helps you use this principle to intensify the color coming at the beginning of your image. The actual description of the garden begins with a picture of brilliant green leaves shimmering in the moonlight. Your previous instruction to imagine gazing at a red sun and then closing your eyes is included only to heighten the green which follows. You'll notice that there is no mention of a green afterimage, per se. It is understood that green will appear automatically by your first imagining its complementary color and imagining closing your eyes. I prefer to see the color in the form of a sun because a sun is of brilliant intensity. The brighter the object imagined, the more vivid the afterimage.

COMPONENTS OF THE GARDEN SCENE

While you get no new colors in this image, you learn to intensify the oranges, yellows, greens, whites, and reds present by imagining them phosphorize in the moonlight. The colors shimmer and glow, almost as if under black light. This is a further extension of your imaginative capacities.

Saturation of the colors varies within the limited range of moonlight. This helps you form more precise discriminations, making you more aware of the subtleties of lightness and darkness.

You are given a new combination of pitch and volume in the soft, low rustling of the leaves in the breeze. In your prior two images you experienced loud, high screamings of gulls and snapping of burning pine logs; loud, low waves pounding the shore; and soft, high wind blowing around the cabin.

Tactile components of temperature and liquidity reappear in the form of the cool, wet pool and warm, dry leaves by the bonfire.

My primary purpose in giving you this image, however, is to beef up your ability to recall the sensory bits composing your memory of taste and smell. Your recalling the aroma and flavor of the sweet oranges and sour lemons serves this purpose.

USING PROPS TO INTENSIFY YOUR IMAGERY

Sometimes you can heighten a given sense or senses in your imagery by plugging in the actual sensory experience while practicing your image. With the *Garden Scene* you can use real oranges and lemons to make your imagery more vivid.

When in the image you imagine smelling and biting into an orange or a lemon, smell and bite into a real piece of fruit you have placed by your side for that purpose. Keep your eyes closed and concentrate on keeping the image intact.

Try using these fruit props the first three days that you practice your *Garden Scene*. You'll find that then you can recall the smell and taste of orange and lemon much more easily. The sensations you experience most recently are the easiest for you to recall. By putting fresh sweet and sour sensory bits into your memory banks you make these sensations readily available for you to recall when constructing vivid imagery.

You can use a prop for any sense you may be having trouble with. John, 26, had been working three years for a large carpet distributor laying padding. Several associates with less company time had already gotten salary hikes while he had been passed by.

I worked several weeks with John, having him *imagine* himself in various encounters with his boss. In each situation John was to imagine himself asking for a raise and then solving in his mind the appropriate response to any objections he might get.

Persuasion is a matter of making appropriate responses. Whether you are trying to convince someone to buy your product or asking for a raise, success is determined by how you handle a series of successive situations. You continue countering objections until your customer or boss can't come up with any more. At that point you've sold your product or gotten your raise.

I asked John to imagine the wildest kinds of objections for a pay increase that his boss could make. No matter how wide a curve his boss threw him, he was to imagine himself coming back with a good counter. You can effectively prepare for any situation by first imagining yourself and the person you want to influence face to face while they create problems for you and you solve each one appropriately.

Most importantly, I advised John to end each practice session by imagining his boss giving him the raise. It was at this point that we hit a snag.

"I can imagine the craziest situations ever," John told me, "but I can't hear the boss say, 'You got the raise.' I can see his mouth moving, but I can't imagine hearing those particular words."

I decided that the easiest solution in this case was to use an audio prop. I asked John to tape record the words, "You got the raise," disguising his voice as much as possible to sound low and husky like that of his boss. Then, at the end of each practice session he was to turn on the recorder. The taped words then played along with John imagining that his boss was speaking them.

After using this "audio prop" for a week, John was finally able to imagine hearing his boss speak the words he wanted to hear. At that point John asked for his raise, and while his boss initially objected, John was able to come back immediately with a good counter. He was delighted to tell me, "I actually *talked* the man into giving me the money I wanted. That's something I never thought of before." You can use a prop temporarily, such as John did, to help you recall a certain sense in your imagery. At that point you can throw away your crutch.

RECHARGING AND MERGING ENERGIES

People often tell me what remarkable results their imagery is having while working. They describe "refresher periods" where they are able to recharge themselves by momentarily slipping into an image.

I always go into these imagery states with my patients and I agree that it's a wonderfully relaxing opportunity to rekindle my energy, but I also believe it makes me more in tune with the other person. I find that any image will take me to this psychic space if my concentration is strong enough; the image provides the means for generating the energy and focus necessary for getting me there. It's as though we each leave the shells of our present existence to enter a shared space we mutually create, a sort of psychic common ground beyond the barriers of conventional thought and reality, a space where we are in essence of one thought, one sensorium, *one mind.* Call it, if you will, a state of spiritual rapport, love in the highest sense—knowing each other completely, breaking the boundary between souls, merging energies. Whatever you call it, it feels divine, limitless, eternal, and complete. It is often the beginning of a yearning, a desire to be *in that state*, the one we create together, forever. I look forward to your having that experience.

FIVE

Pain
Control

☐Anne, a 33-year-old legal secretary on heavy doses of pain medication, married six years to David, 33, a computer programmer, came to me seeking treatment for chronic fatigue, menstrual pain, itching and tender vaginal warts, and headaches. She was also diabetic and required two insulin shots in the stomach every day. Her reaction was amazing the first time I gave her the *Garden Scene*. "That was super," she sighed, coming out of the image. She playfully cocked her head of short red hair that framed her freckled face. "My mouth still feels funny from the lemon." She looked at me blearily, a faraway look in her green eyes.

Then she smiled and rose. In a state she described as "the deepest relaxation ever," she left my office. Here is her account of what followed:

"As I made my way down the hall to the elevator, I felt my energy grow. By the time I reached the ground floor I had an incredible sense of alertness, focus. I remember walking out onto Wilshire Boulevard and hearing what I considered a deafening gobbling sound above me. I looked up and was amazed to discover this clamor was nothing more than the cooing of two doves on the fourth-floor window ledge. It didn't seem possible birds could sound so loud. By the time I crossed Wilshire I was flooded with a sea of childhood memories. I vividly recalled my mother telling me stories around a campfire, how I used to eat the petunias in her flower bed, all sorts of crazy, happy childish antics I used to delight in.

"Suddenly I realized I was no longer walking. I glanced at my watch and saw I'd been standing there on Linden Street over fifteen minutes looking at the sun set through the trees. I swore I couldn't have been there over a minute. Then I realized something else with a joy that took my breath away. My pain was gone!

"I got into my car and headed homeward, driving into the setting sun. I don't know how long I'd been in motion, but I remember becoming gradually aware of a humming around my car. The sound was loud and all around me. It was more exciting than frightening. I was aroused by it. It was kind of sexual, but more electrical, like a surge of adrenaline. Then I noticed a rhythm to it as if it were somehow in pace with the car, like the car's life force.

"The sea of car lights around me appeared as rubies and diamonds, a molten strand of jewels flowing to and from the sunset. My arousal intensified and I felt powerfully female, perspiring heavily, melting into a living ribbon of highway, charged by the heat of the pavement. My energy soared. I felt omnipotent, all powerful. I owned the buildings, the cars, the road. I was hot and wet and charged and nothing else mattered. I was about to discover America!"

The phenomena Anne experienced are things that you too can

expect from practicing imagery: profound relaxation, growing energy, lowered positive sensory thresholds, vivid childhood memories, time distortion, and pain control. You'll learn more about your power to manipulate time in the next chapter. For now, let's focus on your ability to eliminate pain.

I'll discuss with you in this chapter three imagery methods you can use to free yourself of any kind of physical discomfort: 1. Relaxation, 2. Negative Hallucination, 3. Glove Anesthesia. Anne's episode illustrates how you can use profound, concentrated relaxation to raise your sensory threshold to the negative stimuli of pain and lower it to wonderful, new positive things around you. Her soaring, powerful energy, feeling of oneness with the life force of the elements, and absence of pain were a result of her heightened positive awareness induced by the profound relaxation stemming from the *Garden Scene.* By now you are familiar with how you can use imagery-induced relaxation to raise your pain threshold, as Michael used the *Beach Scene* to eliminate the burning sensation in his left foot. However, the second two pain control methods are new to you and we're going to examine them carefully.

POSITIVE AND NEGATIVE HALLUCINATIONS

A hallucination is an image you perceive as vividly as reality. Research shows that your imagery *can* be as vivid as your reality! This amazing fact was demonstrated in a study that labeled this principle the "Perky Effect." Subjects were asked to imagine various objects on a white wall. Then slides of the objects were flashed on the area where the subject was to imagine them. People with the most vivid imaginations couldn't tell their image from the "real" picture.

This is an amazing laboratory demonstration of just how real your imagery can be. The hypnosis literature is filled with accounts of self-induced positive hallucinations, so real in all five senses that they cannot be differentiated from reality. A hallucination can be in one or any combination of your senses.

Further evidence that imagery can be vivid as your reality comes from the research in the field of physiological psychology with electrode implantations in the brain. The only difference between a hallucination or image and what we term reality is the source of the stimulus. We say that reality comes from outside our brains and imagery comes from inside.

However, it was discovered that if you stimulate certain areas of the brain electrically, hallucinations appear that are every bit as vivid as reality and you cannot distinguish the inside from the outside.

Studies in the area of sensory deprivation provide even more data to substantiate that your imagery can be vivid as reality. It was shown, for example, that if you remove the real world (outside), an imaginary (inside) one as real in appearance will soon materialize. Researchers sensorily deprived subjects, removed the outside world, through a series of devices. They put halved ping-pong balls over the eyes to remove vision. The body was bound to eliminate touch. Nose, mouth, and ears were plugged to eradicate smell, taste, and hearing.

Within six hours a whole new experience, graphic in all five senses, materialized. When the world was taken away, subjects created their own! You have the power to imagine so vividly you can't tell your image from reality. This is the first major step to creation. Some pretty fuzzy imagining can produce some quite fantastic results. The most important thing is that you try to make your images as real as possible. Don't worry if your effects are not hallucinogenic.

"Positive hallucinations" refer to your experiencing something that "is not there." They often occur in your everyday reality. They are especially prevalent if you are *expecting* something. If a friend says he'll be over at 8 P.M. you may begin to "hear things" as the hour approaches. You may run to the door several times swearing you heard a car pull up outside or footsteps on the walkway. If the meeting seems important or significant, if it's a passionately awaited lover or a child whose welfare concerns you, the hallucinations may grow stronger as the time passes eight o'clock. You may even hear a knock at the door or the bell ring, so intense is your expectation. The hallucination may not only be audio. You may be certain you see headlights flash on the wall or detect a whiff of your lover's perfume.

Hallucinations can also be "negative." A negative hallucination is your not experiencing something that "is there." You also can induce them hypnotically or experience them in your everyday reality. They commonly occur when you're deeply involved in something. A friend may speak to you repeatedly and you don't hear a word. That's a good example of a negative audio hallucination. Or you may look everywhere for the fountain pen that is right in front of you, unwittingly negatively visually hallucinating it.

What you want to be able to accomplish for your purposes of pain control is the induction of a negative tactile hallucination. You want to not feel a tactile stimulus that "really" does exist, i.e., your pain. You achieve this by imagining that your pain or your body's afflicted area does not exist. This is an example of a specific image for a specific problem.

Margie, 30, a social worker, married to Sebastian, 31, an attorney, with a 3-month-old girl, Sally, had a debilitating case of rheumatoid arthritis. She was on large doses of prednisone and alternating between other medications as well. Severe joint pain and swelling depressed her because of how much she was having to restrict exercise. "I love athletics," she said. "Sebastian and I really go at it. We love to windsurf. But it's been a long time since I've been able to do that. Plus, I'd like to have another baby." Margie felt pain in her shoulders whenever she lay down and raised her arms.

After she had practiced Images 1 to 3 to build her power of imagining, I asked her to imagine herself lying on her back, raising her arms, and feeling terrific. She was to negatively hallucinate the pain in her image, move as if it did not exist. In a little over a week, practicing three times a day, ten minutes each time, Margie noticed she was beginning to be able to do in reality what she was previously imagining—lift her arms without joint pain. Although still not back to windsurfing, Margie today is able to move from any position without discomfort and is planning the second child she and Sebastian so desire.

As always, the key is for you to first imagine what it is you wish to be able to do in reality. Imagine yourself going through specific actions in your life free of discomfort and in time your reality will match your image.

Although I personally prefer the above technique, imagining yourself already being the way you want to be, there is a variation of it so widely used I feel I should include it here for your benefit. In this method, rather than imagining yourself now pain-free, you imagine the pain leaving you. There are many ways to do this. You may, for example, envision yourself floating in a miraculous liquid into which every discomfort of your body drains. Or a beautiful, healing white light may engulf you, cleansing you of all pain. Experiment. See which you prefer.

Another avenue is for you to not only negatively hallucinate your pain, but negatively hallucinate the portion of your body in which it resides. Imagine that your afflicted foot, leg, arm, back, even head, is detaching from you. Since the painful area is no longer a part of you, it no longer has any influence over your sensorium.

When Peter, 67, a retired advertising executive, severed his Achilles' tendon playing golf at his country club he experienced a pain that was "intense, burning, and agonizing." After surgery he stepped out of his car and popped his grafted tendon.

"The pain was excruciating," he explained. "Nothing I do will fix it. I had more surgery to remove neuromas, tumors growing from the nerve. I tried sympathetic nerve blocks. For three weeks I was pain-free with computerized electrodes implanted in my brain for deep stimulation. Then one day, playing golf, one of the electrodes moved in my head and I was right back to square one. The pain is intolerable. No medication works, not even cortisone. I've been to every pain clinic in the country. The only relief I get is at night. Two to three hours after I lie down, it starts to partially subside. I'm telling you, Doc, I've never been a depressed man, but this thing is making me suicidal."

I instructed Peter to practice the *Beach, Mountain Cabin,* and *Garden* scenes, spending a week on each. The relaxation he was able to gain from these images contributed to raising his pain threshold and he reported his leg was feeling better. I then told him to imagine the following specific image as vividly as he could in all five of his senses:

"You are lying comfortably on your back in bed. It's late evening. The room is dark, but you can make out the outline of your body. You feel totally relaxed. Your breathing is slow, deep, regular.

"Now you notice a strange feeling in your left foot, from the heel to your calf. It seems to be detaching from you, drifting off, floating away . . . floating . . . floating . . . floating away. You can see it now. Glowing white. Whiter and whiter. It dissolves, evaporates. It's gone."

Peter was first able to use this image to get a good night's sleep, pain-free. Feeling more rested in the days, he was then able to use it to remove pain when he was sitting up reading or watching television. Eventually, combining the glove anesthesia technique I'll be showing you next, he was able to get back on the golf course and resume a normal life, free of the agonizing pain that had so tormented him.

GLOVE ANESTHESIA

The term "glove anesthesia" refers to your ability to produce numbness in your hand by recalling cold in that body area and then transferring that anesthesia to any region that needs pain control. By developing this technique, you are in essence learning to control the flow of your blood; your recalling cold causes blood to leave a given part of your body while your recalling heat results in blood congesting in that particular area. This is the procedure most often found in the hypnosis literature to alleviate pain and the one I personally have discovered most effective in treating my clients.

There have been thousands of operations done using hypnoanesthesia, surgery without medication in which the patient feels nothing. James Esdaile, a Scottish surgeon practicing in India, reported hundreds of painless operations between 1840 and 1850 when they ran out of quinine and had no anesthetics other than mind control available. In 1849, Crawford Long, who pioneered the use of ether in America, reported many reputable physicians were recommending hypnosis for pain relief during surgery.

The patient using hypnoanesthesia is totally aware of what is going on during his surgery, he doesn't even feel groggy. He simply doesn't feel the scalpel. He may even carry on a conversation with the surgeon. The early martyrs were said to be experts in this phenomenon, laughing at their tormentors as they were burned at the stake. They transcended the pain threshold and felt nothing as they were burned alive. The glove anesthesia technique is invaluable for healing, pain control, and shutting out all negative physical stimuli. Its emphasis on your control of the circulatory system is the beginning of your gaining more control of all your bodily functions.

MOUNTAIN CABIN SCENE II

The following image will show you how to induce numbness in your right hand and then transfer that anesthesia to your cheek and back to your hand again. Practicing the transfer of anesthesia can be as valuable as learning to induce it. You begin mastering pain control by inducing anesthesia in areas of your body where you have most often experienced it already. You know what it feels like for your hand to go asleep or your cheek to be numb from novocaine, so you start there, imagining cold numbness in your hand and cheek.

It is almost always easier to recall a sensation in an area where you've felt it before. If, for example, you suffer from low back pain, an area of your body where you have probably never before experienced numbness, the procedure to use is for you to induce numbness in your hand first. Then transfer the anesthesia from your hand to your back. Once you have practiced *Mountain Cabin Scene II* three times a day for a week, you are ready to transfer the numbness you induce in your hand to any place in your body you have pain. You practice the hand-to-cheek numbness transfer only until you learn to accomplish a transfer.

In order to induce glove anesthesia you return to your second image, the *Mountain Cabin Scene,* and modify it to incorporate the anesthesia.

MOUNTAIN CABIN SCENE II:

"You are in a cabin in the mountains. It's midnight. Outside the wind is howling. Inside you are sitting in front of a fireplace, staring intently into the flames. Feel the heat from the fire against your skin; feel the warmth from the flames upon your flesh. There is a prickling, almost itching sensation in your thighs, the heat on the front of your body is so intense.

"Smell the smoke from the burning pine logs. Hear the crackling of the logs as the sap hits the fire. See the flickering shadows on the wall. The only source of light comes from the fire. The rest of the cabin is in darkness.

"Now you get up. You are going to go outside. Bundle up. Put on boots, a coat, gloves. You go to the door. Feel it give way against the pressure of your hands. It opens. You take a deep breath of clean, crisp, fresh, pure mountain air. Your entire rib cage collapses in total relaxation. It feels so good to breathe. Smell the pine.

"The night is clear, the sky filled with stars, the moon full and silver. Everything has a bluish tinge to it. Even the snow looks blue. You begin walking down a path on either side of which are tall evergreen trees laden with snow.

"Ten minutes pass . . . twenty minutes . . . thirty minutes. You stop. You take the glove off your right hand. Thrust your right hand into the cold snow, making a fist, compressing the snow into a ball of ice in the palm of your right hand . . . a numb, woodenlike sensation beginning in the palm of your right hand . . . first the size of a pinpoint, then a dime, then a half dollar, spreading like ripples on a pond.

"When you feel that numbness in your right hand, place your right hand upon your right cheek. (Really do this.) Now let the numbness in your hand drain into your cheek. Cheek is becoming numb, just as if novocaine had been injected into it. When all the numbness has drained from your right hand into your right cheek, place your hand again at your side. (Do this physically also.) Now place your hand again upon your cheek. (Do so.) Let the numbness in your hand drain back into your cheek. Cheek is becoming numb, just like a log with nails in it. When all the numbness has drained from your hand back into your cheek, place your hand again at your side. (Do so.)

"Now you put the glove back on your right hand. You turn around. You begin retracing your footsteps through the snow. Ten minutes pass . . . twenty minutes . . . thirty minutes. You are back to the cabin. You go inside. It's warm.

"Walk over to the fireplace. Hold your hands over the fire. Feel the warmth return to them. Lie down by the fire on a bearskin rug. The smell of smoke . . . the crackling of the logs . . . the howling outside of the wind . . . all those sights and sounds and smells getting very, very far away as you drift and float and dream in that cabin that winter's night."

REACTIONS AND USES

Anne practiced the above image for a week, till she learned to induce numbness in her hand, transfer it to her cheek, and transfer it back again. At that point, whenever she had a headache or vaginal pain, she induced numbness in her right hand by recalling the *Mountain*

Cabin Scene II with one modification. Instead of transferring the numbness from her hand to her cheek, she transferred the numbness from her hand to her head or vaginal area. In a week her headaches were gone although some of the vaginal pain persisted.

In time, you may find that you no longer need the whole image to anesthetize yourself. After you have the procedure down you may need only to recall making a fist full of snow to induce the numbness. Eventually you may become so adept at recalling numbness that you can recall and create it directly in the area you wish to be free from pain. Anne did this on her own. "After a while I started imagining that my whole body was lying in the snow all numb. It was so easy I couldn't believe it. I would just lie there and wait for it to happen. It works permanently. I have no more headaches, no more menstrual pain, no itching. I'm off pain pills." The accumulated effects of relaxation from the *Beach, Mountain Cabin,* and *Garden* scenes and glove anesthesia from the *Mountain Cabin II Scene* helped Anne to become pain free. I was amazed at the rapidity of her progress. Creating numbness in your hand, using glove anesthesia, and then developing transfers are effective tools on your road to mastery of pain.

Peter also used glove anesthesia to put a cap on his pain problem. By using imagery-induced relaxation, coupled with imagining that his left leg from his calf down was detaching and evaporating from his body, Peter was able to be pain-free lying flat or sitting up. His Achilles' tendon area still caused him extreme pain, however, when he was standing. "My doctors advise me to get as much exercise as possible," he told me, "but how can I when it hurts so much?"

Peter practiced the image for glove anesthesia for a week. Then he modified it, transferring the numbness from his right hand to his right calf rather than his right cheek. He performed this procedure while he was sitting, relatively pain-free. It's easier to learn this technique if you practice anesthetizing the area of concern when it feels the best rather than the worst. Once Peter was able to transfer anesthesia from his hand to his calf, in a sitting position, he practiced doing it while standing.

Since Peter's pain increased the longer he stood on his leg, he had a built-in hierarchy for practice. Initially he'd transfer the numbness as soon as he stood, then he'd allow progressively longer periods of standing before transferring anesthesia. Soon he was able to use glove anesthesia to eliminate pain when he was walking. The moment he felt a twinge, he'd imagine the scene and induce numbness in his right hand. Then he'd bend down, placing the palm of his hand firmly over his right calf. He'd imagine the transfer of anesthesia and be back up and about in less than a minute. His effects at first lasted about an hour, but the longer he used this technique the longer his pain-free periods became, till finally he could do an entire round of golf with just one fix of glove anesthesia.

Donald, a 63-year-old carpenter, had chest surgery for lung cancer he developed from an asbestos problem on one of his former job sites. His doctors pronounced his surgery a success and he was now undergoing chemotherapy. However, he continued to experience pain in his chest unless he was at rest. He quickly learned to use glove anesthesia to transfer numbness to his chest whenever he was in pain.

You can use the glove anesthesia procedure for a wide variety of pain and pain-related problems, many of which don't respond well to common medical measures. You may even find it an effective combatant against heartburn and nausea. In both of these cases, the technique is to transfer the anesthesia from your hand to your chest and stomach area. Heartburn is especially responsive.

Glove anesthesia also has some beneficial uses that aren't pain-related. Of special note is its use in weight control. While dieting, you can use it to eliminate hunger by transferring anesthesia from your hand to your stomach to "freeze" the hunger pangs. Jill, a 50-year-old overweight waitress, lost over forty pounds using glove anesthesia. The bulk of Jill's weight problem came from the "munchies" that overwhelmed her in the late evening hours when she was watching television. "I don't seem to have any resistance at that time," she said. "I'm so beat from the day, I just give in." I told Jill that whenever she felt an attack of the munchies she should induce glove anesthesia using the *Mountain Cabin Scene II* and transfer that numbness to her stomach to put the munchies out of commission. "It's amazing," she reported. "Once I deaden my stomach, I don't feel anything there. Not even hunger. It's great!"

The more vivid your imagining, the more real you make the cold in your image for glove anesthesia, the stronger will be your results.

WHAT MAKES AN IMAGE REAL?

To make an image seem real, you should experience it in all five senses. Reality comes about through your five senses. The only difference between an image and reality is the *source* of your stimulation or data. Reality comes to you from outside your head. Images come from inside. You can perceive both with identical vividness.

When you create an image, you draw on past sensory data which has been recorded in your cortex. You can retrieve and play data from this sensory memory bank in a staggering array of new combinations and permutations. It does not have to be projected back into consciousness in the same sequence or in the same combinations that it entered. For example, you can play back the reality of a white bird sitting on a blue table as twenty winged white tables setting in a row with no bird present. Fantastic as the image seems, it does have a basis in your reality.

As your range of experience in reality increases so does the amount of information at your disposal for creating new images. Retrieving a bit of sensory data to make an image feels no different than *trying* to remember a fact or a figure. If your image calls for you to be in a mountain cabin, work at recalling what it felt like to be in such a cabin. If you've never been in such a place, recall fire, snow, howling wind, and the taste and smell of pine from other separate experiences, put them together, and *create* a memory of a mountain cabin. It's that simple! You can reorganize bits from your past any way you desire.

To make an image real, therefore, focus on the sensations called for in its production and *remember* times when you actually had these sensations. The process of remembering will trigger the recording. Sometimes this takes considerable energy. Remember the time you struggled to recall a certain date? At first it was buried somewhere, but with determined effort the material surfaced. Your retrieval of a certain smell or sound goes through the same process.

If the sensation you're trying to create in an image is giving you difficulty and it's available to you in reality, search out the real thing. Then try to remember it. For example, if you're trying to anesthetize your right hand by imagining thrusting it into icy snow and you cannot remember what this feels like, do precisely that and immediately attempt to recall the feeling for your image. Or, take an ice cube, clutch it in your hand, and concentrate on the cold numbness that ensues. Then put the ice cube down and immediately try to recall what it felt like. Sensations you've experienced most recently are the easiest to retrieve.

WHAT IF I DON'T GET IT?

Relax. You will. In time. The images always become more real with practice. I suggest you tell yourself that it's not important to get it, that it's okay to totally fail. Even if mastering a particular image to eliminate a certain problem is more important to you than life itself, *tell yourself* that you do not care whether the image seems real or not. This is a hard lesson for many people to learn, but it's at the point where you let go, where you do not force it, that it will all come together. Don't allow yourself to make it too important. That is part of your exercise.

Take the case of Doug, 45, a construction foreman suffering from constant low back pain caused by a job injury when he tried to lift too much weight. Several surgeries and nerve blocks later he still had pain when he lay flat. He'd been on medication for years and "couldn't live without it." His internist, fearing he was becoming addicted, was gradually cutting his dosage and Doug was certain he couldn't go on. He told me that imagery was his last hope. If it didn't work he was going to kill himself.

For several months Doug worked at imagining his hand immersed in ice, numb from fingertips to his wrist. Occasionally he would experience a tingling, the beginning of anesthesia, but then he would lose it. Finally he came in and said this was to be his last visit. I told him to lie down on the couch as there was one more image I wanted to try on him. He refused, saying he'd only come today to announce to me that he was quitting. Treatment of any kind was hopeless.

"I agree," I replied, "but I don't know how else to finish out the hour. You want your money's worth, don't you?" Reluctantly Doug gave in but still insisted he knew it wasn't going to work. I went along with him totally. "Great," I said. "It isn't going to work. Good. Who cares? It's your last visit, anyway."

I'm sure you can guess the end to this story. Doug's back went numb as a rock in the first five minutes. It went numb because he let go and let the image take over.

There's a fine line between trying and pushing. Imagery *does* take energy, it does take work. You can't just lie there with the tape going and doze off, as many of my clients have tended to do. But you also cannot force the issue and will the image to become real. Active recall, not brute force, will make your image materialize. Don't grit your teeth and flex your muscles to get an image going. Direct your total attention to the immediate sensations of the image, not the goal you wish the image to achieve. Don't anticipate. Without anticipation there could be no worry. Without worry it will all happen.

HOW "REAL" MUST AN IMAGE BE TO GET RESULTS?

Not very. This may seem surprising to you since I'm now stressing that you make your images as real as possible to get good results. While it is true that stronger imagery produces stronger results, I am continually amazed by clients who claim they "can't see a thing," yet are able to achieve outstanding results from practicing their images. Obviously something is being shaken up in their heads when they do these exercises, even though it may not *seem* so at the time. Though their images may seem weak, they are nonetheless no longer smoking, drinking, overeating, ejaculating too soon, or whatever. Even if the images are weak, you can conquer many problems. A little relaxation and a barely perceptible image of the *right kind* will take you a long way.

HOW DO I KEEP THE IMAGE FRESH?

Repetition is the key to your learning and you may have to rehearse some images several times before they take effect. There is no set number of times to go over an image you are using to treat a particular problem. Practice until you get results, once or a hundred times. While you may continually modify your images in order to keep their freshness, you may also keep them from going stale by altering your perception rather than the image. You have the power to maintain the "illusion of the first time."

The key to this is, *don't anticipate*. Stay in the now. Concentrate only on the senses involved in your image at the time. Just as a good actor never contemplates his next lines while delivering his present ones, a good imagery subject never flashes on the future while conjuring the present. Rehearse an image *as if* it's the first time you've ever done it. You have no idea what's coming next. That is the exercise!

If you're still having trouble recalling cold vividly enough to induce anesthesia after I've given you all these tips for making your imagery more real, take heart, there is yet another way you can use imagery to create anesthesia and eliminate your pain.

DESERT SCENE

The *Desert Scene* teaches you to induce anesthesia by recalling physical pressure. Sensory recall of cold and/or pressure leads to blood vacating the area of your body that you are focusing on. Remember how, when you sat too long in one position on your leg, it went numb? Or how your arm went wooden from sleeping on it? In both these cases, pressure cut off your circulation and gave you a sense of anesthesia. Just as real pressure can produce numbness in your body, so can imaginary or recalled pressure.

DESERT SCENE:

"You are standing, gazing at a smooth, white wall. Stare fixedly into the white. See nothing else.

"Now you turn around. See a brilliant blue sky, blazing yellow sun, and flat, cracked clay clear to the horizon line. Feel the hot, dry clay beneath your bare feet. There are no trees, no plants, no hills. There is nothing but dried, cracked clay all the way to the vanishing point.

"Feel the warmth from the sun against your face. Feel the heat from the sun's rays against your skin. Begin walking. Your lips feel dry, throat is parched, tongue is thickening. Experience difficulty swallowing. As you go farther and farther, you become thirstier and thirstier.

"Suddenly before you is a clear, freshwater sea. Take off your clothes. Glide into the pure, cool liquid. Drink. Quench your thirst. Float buoyant on your back looking up at the sky. Hours pass. Night falls. The sky is clear, filled with stars.

"Now get out of the water. The cool night air touches your wet skin, sends shivers down your back. Gooseflesh appears. Walk along the shore. Feel the warm sand beneath your feet. The sand is still warm from the day, still retains the heat from the sun.

"Lie down in the sand. A soft, high-pitched wind begins blowing sand over you. Feel the ever-increasing *pressure* as the sand covers you, layer by layer. You feel safe, secure, protected, in a warm cocoon of sand under the desert sky."

REACTIONS AND USES

"I feel so different, it's incredible!" exclaimed Emma, 62, a retired guidance counselor who suffered pain in her right leg after a bad fall. "That sand pressure was nice. My leg feels fine. Tremendous. That's the best I've ever done, although the sky was too low at first. I love to swim, to float. The cocoon of sand was terrific. I really felt protected."

Surprisingly, Emma's pain in her right leg didn't begin until she started physical rehabilitation to regain motion in her paralyzed left leg. She evidently had used her good leg to buffer her fall when a stroke paralyzed her other leg, rendering both legs useless for walking. "I'm so depressed," she told me in her first session. "My husband and I used to do everything, go everywhere together. I painted, studied classical piano, had tons of friends. How I used to entertain! We traveled—a different country every year. We met so many wonderful people on our travels. Now I can't go anywhere. I can barely get out of my wheelchair."

Emma's pain was so severe that she cried through most of our first few sessions together. I first tried using relaxation and glove anesthesia, but she had trouble recalling cold and it wasn't until the *Desert Scene* that she started to respond. Gradually, her recall of "that sand pressure," as she referred to it, led to an end of the pain in her leg.

Unlike the glove anesthesia technique, recalling physical pressure for pain control involves no transfers of sensation. You simply imagine a pressure building in the area where you have discomfort. The *Desert Scene* is especially effective because imagining your body being covered with sand, layer by layer, with ever-increasing pressure, eventuates in anesthetizing nearly all of you. If you wish to focus on one particular area, modify the image to imagine sand gradually covering only the area that is causing pain. If, for example, you wish to eliminate the pain of a stomachache, suggest at the appropriate place in the image, "A gentle breeze is beginning to cover my stomach with sand. I feel the ever-increasing pressure as the sand covers my stomach. Layer by layer . . ."

ENURESIS

You can use the recall of pressure demanded in the *Desert Scene* not only to eliminate pain, but to achieve bladder control. Many cases of enuresis, bedwetting, especially in children and adolescents, are due to the enuretic's not being sensitive enough to the pressure exerted by his full bladder to wake before wetting. He must therefore be trained to lower his sensory threshold to pressure in his bladder area.

You can develop a finer discrimination and lower threshold in any sense modality simply by directing more attention to it. I'm sure you're familiar with the acute hearing of the blind man, the fine color discrimination of the artist, the sensitive taste and smell of the wine taster and gourmet cook, and the precise touch of the sculptor. These are all examples of how you can further develop specific senses through training and concentration. The enuretic is trained to develop greater sensitivity to pressure in his bladder.

Eric, 14, a shy, nervous high-school freshman, came to me to be treated for bedwetting. "I can't believe I'm still doing it," he said, turning red with embarrassment. "Mom always said I'd grow out of it, but here I am. I can't have friends over to sleep with me. I can't go to camp or stay overnight with the guys in a tent. I can never sleep in the same room with anyone. It's mortifying."

I told Eric, "Your only problem is you're not sensitive enough to the pressure in your bladder to wake up before it's too late. I'm going to show you how to become more aware." I asked Eric to practice the *Desert Scene,* concentrating particularly on the growing pressure in his bladder area as the sand covered him, layer by layer. Focusing on the growing sensation of pressure in this part of his body heightened his sensitivity to his bladder pressure and after a couple weeks of practice, Eric's frequency of waking up to urinate began to increase.

CLEAR SKIN

Another element contained in the *Desert Scene* that you can use to effect healing is that of extreme heat. Images involving the recall of heat on your skin can be very effective in relieving dermatological disorders. You already saw how Sandy used the recall of heat from imagining sitting near the fireplace in the *Mountain Cabin Scene* to clear up her psoriasis. When I gave Paul this image to help him continue working upon his acne, he said, "The sun was burning my eyes . . . I felt so hot." Combining his recall of extreme heat on his skin from the *Desert Scene* with the relaxation he had already derived from the earlier images, he was able to eliminate his acne permanently. If you too suffer from acne, psoriasis, or a related skin disease, try practicing the *Desert Scene,* focusing especially on recalling the extreme heat of the sun against the areas of your skin where you have eruptions.

STOPPING SMOKING

You can also use the recalled heat of the *Desert Scene* to stop smoking. Modify the image to imagine you are walking the desert, smoking a cigarette. Concentrate on the taste and smell of the tobacco. Pair the dry, parched, hot, tongue-thickening, throat-constricting sensations therein with the act of smoking. When you put your cigarette out, the freshwater sea appears as your reward for stopping smoking, your thirst is quenched and taste freshened. You can also add suggestions such as, "Every puff I take, it gets hotter and hotter . . . every taste I take, my throat gets drier and drier."

LIFTING THE PAIN OF DEPRESSION

The *Desert Scene,* in effect, requires you to imagine yourself in a deprivation state, one of extreme thirst. The positive result of this is that it heightens the reinforcing quality of whatever satisfies this state, in this case your drinking water. You can use your ability to self-induce the sense of a deprivation state to dispel the apathy of depression.

When you are depressed, nothing is rewarding or worth your effort. If, however, you were truly parched with thirst, water would definitely motivate you, no matter how depressed you were. Using imagery to induce a deprivation state makes you want the thing you imagine being deprived of more in reality. It increases your drive, your motivation. Since drive is incompatible with depression, this imagery banishes the ennui of depression. You cannot be charged with energy and depressed at the same time.

Marcia, a 32-year-old physical therapist overcome with depression due to the loss of a job, divorce, and a dying father, told me, "There's nothing in the world I want to do. Everything's an effort. I have to force myself to get out of bed in the morning. Even things I used to enjoy, like movies and talking to friends, are a drag. I haven't an ounce of energy." Marcia needed to learn what it felt like to have a drive again, to really feel like doing something, anything.

Hunger, thirst, and sex are our three basic drives and an image incorporating any of these will give you motivation. After Marcia practiced the *Desert Scene* for a week she reported, "I'd forgotten what it felt like to really want something. But that image sure made me want water. Boy, how I wanted it! I forgot all about being depressed. It felt so good to experience a drive again. Now, whenever I find myself feeling blah and apathetic I recall this scene and the feeling of desperate thirst it evoked. That drive dispels my apathy. It also helps me to remember how good I felt when I satisfied that drive." Depression and satisfaction cannot coexist. If you recall the latter, you eliminate the former.

SEEING "NOTHING" CAN HEIGHTEN YOUR IMAGERY

You'll remember I said that sensory deprivation leads to vivid hallucinations in all five senses. If you plug a person's ears, mouth, and nose, cover his eyes, and wrap his body in heavy cloth, within six hours he'll create a hallucinated world every bit as vivid as the "real" one he was deprived of.

Covering the eyes is usually accomplished by placing two halves of a ping-pong ball over them. The visual effect is called a "ganzfeld," an area with no visual discrimination. You would see only a field of white, with no type of distraction. A few hours of viewing this white leads to brilliant visual hallucinations.

Drawing on the fact that the same principles that apply in your reality also apply in your imagery, it is possible for you to use an *imaginary ganzfeld* to give yourself brilliant hallucinations or imagery. If you first *imagine* a field of white, free of distraction, before each of your images, that which follows will be more vivid to you. By first imagining that you are visually deprived, you can then experience more intense imagery.

You used this principle at the beginning of the *Desert Scene* when you gazed into the white wall, which served as a ganzfeld or area of minimal stimulation. Depriving yourself of visual stimulation serves to induce visual hallucinations or imagery. So initial concentration on the white subsequently enhances the blue sky, yellow sun, and landscape of clay.

You can use the principle of the ganzfeld whenever you wish by simply spending a minute or two imagining you are staring into white before you commence to conjure the image of your goal.

COMPONENTS OF YOUR DESERT SCENE

I deliberately kept at a minimum the sensations you were asked to recall in this image, so that you could intensify and focus on your recall of pressure. (You will see further along that your facility for recalling the sensory component of pressure has many valuable uses, including controlling circulation, creating sexual arousal, and clearing up skin disorders.) Visual cues were few: blue sky, yellow sun, and cracked clay. There was almost no detail for you to attend. The only audio component you were asked to produce was a soft, high-pitched wind. Taste and smell were not included at all. All three tactile components of temperature, pressure, and liquidity were present, but *pressure* was your definite area of focus, concentrating on various gradations as the sand covered you.

OTHER BENEFITS TO PAIN CONTROL

I'll bet you think that being pain-free is reward enough for practicing images. That is certainly the case, but you are also in for a bonus. In cybernetic terms, pain is noise in your system. It not only brings you down and makes you feel awful, it competes with wonderful, positive stimuli for your attention, and usually wins.

You don't smell the roses because you are too busy thinking about your headache. A delicate new seasoning eludes you completely because your feet hurt. Subtle variations in a symphony go unnoticed because your attention is on your arthritis. Your lover's touch feels like nothing because it's in competition with a skin rash. You totally miss the beauty of a sunset, your mind is so attuned to your backache. Pain, in essence, makes you miss the beauty of your world. It competes for your attention in all five senses. You can only process so much information at a time and when all your channels are on the pain network, there is no room left for pleasure.

Eliminating pain clears your channels. You suddenly have a whole new set of positive stimuli at your disposal to process. Sights, sounds, feelings, tastes, smells suddenly come into a blazing new clarity. The world looks young and new again because you are receiving it fresh, uncolored by the negative signals of pain. Your positive sensory thresholds lower. The range of your perception in all five senses increases. You can taste and smell things you never could before. Colors become vibrant, alive and in shades you've not seen for a long time, or possibly ever before. Your discrimination of sound is remarkable and you can pick instruments out of a musical piece you never heard before. All sorts of new textures and feelings related to temperature, wetness and dryness, lightness and heaviness appear in your sensorium. This is only the beginning.

If you're really good at clearing pain and negative noise from your consciousness, you'll have created room to process even *more* than your five senses. You now have space for "extra" senses. Please remember that I discovered all this stuff on my own, working on hypnosis and imagery with patients. It was not my original intent to eliminate pain in order to make way for the development of senses beyond the common five. It simply evolved, a natural result of practicing these images. I'd like to backtrack a moment to the first time I became aware imagery could be used not only for pain control and the enhancement of positive sensation, but to develop faculties beyond the five senses.

I was 27 years old and in my second year of practice. Many of my patients reported heightened intuitive powers from practicing their hypnosis and imagery, but I didn't regard it as significant because I really didn't know what they were talking about. I supposed they meant they were able to figure things out better or come up with better guesses.

Then Anne shared something interesting with me. It was at the session after the one where I'd given her the *Desert Scene*. She'd been practicing this image a week and seemed excited when I ushered her into my office. "'I had the greatest experience," she said. "My mother phoned and told me Dad had made a ghost figure with a pumpkin head for Halloween. And I said, 'Yeah, I know.' It's amazing! I really knew that before she told me! Is the hypnosis doing that to me?"

I was later to discover it was more a product of the imagery than the hypnosis, but at that moment I felt it was purely a figment of Anne's imagination. Yet I couldn't help being intrigued by her positive energy and her delight about the whole thing. I'd heard of psychic phenomena, of course, but I was skeptical and not particularly interested. There was something about this singular incident, however, that got a grip on me. It didn't make me a believer in telepathy, but it did cause me to open my eyes to areas I'd been conditioned to overlook. Sure enough, I found things I never knew were there.

Come along. Your mind is clearing. Since you now have room to process extra senses, let's begin by experimenting with what is often called an extra sense, time.

SIX

Time Control

Haven't we all, at some wonderful moment in our lives, sighed, "I wish this time could last forever?" Everyone's life has good times as well as bad; it's only natural to want the positive periods to linger. You wake up one glorious morning feeling more refreshed than you have in years and you want that feeling to last. A certain episode of lovemaking is incredibly passionate and exciting and you never want it to end. You suddenly find yourself in a good mood one particular Monday afternoon for no special reason and you don't want to let go of it. Or perhaps a nagging headache or backache suddenly lets up and you want to hold the moment of relief. Maybe that terrible urge for cigarettes, drugs, or alcohol is gone for a while and you wonder if something can keep this craving-free time from passing. These are just a few examples of the good moments you can prolong using imagery to induce the marvelous time-control phenomenon called "time expansion." If your good times pass too quickly and your bad times stay too long, this chapter is especially for you.

TIME EXPANSION

Time expansion is the ability to cause time to elongate, to make it seem that more time has passed than actually has. You get time expansion normally, in everyday life, during a negative period. If, for example, you're waiting for a taxi, and you're late, and it's raining, time drags. If, on the other hand, you're at a party having a marvelous time, time flies by. What you want to be able to accomplish is to reverse this normal process, to have the good times last forever and the bad times speed by. Fortunately, time expansion is one of the easiest, as well as most dramatic, phenomena inducible with imagery.

The reason you are able to create time expansion so easily is that time doesn't really exist. Time is a psychological construct. You get your "idea" of time by the number of events that transpire between one event and another. If, for example, I froze you solid for a hundred years and then unthawed you and asked, "How long does it seem since last I spoke to you?" you'd say, "A second," because nothing has transpired in your brain for a century. Brain activity produces your sense of time. Time as a real thing with substance, composed of matter, does not exist. It's not something you can put on a plate or look at under a microscope. Because time is a psychological construct, literally a figment of the imagination, you can manipulate it psychologically, or imaginally, using imagery.

SPACE SCENE

The image that follows, *Space Scene,* shows you exactly how to create the sense that time is lasting longer. As with the other images, you may practice it from memory, or you or a friend may read it into a tape recorder and play it back. Again, always follow the mind clearing procedure described in Chapter One before recalling this image. I usually ask my patients to recall this image three times a day for a week before going on to the next image in this series, but you may get actual results from your first practice. Keep working on the scene until you get the desired results. How to apply these results to make your life better will follow. First, though, I want you to have the experience!

SPACE SCENE:

"One minute of actual time will seem like ten minutes to you. Time will go by very, very slowly. It will seem like an eternity.

"You are lying on a large, round bed in a huge, circular, black marble room. It's midnight. You are looking up at the ceiling. The ceiling is a glass dome, a clear, transparent bubble. The night is clear, the sky filled with stars.

"Suddenly you notice that the room is beginning to turn, ever so slowly at first, gradually picking up momentum, revolving like a turntable on a record player . . . going round and round and round and round and round and the room is spinning. You hurl off the bed. The bubble opens. You shoot upward and outward into space, traveling at an incredible rate of speed, faster than the speed of light.

"Flashes of light pass you by as you go by other planets, other solar systems, other galaxies, traveling through space . . . beautiful, beautiful trip.

"Now you are beginning to fall. You are falling through space. . . . You are back to your source, but there is no bed, there is no Earth. The Earth has long ceased to exist. You have been gone over a billion Earth years. You are hanging in space, in a vacuum. No touch, no sound, no smell . . . suspended animation throughout eternity."

WHY THE IMAGE WORKS

Before we get into all the great things you can do with time expansion, let's see *why* this particular image should make you feel that time is going more slowly. There are two reasons: First of all, the image begins with the affirmation, "One minute seems like ten minutes. Time is going by very, very slowly. It seems like an eternity." The deep state of relaxation you achieved from the clearing procedure is also a state of heightened suggestibility. What you tell yourself in this state bypasses the criticalness of your conscious mind and goes straight to your subconscious. Your conscious mind is not there to negate your affirmation by saying, "What are you talking about? What is this time expansion nonsense?" Instead, you accept and *believe* as truth the statements that time seems to be slowing.

Secondly, the amount of imaginal time far exceeds the amount of real time that has passed. That is to say, the elapsed time in your image is greater than the time it takes to practice the image. Over a billion years go by in the *Space Scene,* yet it will only take you about five minutes to imagine this, even if you take it very slowly as I recommend.

If the image seemed totally real to you and I asked you upon its completion how much time you thought had passed, you'd say, "A billion years." Naturally, it won't seem *that* real, but the more real it does seem, the more time you will think has passed. Whenever you want to slow time, the trick is to imagine more time passing than actually is, as you did in the *Space Scene.*

IMPROVING YOUR LIFE WITH TIME EXPANSION

After you have practiced this image a few times, try using it to improve things in your everyday world. Find an experience in your life that you would like to prolong. This may take some ingenuity on your part at first, but you'll soon get the hang of it. Start with simple things. For example, you may just love the wonderful, soothing sense of relaxation that comes over you in the bath or hot tub at night after a long day's work. While you are sitting in the tub, enjoying the comfort of the moment, repeat the suggestion for time expansion quietly to yourself. Really say, "One minute seems like ten minutes. Time is going by very, very slowly. It seems like an eternity."

You'll notice that you don't need to recall the *Space Scene* while prolonging your positive moment, but only give yourself the affirmation for it. This is because the suggestion alone is now sufficient to produce time expansion because it has been *paired* with the image. Through classical conditioning the suggestion will now trigger the effects of the image because you practiced the suggestion and image together. You may remember how the Russian psychologist Ivan Pavlov got a dog to salivate to a bell by pairing it with food. Now you can condition intensified time expansion by pairing the suggestion for it with the image for it and then using the suggestion alone.

You will also probably notice that in your endeavor to expand the comfort and relaxation of your bath or hot tub experience, you are telling yourself just the opposite of what you would normally be thinking in such a situation. Usually when you're really enjoying yourself thoughts such as "Time is sure flying," "I can't believe it's so late already," or "Where is this night going?" are buzzing through your head. These normal thoughts only make your good times speed by even more quickly. You may want to invent more time expansion suggestions of your own to pair with the *Space Scene*. Suggestions such as "I can't believe how long I've been here," or "This seems like forever," or "Time is sure dragging," are all good to give yourself during positive moments, rather than the negative ones you would normally be most apt to give yourself.

Also, you may already have found yourself experiencing time expansion before coming to this chapter. When you begin expanding the world of your mind through imagery you will likely find your sense of time changing. Time expansion is a natural byproduct of working with imagery.

To provide a better understanding of all the wonderful uses you can put your imagery-induced time control to, I've included the experiences of several of my cases. They offer a variety of innovations you should find most instructive.

EXTENDING SEXUAL PLEASURE

One of the most common uses for time expansion that I see in my practice is to lengthen the period of sexual arousal for both men and women. You can vastly improve the quality of your sex life by giving yourself suggestions for time expansion during actual love-making.

Allison, a 25-year-old bank teller, is a perfect example of a woman who used the *Space Scene* to put spice back into her marriage. Every time she had sex with Derek, a 28-year-old systems engineer, she would think, "Here we go again at the same old thing," and although she loved him she felt her marriage was in jeopardy because she couldn't return the sexual feelings he showed for her. "It's not that I can't reach a climax," she explained. "I can. It's just that I have to work at it so hard. Sometimes it even gives me a headache. I thought sex was supposed to relax you. And it's not that I don't find Derek attractive. I do. He's a great looking guy. And he does turn me on, but only for about the first five minutes. By the time he gets down to business and is inside me, I've lost interest. I don't even lubricate then. What should I do, eliminate foreplay entirely and tell him to jump me quick when I'm not looking?" Allison made a joke about her poor sex life, as many women do, but I could easily see by the telltale sadness in her brown eyes that it was no laughing matter.

"I know a way to turn those five good minutes into fifty," I told her. I asked her to practice the *Space Scene* three times a day for a week. Then the next time she and Derek made love, she was to immediately, during her initial five-minute arousal, give herself the suggestions for time expansion that began the image, but go no further with the image. After the fifth time of inducing time expansion while making love to Derek, Allison reported, "It's amazing. The first couple of times I didn't see any difference at all. But now I can honestly say my interest is sustaining. I'm still aroused by the time he penetrates me. God, what a difference that makes." It took Allison four months working with time expansion before she was able to expand the good sexual moments to encompass their entire period of lovemaking.

Any positive moment, no matter how brief, can be expanded. Good times do not have to be fleeting. Sexual interest need not fade. If it ever existed, if there was ever even a spark of sexual interest, you can develop and expand it into a flame.

I once worked with an attractive woman, Ally S., 41, an office administrator for a lighting company, married three years to Ben, 45, an electrician, who complained she had never been able to reach a climax other than by masturbating herself in private. "I'm just too nervous with men," she explained. "Maybe I waited too long to get married. I was 38 and a virgin. All my life I'd been told sex was bad. In convent school the nuns made us change our underwear under our clothes, that's how opposed to nudity they were. I thought I'd get over it. I thought if I met a man I really loved, like I do Ben, sex would be okay. It's funny, I can get really aroused just looking at him, but as soon as he touches me I clam up."

Ally didn't realize it then, but she had just given me the key to releasing her sexuality. What we needed to do was expand that period of sexual electricity she experienced looking at her lover over a longer time frame, making it last throughout intercourse. "How do you feel when he kisses you?" I asked. "I like it," she laughed. "It's not really until he touches me down there that I tense up." I suggested that Ally ask Ben to increase the time they spent in foreplay, especially kissing. During the kissing, Ally periodically gave herself suggestions for time expansion to make it seem her arousal was lasting a very long time. This served to intensify her sexual feelings to the point they overpowered her inhibitions. A stronger response always gains precedence over a weaker one and when her sex drive reached an intensity greater than the anxiety that was blocking her from feeling arousal when her genitals were touched, she was able to let go and experience a satisfying sexual climax.

As you can see, using time expansion to prolong a drive such as sex also intensifies it. That is the nature of drives. The longer they are experienced without being satisfied, the stronger they become. Prolonged hunger without food makes you starved, a protracted period of thirst without drinking causes you to parch, extended sexual arousal without satisfaction intensifies the drive to such an extent it can overpower all competing feelings including inhibitions, anxiety, and fear. Your ability to control your drives using the appropriate imagery has many uses in ending addictions and lifting the apathy of depression.

Men, also, can use time expansion to intensify their sexuality and eliminate any negative competing responses that may be causing them impotence. For years Adam, 35, a host for a TV game show, bounced from woman to woman because, as he put it, "I just can't get it up after the first date or two. I seem to lose interest." Then he met RoxAnne, a cosmetician on the set, and he fell madly in love. Now Adam worried that he would lose sexual interest in her just as he had with all the women that had come before. I told Adam, "As long as you keep your attention focused on your sexual feelings while

making love to RoxAnne and are not distracted by negative competing thoughts, such as you might fail or lose your erection, you will
continue to be potent with her." I taught him to use the *Space Scene*
to set up suggestions for time expansion to give himself when making
love to RoxAnne. Here again you can see how intensifying your
sexuality using time expansion takes your focus off negative competing thoughts during sex and keeps you sexually interested in your
partner. I am happy to say that Adam and RoxAnne are still together:
"When I was able to concentrate on her rather than my fears that I
would lose interest in her, I never did lose interest!"

Men can use time expansion not only to strengthen their sexual
feelings, but also to bolster self-confidence in their sexual prowess,
especially if there is a problem with coming too soon, premature
ejaculation. Marty, 53, an accountant, came to see me with his wife,
Maria, 42. Marty was upset at his wife's "sexual demands." "I can't
understand it," he exclaimed. "Twenty years of marriage and not
one complaint. Now suddenly she wants me to be Superman. This
sex revolution is no good. She's been reading too many books." I
learned from further discussion that Marty was premature, never
lasting longer than 30 seconds before ejaculating inside Maria, who
was never able to reach a climax. "Sometimes I fake an orgasm,"
Maria admitted. "Sometimes he's able to make me come using his
hands or mouth. But I want to be able to reach a climax with him
inside of me."

It wasn't until the third session that Marty revealed an incident
that caused him to lack sexual confidence since puberty. "I was
about fourteen at the time," he recalled. "A friend had a group of
about six of us guys over to his house one night. His parents were
out and this girl was there. She was making it with all my friends
and I got so excited I came in my pants. When it was my turn I
couldn't do anything. All the guys laughed. I had trouble lasting
sexually ever since." I explained to Marty how the trauma of this
event had set up his expectation that he would not be able to control
his climax in the future and he would come too soon. He needed a

new expectation, a belief that he could delay his climax as long as he desired. To instill this belief I taught him the *Space Scene* and told him to give himself the suggestions for time expansion during the interval he was inside his wife. The effect of this procedure was to make Marty believe he was lasting longer than he actually was, thus building his sexual confidence. The belief he was lasting longer, even though it was an illusion, set up an expectation of more time before his climax, which then actually caused Marty to delay more and more to the point he climaxed when he wished, after Maria had been satisfied.

It is my goal for you that you learn to use imagery-induced time expansion to enhance your own sexual fulfillment. When you can prolong and intensify your moments of sexual joy you will have gained control over a tremendous energy source, one you can channel into ever-higher realms of experience.

EXPANDING PERIODS OF RELIEF

In this section you will see how you can use time expansion to prolong not only periods of pleasure and happiness, but also times that are simply free of unwanted or negative feelings. These can be times when you are free of pain, an urge to smoke, a desire for fattening foods, a craving for drugs or alcohol, or a particular fear or negative train of thought. You want to be able to expand the time between your negative feelings and condense the times you are immersed in them. Shortening your sense of negative experience, time concentration, is something you'll learn to do in Chapter Seven.

No experience is as negative as the one we label "pain." You can combine the techniques learned in Chapter Three for pain control with time expansion to lengthen the periods you are pain free. If you are troubled by recurring pain of any kind, time expansion is effective at prolonging the soothing periods between your episodes of discomfort.

The story of one of my patient's recovery from cancer surgery provides a good example of how to use time expansion to prolong your pain-free periods. Winston, a 62-year-old jeweler, successfully underwent an operation and radiation therapy for colon cancer. His spirits were high and his outlook bright. He had only one complaint. "I get these stabbing pains in the rectal area," he explained. "It's not so bad when I stand, but sitting down can be excruciating and sometimes sleeping is difficult. It's hard to get a good night's sleep. I never feel rested." Winston's doctors diagnosed his complaint as "phantom pain," a not uncommon condition where pain is felt in tissue that has actually been removed, as in the well-known phantom limb syndrome where amputees complain of pain in a leg that has been severed. I taught Winston time expansion using the *Space Scene* and then explained to him, "Your pain runs in cycles, as you've already told me. It comes and it goes without much particular pattern to it. I want you to use time expansion when you *don't* have pain. Tell yourself that time is going very slowly when you are feeling your best. You don't need to actually do the whole *Space Scene* during these times, just the beginning with the suggestions for time expansion." By using the images to recall cold and pressure described in Chapter Three to eliminate pain, combined with time expansion to prolong periods between pain, Winston was able, in a couple of months, to reach a state of physical comfort. "I sure learned one thing," he laughed. "I was looking at the wrong end for the cure. The pain was in my head all along."

You may want to lengthen the time between unwanted urges as well as physical pain. If you're a smoker trying to overcome the mental pain of craving cigarettes, you can use time expansion to prolong the time between these overpowering desires, and thus progressively decrease the frequency of your smoking. To begin getting your habit under time control, I suggest the following strategy which I recommend to all my clients. Buy a small pocket notebook, one you can easily carry with you at all times. Whenever you have a cigarette, write down the *time, place,* and *activity.* Write the time of day you smoke; where you are—the kitchen, bedroom, car, office, garden, wherever; and what you are doing at the time you have the cigarette, i.e., talking on the phone, finishing a meal, driving to work, watching TV, reading a book, having a drink or cup of coffee. Most importantly, record the cigarette *before* you smoke it. Some people hate paperwork so much they stop smoking just to avoid this charting. No matter how much you may detest keeping a record, I can't overemphasize how tremendously beneficial it is to eliminating any unwanted habit.

After you have charted your consumption of cigarettes for at least a week, take a careful look at your data. Find the time of day, on average, that you go the longest between cigarettes. Then, for a week, repeatedly give yourself suggestions for time expansion during this time frame. For example, if your charting reveals you are less likely to smoke between 2 and 3 P.M., then give yourself time expansion suggestions every few minutes throughout this hour. Do this only after you have practiced the *Space Scene* at least five times. Remember that practicing the image empowers your suggestions by being paired with them. You will find that the time between your early afternoon cigarettes will measurably increase as a function of your practicing time expansion between them.

Dolores, a 40-year-old supervisor in an upholstery factory, smoked least in the early evening between 7 and 8 P.M. "I'm fine when I first get home from work at seven," she said. "As long as I have things to do I'm okay. I put my stuff away, change my clothes, read the mail, check my answering machine for messages, make calls, fix my meal. It isn't till I sit down to eat that this wave of loneliness comes over me and I feel I need a friend. That's what a cigarette is—a friend, a companion to keep me company."

I asked Dolores to give herself suggestions for time expansion as soon as she got home in the evening, to prolong the positive state of mind she had before allowing loneliness and cigarette urges to set in. As the weeks went by, she found she wasn't smoking until later and later in the evening. "Time expansion not only puts off my urge to smoke," she said, "it puts off those terrible feelings of loneliness. I suddenly realize that if I have the power to put these negative feelings off and delay them, I have the power to not feel them at all. This whole cycle of self-indulgence is just stupid. I don't have to feel deprived and lonely if I don't want to, and I definitely choose not to."

It you have trouble controlling your eating and are plagued with overwhelming urges for food, sometimes even when you're not hungry, you can overcome these urges using time expansion in much the same way just described for smoking. First of all, do as Sonia did to lose weight in Chapter Four. Chart everything you eat, along with time, place, and activity, writing it down *before* you eat it. After a week, study the data, looking for the time you are most likely to stay on your diet—and least likely. Begin by practicing the *Space Scene* at least five times and then giving yourself suggestions for time expansion during the time of day it is easiest for you to diet. Later, pinpoint a positive time closest to your downfall, the time you are most apt to break your diet, and give yourself time expansion suggestions then to delay, postpone, the negative time of nondieting.

You can see the effective use of time expansion for weight control in the case of Marilyn, 32, secretary for a firm that makes baked goods. "It's crazy," she proclaimed. "All day long I'm surrounded with chocolate cakes and jelly doughnuts and it really doesn't faze me. Especially in the morning I don't even notice it. I even skip breakfast. But late at night, hours after I'm off work, I'm suddenly struck with the munchies. I nearly tear the door off the fridge trying to get in. You'd think I hadn't eaten in a month." As we saw with Jill, late-night food cravings are common. I knew Marilyn could learn to overcome them, but first I wanted her to work on her best period, the morning, with a modification. "I don't want you to miss breakfast," I told her. "Meal skipping, especially the first meal, is the thing I see most often in people who have a weight problem. You need to learn to eat when you are *not* hungry, on a schedule, and not dependent on uncontrollable emotions.

Regular meals three times a day are the best way to put control back into your eating." Marilyn did well with imagery and was easily able to induce time expansion. I told her to give herself time expansion suggestions in the morning after breakfast, the time she felt least like eating, in order to prolong these feelings that were conducive to weight control. Next, we pinpointed that the last positive time frame before her downfall of nightly munchies was between 10:30 and 11 P.M. "I always seem to be famished right after the news," she said. I asked Marilyn to give herself suggestions for time expansion repeatedly at five minute intervals between 10:30 and 11 P.M. to prolong her period of non-craving and delay the onset of the munchies. After two weeks she reported, "If the food goblins are coming at all, it's after I'm asleep. I'm sure not aware of them anymore." Two months later, when Marilyn reached her ideal weight, I knew the time expansion had gotten through to her.

You can treat unwanted periods of craving for drugs or alcohol with time expansion in the same fashion you would work on cigarettes or non-dietetic foods. Chart when you drink or abuse a drug and use time expansion to prolong the time you are free of urges in order to delay the onset of the craving. You will be happy to find that you can expand periods of relief from the habit to the point you are free of it.

BENEFITS OF TIME EXPANSION ITSELF

Time expansion feels good. It is a sense you have all the time in the world to do whatever you want. With this sense you wind down, you relax, you center and experience the wondrous beauty of a five-sensory world. You wake up and smell the roses!

Anything that makes you feel better is therapeutic. The winding-down relaxation of time expansion counters your anxieties and improves all your problems. No matter what ills you may be experiencing, when you reduce your anxiety level, your maladies have a way of fading. You automatically smoke less, fear less, hurt less, and assuredly are more happy. You are able to rise above your problems, come from a different space, as it were, where problems diminish relative to the beatific state you are now experiencing.

This wonderful winding-down quality of time expansion renders it excellent treatment if you have any sort of gastrointestinal trouble. Ulcers, colitis, emotional diarrhea, involuntary vomiting, and even constipation and gallbladder dysfunction respond favorably to time expansion therapy. All you need to do is continue practicing the *Space Scene*. Your concentrating on the image will give you a sense of time expansion. This sense will linger long after the image is over, pervading your normal everyday life. This is especially true if you parcel out your practice in equal intervals three times a day. You will find that as you continue to practice, your sense of time expansion will intensify, carrying over for longer and longer periods of time. If you work at it diligently you will attain that expanded awareness and slowing of time throughout your entire day. To your joyful surprise you will discover you are able to accomplish more, not less in this state. Anxious hurriedness only impedes progress. Relaxation is the key.

Mel, a 31-year-old journalist for a major newspaper, developed a bleeding ulcer that gave him such pain he would find himself doubling over at work. The chronic stress from his treadmill of schedules and deadlines had finally taken its toll. "There just aren't enough hours in the day," he stated. "I'm always behind, always rushing, always pushing. There's always something new that needs to be done before the final edition goes out. At the end of a day I crash. Some nights I just fall into bed with my clothes on. I'm even too tired to eat. Besides, who's got the time?" I smiled at him. "But things always get done, don't they?" I asked. "Yeah," he sighed, "but what a price to pay!" "And what an unnecessary price," I added. He looked at me perplexed, not seeing what I was driving at. "The fact you get the work done shows that what you need isn't actually more time, but the *feeling* you have more time. With that feeling you could relax, do the same amount of work, if not more, and not have an ulcer."

It took Mel longer than the average, three weeks to be exact, before he was able to get a sense of time expansion from the *Space Scene*. But he did get it. "It's great!" he said. "I feel like I have plenty of time now. Once I got that feeling of time expansion I was able to bring it on anywhere, anytime, just by remembering it." As it did for Mel, the image will teach you how to experience a new sensation, that of time expansion. Once you have that experience, it is recorded forever in your memory banks. You have only to recall it when you need it.

If you or any of your friends or loved ones have a speech problem, pressured speech or a stutter, you may be pleasantly surprised at how well this disorder responds to time expansion. Time expansion grounds you in the moment, preventing your thinking ahead to what's next before you even get there. You'll recall my mentioning in Chapter Three that expectation or "intent" to speak often produces anxiety and blocks speech, which is why a stutterer usually has no trouble reading a passage out loud from a book or even reciting a memorized script. What's coming next has been precisely mapped out for him and he doesn't have to worry about it. Jumping ahead in time, in mind, causes a stutter if you are worried about speech. Staying here, in time, in mind, allows you to speak normally with no pressure to get ahead of yourself.

Experiment by speaking out loud immediately after practicing the *Space Scene* and notice how much more relaxed your words are, how they aren't forced or pressured. Even the tonal quality of your voice will improve. You'll hear more resonance, more timbre, and usually it will be lower, modulated, and free of stridency. Continued practice of the *Space Scene* leads to a growing sense of time expansion throughout your day and along with it, greater fluency of speech. If a particular situation arises where your speech is likely to be more strained than normal, such as an important job interview or meeting new people, you can give yourself suggestions for time expansion immediately beforehand and, once you become adept, during the actual situation itself.

When Travis, 24, interviews with a casting director he finds himself stuttering and fumbling over words that usually don't give him a problem. "It's outrageous," he said. "Why don't they just give me a script and let me read? I'm great at that. Isn't that what acting's all about? Why do they make me sit and chat like I'm at some damned tea party?" "What makes you so nervous on an interview?" I asked. "They never give you any time," he answered. "How can they really see what I can do in only thirty minutes?" I explained to Travis how it was his *belief* that he didn't have enough time that was creating his speech disorder. In reality he had all the time he needed. Other people were cast from thirty-minute interviews. What Travis needed to do was change his attitude toward time, to feel he always had enough of it. Once he experienced time expansion by practicing the *Space Scene,* a feeling he had all the time in the world, he was able to recall it when he was talking and no longer stammer and stutter out of a need to rush ahead.

You can also use your perception of added time with singular effectiveness in excelling at sports. Athletic maneuvers requiring split-second timing and minute specificity can be perfected using time expansion. Any golf swing, tennis shot, basketball throw, football kick, baseball hit, ice figure, high jump, or other physical motion is more precisely executed under the influence of time expansion. Practice the *Space Scene* enough times to familiarize yourself with the feeling of time expansion. Then at any time in your sport where there is a need for precision maneuvering, quickly give yourself a simple time expansion suggestion such as, "Time is going very slowly." This will only take you a few seconds to do and the rewards will be significant. Not only will you relax and perform better, free from the competing noise of anxiety, you may even notice a perceptual change, like a world in slow motion, where you can literally do more in each time frame than you could before.

Norman, a 28-year-old tennis pro who complained of trouble

returning serves, described such a slow-motion phenomenon using time expansion. "The ball actually looked like it was in slow motion coming over the net," he stated. "I've never seen anything like it. Amazing. It was like it gave me more time to return the serve." Norman had only been practicing the *Space Scene* for a week when he was able to accomplish this remarkable feat. "I waited until the guy was about to serve," he explained. "Then I said to myself, 'One minute seems like ten. It seems like an eternity.' Sometimes I got more specific, modifying it to, 'The ball is taking forever to come over the net.' "

While the feeling you can get more done in a given time frame is valuable in athletics, you can also use it to your advantage to improve your memory and concentration. Inducing time expansion before reading a manuscript or studying for an exam relaxes you and enables you to assimilate more material. It facilitates not only your absorption of new material, but also your retrieval and can be induced during your actual taking of a test as well, simply by your giving yourself suggestions for it before and during the exam.

Because time expansion feels so good and because its effects are in some respects similar to those produced by many drug states, you can, if you have a drug dependency, substitute the reinforcing sensations of time expansion for the drug state, once you have mastered the *Space Scene*. A "rush" similar to that experienced from heroin is often reported by patients from imagining speeding through the galaxy as called for in this scene.

The procedure is to immerse yourself in the *Space Scene* whenever desire for the drug is intense. The resultant relaxing time distortion will take the edge off withdrawal as well as provide a pleasing, safe substitute for the effects of the drug. In later chapters you will see how additional feeling components of drug states such as time condensation, dissociation, hallucinations, color intensification, form distortion, and body rushes can be combined with time expansion to "shape up" the perceptual equivalent of a drug state to substitute safely for the real thing.

Eve, a 42-year-old beautician, had been smoking marijuana on and off since she was eighteen. "I was one of the flower children, you know. Everything was so beautiful then and grass made things so profound . . . I loved it. Maybe I loved it too much, because with all that lofty thinking I forgot to apply myself to the realities of schoolwork and I flunked out my junior year. I switched to beauty school and got a job. I didn't touch the stuff for at least ten years. But then during the sexual revolution of the late seventies I kept hearing my women clients raving about how good it made their sex. I'd been a washout in that department since my divorce two years back and I thought a little pot might loosen me up. It did. It made me a real sexual animal and I loved it! The first few years I only used it for sex. But then my job was getting to be such a bore I thought some THC might liven that up like it did my sex life. I was right. Work became much more interesting, a real experience. I know I lost some customers because I got careless, but it didn't bother me at that point.

"In the last two years I've used grass on a daily basis, a hit to get me out of bed, a hit to buck the freeway, a hit to do a difficult customer. The only problem is I'm becoming more preoccupied and distracted. I can't concentrate. Nightmarish thoughts I've never had before pop into my mind and I can't get rid of them. I have to stop now, cold turkey, before my mind drifts off altogether." It was a struggle. Eve went off the wagon many times, but in six months she was finally drug-free. "I think what helped most was the time expansion," she said. "It gave me such a drifting, floating feeling of suspension. It helped me rise above my problems and relax without the grass. The feeling was almost spiritual."

IMAGINING WIDE OPEN SPACES

Although the *Space Scene* was designed primarily to help you induce time expansion, I've discovered over the eighteen years and nearly three thousand cases I've taught it to that it has other useful applications as well. One of them is in the elimination of phobias involving anxiety or fear attached to physical restrictions. The most common of these, of course, is claustrophobia, a fear of closed or cramped spaces. However, you can effectively use the *Space Scene* to decondition panic attacks to any situation entailing restricted movement such as crowds, elevators, airplanes, the back seat of cars, freeway traffic, wet suits and scuba gear, and even tight clothes.

The *Space Scene* takes you through the greatest expanse there is, the cosmos. It is impossible for you to be claustrophobic when your mind is attuned to this image. Therefore, if you experience anxiety in situations that spatially constrict you, practice this scene for about a week, firmly implanting the imagery of wide open spaces in your head. You should find a reduction in anxiety from this phase of the treatment alone. Then, the next time you start to tense in a claustrophobic circumstance, put yourself imaginally in the *Space Scene,* taking your mind off your closed-in environment and focusing on one of limitless space. It is not necessary to give yourself the suggestions for time expansion at the beginning of this image when working with a phobia. You need only envision yourself traveling freely through infinite space.

When Lucy, a 27-year-old theatrical agent, developed a phobia for crowded restaurants, she was afraid that her career was over. "What am I going to do?" she asked. "If I can't schmooze my contacts in the film business, I'll never be able to get my clients work. Half my day is spent in restaurants. Sometimes I even double lunch, meeting a producer at Le Dome from 12:00 to 2:00 and then dashing over to the Ivy to court a director." She explained how her first claustrophobic panic attack occurred in college when she was forced to ride in the tiny back compartment of an MG on the way to a party. "I kept thinking, 'I can't get out. The only way out is if the driver stops the car and he and the other passenger get out first. I can't wait that long. I need to be able to get out now.' The fact that the car was moving and I couldn't jump out immediately didn't bother me. It was knowing I had no immediate exit that drove me crazy." As is often the case, Lucy felt fine as soon as the MG arrived at the party and it was several years before the occurrence of another attack in a crowded elevator.

"One night I was sitting in a restaurant with clients, at the far end of the room away from the entrance," Lucy went on. "I found myself watching the people pour in and the waiter moving the tables closer together. I thought, 'I'm not going to be able to get out of here unless those people get up from their table and let me by.' Then the panic started. Now I won't enter a restaurant unless I can sit by the entrance and even then I'm fearful. Do you know how hard it is in this town to specify where you want to sit? You're lucky to get a table at all. It's so embarrassing making your friends wait hours so you can sit in a place that won't drive you into a frenzy." I suggested Lucy practice the *Space Scene* a week and then, when she was in a crowded restaurant, periodically recall the scene, concentrating on the image of wide open space rather than the thought of how restricted she was. It worked. In less than two months she was double lunching again.

FARM SCENE: A SECOND IMAGE FOR TIME EXPANSION

I'm showing you two images for time expansion because even though they will give you similar results, they do it in somewhat different ways and their combination is a powerful package. Because the *Space Scene* is filled with great adventure and drama it involves you instantly, riveting your attention. You hurl through a cosmic phantasmagoria faster than the speed of light, gone for over a billion years. However, its strongest asset is also its greatest liability. The intense drama of this image renders it less identifiable; it's far removed from anything you have actually experienced. To compensate, I give you the *Farm Scene,* lacking in drama, but high in identifiability. It's a series of sensations you are much more likely to have encountered than those you conjured in the *Space Scene* and probably easier for you to make real, although it definitely is not necessary that you have had the experiences you are imagining. You can create anything in mind. Instead of a billion years passing, you imagine the lapse of 6½ hours, from 5:30 A.M. to 12 noon. But again, this amount of time you imagine passing far exceeds the approximately 6 minutes it will take you to do the image, thus creating the effect of time expansion.

FARM SCENE:

"One minute of actual time will seem like ten minutes to you. Time will go by very, very slowly. It will seem like an eternity.

"You are lying in bed. It's very early morning. Feel the heavy quilts over your body. You are in a farmhouse, a farmhouse in Kansas. It's late August, 5:30 in the morning. Hear the crow of a rooster. You doze off back to sleep.

"Suddenly you are awakened by the shrill sound of an alarm clock. You look up. It's 6:00. You get out of bed. Go to the window. The sun is just beginning to rise. Every breath you take the sky gets bluer and bluer, every breath you take it gets warmer and warmer.

"Now you go into the kitchen. There on a table is a blue plate with a stack of crisp bacon. Next to it, on a white plate, are squares of fresh corn bread covered with melted butter. Bite into the bacon. Feel it crunch between your teeth. Taste the smoky flavor. Next, you eat the corn bread. Feel the coarse texture. Taste the rich, creamy butter. Finish eating. It's 6:30 in the morning.

"Now you go out onto the porch and sit down in a rocking chair, rocking back and forth, to and fro, listening to the creaking of the porch boards beneath the weight of the rocker. Look out over the farmyard. See the mud yard with ruts from the tractor, a white henhouse, red barn, a garden with radishes, squash, pumpkins, lettuce, cabbages, tomatoes . . . then a ditch, a gravel road, bright green cornfield, brilliant blue sky, a lazy summer day in Kansas.

"Suddenly off to your left you hear the voices of children. You turn. See three boys, age 8, hurrying off to school. They're late. It's five minutes to nine. They run up a hill to your right and disappear into a white schoolhouse. You continue rocking.

"Now you are getting hungry again. You get up. Go back into the kitchen. There on the table is a blue plate with a piping hot stack of blueberry muffins fresh from the oven. Bite into a muffin. The plump, ripe blueberries burst in your mouth. Taste their sweetness. Finish the muffins. It's 10:30. Go back out onto the porch and continue rocking, getting warmer and warmer, lazier and lazier.

"Get up from the rocker. Walk down the porch steps, across the farmyard, down the ditch, over the road, and into the corn. Feel the corn rustle against your body. Next you come into a patch of sunflowers, huge golden flowers with large, round, brown centers against the deep blue sky.

"Now you find yourself in a field of clover. The smell of honey is in the air. Butterflies dart among the clover blossoms. Lie down in a bed of clover, the smell of wet earth beneath you, the smell of honey around you, the sun straight above you. It's high noon. Gaze at a wisp of a cloud in the sky. You drift, you float, you dream, a lazy summer day in Kansas."

REACTIONS AND USES

Just as the *Farm Scene* is less dramatic and more identifiable than the *Space Scene,* so are most people's reactions to it. Typical reactions to the *Space Scene* are: "I feel good, weird. Interesting phenomenon . . . feel spaced out, like I was out there a long time," or "I had a feeling I would take off. How long was that?" Anne had a similarly dramatic reaction. "Those lights were unbelievable, could you have lived before to see that so well? A kaleidoscope . . . just unbelievable." A typical reaction to the *Farm Scene* is much more down to earth: "I enjoyed the blueberries," said Marie, 31, a stenographer learning time expansion to improve her work efficiency by making her feel she had more hours in which to get her job done. "They had a tart taste. Mmmm . . . I liked the bacon and corn bread too. It seemed like I was there over a half hour." Marie had been in her image seven minutes and had achieved a fivefold sense of time expansion. Your affirmation is for a tenfold expansion, but if you get any increased sense of time at all, it is excellent. You are gaining control of your time sense.

You can use time expansion you achieve with the *Farm Scene* for the same practical applications you used the *Space Scene:* prolonging and intensifying your sexual feelings; a substitution for drug states; staying in the now, thus avoiding any intent to misspeak if you have a stutter; extending the time between pain or undesirable urges for food, alcohol, cigarettes, or drugs; feeling you have more time to execute a precise athletic maneuver; winding down and relaxing; and if you are a man, restoring sexual confidence through believing you are maintaining an erection longer than you actually are.

You'll find that after you've practiced the time expansion images several times, you'll only need to say quietly to yourself, "Space," or "Farm," to trigger the whole sense of time expansion it previously took you the 250-word image to create. You won't even need the affirmations that time is lengthening. One word now cues, by its association with your experience of time expansion, a result it initially took you the whole image plus affirmation to produce.

Like the *Space Scene,* the *Farm Scene* has uses not related to time expansion as well. You can use the recall of the delicious, savory bacon, corn bread, and blueberry muffins to induce hunger if you are anorexic or need to gain weight. You can also use this induction of your hunger drive to dispel the apathy of depression and experience a desire again as Marcia did to feel like getting out of bed once more. Recalling the strong heat from the midday sun on your skin at the end of the image will help you clear up skin problems such as acne or psoriasis. You may also discover this to be an excellent image to do right before bed to help you sleep as it ends with your dozing off: "You drift, you float, you dream, a lazy summer day in Kansas."

OTHER REWARDS

Increased self-control comes from your learning to control your time sense. This leads to your having a better self-image and more confidence in general. Many who practice imagery find themselves slipping into positive altered states automatically, without working to induce them. They are more aware, not less aware, in these states and can perform work much more effectively, along with feeling better. In addition, they report better memory, energy, positivity, and feelings of power. These are common benefits many people receive by this stage in the imagery progression. You may expect them also.

Since the images require your increased concentration, better memory is an almost immediate reward. One woman explains, "I am now seeing myself as a force, no longer a victim to be acted upon, but someone capable of doing my own acting, creating my own effects." Your powers of insight and intuition are on the rise, along with a feeling of limitless possibilities. "I feel I have all the time I need now for anything," people frequently tell me. Others happily recount, "Sex is better, not rushed." Learning time expansion can even lead to a personality change as evidenced by a man who said, "I feel independent. I've stopped complaining."

Your sense of your body may modify. Anne reported that after practicing the *Space Scene* on her own at home, she had an exhilarating experience during which her perception changed. "I was driving home from work one evening when suddenly my eyes felt two yards wide. I blinked tight and then opened them slowly. The headlights of oncoming cars looked like snowflakes. They pulsated. In fact, they were pulsating in time with the car blinkers. My time expansion is sure getting better too because this seemed to go on for several minutes, but when I looked back at my watch, the whole episode had only been a matter of seconds."

Boundaries and limitations begin to break, including your sense of self and world as separate. Your perception expands. Your sense of time, space, and motion are inseparably linked. You cannot alter one without experiencing changes in the others. Two days after Anne's perceptual alteration of the car headlights she had the following experience which further illustrates how changing your time sense leads to alterations in your senses of space and motion: "David and I went to a swap meet. It was a beautiful day and we were having a great time. I found myself becoming transfixed by the carved figure of a snake on an obelisk. I don't know why I found it so fascinating because I'm deathly afraid of snakes, but I couldn't take my attention off it. Suddenly the figure began to grow. It got bigger and bigger, coming toward me, till it was all that existed in my view. Then suddenly everything went back to normal, except for one thing. I'm no longer afraid of snakes. Isn't that amazing?"

You could say that Anne went through a standard desensitization procedure here, pairing the profound relaxation associated with her fixation and the snake to countercondition her phobia. What I found most exciting, however, was not her desensitization experience, but the alterations in space and motion she encountered.

The figure on the obelisk grew, spatially changed to fill her entire visual field, and moved in the process of doing so. Growth out of space, time, and motion is impossible. Inherent in growth is movement through space and time. Your perception of time, space, and motion will continue to expand as you progress through the imagery sequence. In time you will come to see that these three phenomena are illusion, a function of your limited perception. As your perception becomes limitless, time will be no more. Great things are in store.

SEVEN

Lightening Up

Remember those wonderful moments in your life when you were so exquisitely relaxed you felt like you were floating, disembodied, drifting cloud-like through space? Perhaps it was a magic summer night under the starry sky in a hot tub, the sound of gurgling water and silken liquid caressing your senses till you felt sublimely detached from everything. Or maybe you recall an other-worldly feeling you sensed in that hypnopompic state between sleep and wakefulness, the twilight period between a restful night's sleep and the clarity of waking refreshed to a beautiful day.

Then too you might recall a time, when after a really hectic day or week, you just suddenly shut off, and found yourself numbly staring into space, eyes wide as saucers, captivated by a wondrous, seductive state of separation from all that had preceded it. Or there are those special interludes after lovemaking when your spirit seems to soar, taking you to an ecstatic plane of being, independent of your body and earthly concerns, a world beyond your five senses. Wouldn't you like more times like these? A constant dose of this state of mind would surely take you closer to paradise. Come with me. There is a way.

DISSOCIATION

The marvelous state of consciousness I've just described is called "dissociation." By this is meant a feeling of separation of mind and body. It may be as simple as a feeling that your legs are crossed when they aren't or that your hands are on your chest when they really are at your sides. Or it may feel as if your body is arched a few inches in the middle. It may even feel as if you are floating above the couch or to the ceiling. In more extreme forms, dissociation may be termed an "out-of-body experience" where you feel as if you are actually traveling, leaving your body behind to journey to the next room, house, or farther. In any event, it is a change in your sense of location without your physically moving, and it feels wonderful.

The feeling associated with dissociation that will impress you immediately is your incredible sense of relaxation, as if you'd been all day in a sauna, or just had an hour-long massage. This relaxation dramatically lowers your positive sensory thresholds, making you more sensitive to pleasant stimuli, while raising your negative sensory thresholds to make you less aware of unpleasant stimuli. Your resulting heightened sensitivity to pleasure creates a wonderful sense of permeating sensuality.

It may seem odd to you that a state in which you feel separated from your body can also make you more aware of your bodily senses. The reality is, however, that while you *feel* detached, your senses are more sensitive, more receptive, such that if you expose yourself to beautiful things or have sex in this state, your resultant feelings are ecstatic.

As your dissociative state deepens, becomes more profound, your heightened sensuality gives way to new experience, beyond the realm of your present five senses. It is in this domain you may enjoy the feeling of trips "out of body" or "astral projection." But there is even more beyond this.

For centuries, philosophers have lamented the fact that we can never really know the great truths of our universe because we are limited by our five senses. Our reality is so filled with, so much a function of, our sensorium, we are unable to know what else there is. We force our senses upon the universe and call that reality; but what of the true nature of the cosmos, independent of our receptor organs of sight, sound, touch, smell, and taste? What is the *true* nature of reality?

Dissociation, if you continue to develop it, can be a beginning to your transcending the philosophers' lament, to rising above the limitations of a body with only five sensory modalities and experiencing a greater truth. As your facility for dissociation grows, you pass from deep relaxation and heightened five-sensory reality through a sense of out-of-body motion in your five-sensory world into a transcendent reality, independent of your body and its organs of sensory reception. You will learn in the final chapter how to use the phenomenon of the negative hallucination to further enhance your dissociation to transcend the limits of your five senses to find your greater knowledge and truth that lies above. Let us begin.

JUNGLE SCENE

In your eighth image your body disappears completely. Only consciousness remains. Really try to concentrate on the sensations called for, such as the warmth of the water and smell of sulfur, as this will increase the reality of your image and make your resultant sense of dissociation more complete. As with the other images, try practicing it three times a day for a week.

You can tape record the self-hypnosis technique and the image exactly as written and simply follow its direction on playback. If you choose to rehearse the image from memory, however, it's important that you not verbalize it. For example, when you are practicing the *Jungle Scene,* don't say to yourself, "I am cutting a path through the jungle with a machete." *Just be there.* Feel yourself there. There's no need to say, "I am there." When you remember a past good time at a party, the memory doesn't speak to you saying, "I am once again at that party." You simply remember it.

In working with the self-hypnosis technique, however, it is all right to say it to yourself in the form, "I am now feeling a sense of relaxation moving up from my toes. . . ."

JUNGLE SCENE:

"You are in a sleeping bag. It's very early in the morning. The air feels hot, close, humid. You can hear insects humming around you. Now you sit up. You see that you are in the middle of a dense jungle, a tropical rain forest. Sunlight is just beginning to filter through the canopy of leaves above you, casting a lace-like pattern of light on the jungle floor. Birds are cawing. Monkeys are chattering.

"You get up. Begin making your way through the dense undergrowth, cutting your way through with a machete. Beads of perspiration run down your face, armpits, the small of your back. Hair is matted to your forehead. Eyes sting from the salt in your perspiration. Getting warmer and warmer, hotter and hotter.

"Suddenly you come to a clearing, a grotto, a mineral hot spring. The grotto is composed of a white, chalk-like substance resembling coral. It crunches beneath the weight of your feet. The smell of sulfur is in the air. Interspersed in this white, chalk-like substance are pools of aqua-blue mineral water.

"Walk over to a pool of boiling water. Feel the hot, wet steam condense against your skin. Now you walk over to another pool of water, hot but not boiling. Remove your clothes. Glide into the hot mineral water. Muscles become soft and pliant as if in a sauna.

"Now you notice a curious thing. The pool is getting larger. First the size of a baseball diamond, then a football field, then a small lake. You look up. You see that the trees are miles high into the sky. You realize that the pool has not been getting larger, you are becoming smaller . . . shrinking . . . growing smaller and smaller. . . .

"A large, orange Monarch butterfly lights beside you. You crawl onto his back. He flies high up into the blue sky above the green jungle, dipping and soaring like a roller coaster. And you continue to shrink till finally there is nothing left at all."

REACTIONS AND USES

The most common reactions to the *Jungle Scene* center around feelings of deep relaxation and lightness: "Ooooh . . . I feel so relaxed, I want to stay there forever." "My body feels so light . . . like a feather. I feel like you'll have to hold me down to keep me from floating off the couch." "I feel like air. It's wonderful. I can go anywhere." Sometimes your first experience with dissociation can be even more dramatic as you can see from the following man's reaction: "I saw something lifting out of my body . . . a body lifting out of my body. I was still in my physical body, as if I was an observer of what was lifting . . . it looked like a body within a body. It was clear, clear skin and bones. It had a spatial shape."

You will also more than likely experience a sense of time distortion when you start to work on producing dissociation. Dissociation is an altered sense of space and you cannot alter your sense of your body space without also feeling a change in your senses of time and motion. Remember that your senses of time, space, and motion are interlocked. Changing one changes the others.

Anne's reaction to the *Jungle Scene* illustrates how this image can produce time distortion: "That's strange. I really felt the shrinking, enormously so. The orange butterfly was blinding. I felt wilted and relaxed when shrinking. I got down to nothing and then grew back when you counted to 3. I felt like a flower blooming. I was out of this world. The time expansion was amazing. It felt like hours and hours to get small and then get large again. Two weeks ago I wouldn't have believed this could happen."

Practicing the *Jungle Scene* may also lead to your experiencing a sense of motion. "I felt like I was traveling very fast," explained a young housewife of twenty-two. "It scared me and I stopped it. Now I wish I'd gone with it and seen where it would take me." There is nothing for you to be afraid of. The feelings you are discovering are positive. Go with them. They will take you ever upward.

Learning to literally lighten up your sense of weight by inducing dissociation leads to your lightening up emotionally as well. You feel free and unfettered. After practicing the *Jungle Scene* for two days, Joyce, a 32-year-old real estate broker who was feeling depressed and unloved in her marriage, recounted, "I felt out of my body. Like I was just floating there a few inches above the couch. It was great. My whole attitude's lightening up. My husband is being much more adoring."

Since dissociation is a state of profound relaxation, and relaxation makes you more sensitive to all positive stimuli, heightened sensuality is one of the first benefits you'll derive from inducing dissociation. You can use it almost immediately to enhance your sex life. After Allison had used time expansion to expand the five minutes of good sex she experienced with Derek to encompass their entire lovemaking she combined it with dissociation to elevate their good sex to great sex. I told her to practice the *Jungle Scene* three times a day for a week. Then, during sex, she was simply to say to herself, "Jungle." This word now triggered a sense of heightened sexuality and dissociation as a function of its prior association with the inducing image. Allison's sex with Derek was no longer boring.

Mark also was able to improve his sexual functioning practicing the *Jungle Scene* and using a trigger word. He built on the dissociation he'd already learned to create from the *Beach Scene* to intensify his sexuality and stop feeling old. Combining this dissociation with the recall of heat in his genital area that he'd learned to do using the *Mountain Cabin Scene,* he was able to further extend the period of his erection while he was inside a woman. Once you've practiced the *Jungle Scene,* you too can use "Jungle" as a silent trigger word during lovemaking to enhance the effects of lovemaking.

Dissociation, a feeling of separation of mind and body, is also an extremely effective weapon to add to your arsenal of techniques for pain control. You can get good results here for eliminating any kind of discomfort, regardless of its source. When you imagine your body shrinking till there is "nothing left at all," there is nothing left to hurt.

Jane, a 38-year-old receptionist, developed an excruciatingly painful case of internal shingles when she fell hopelessly in love with Simon, a married attorney in the law firm where she worked. They'd had a two-year affair during which Simon continually promised he would divorce his wife, Shelley, whom he said he detested. As time passed, it became increasingly evident to Jane that whether Simon detested Shelley or not, he was making no moves to sever their marital contract. Jane felt betrayed, a dupe and a fool, yet she kept hanging in there hoping.

While I still haven't been able to get Jane to focus on another man, I was able to get her over her shingles. Jane had tried several treatments: mainstream prescription drugs, herbal homeopathic drips, acupuncture, and chiropractic. Some provided initial relief, but her condition always returned. It was particularly resistant to treatment because the sores were inside her body and not easy to medicate.

I decided to start Jane with the *Jungle Scene* rather than glove anesthesia because her pain was so pervasive, extending through virtually all of her body. I told her to practice the image three times a day, on a regular schedule, whether or not she was experiencing pain at the time. The residue from these anesthetic fixes lasted longer and longer, and in about five months, Jane was able to control her pain. "It still bothers me occasionally," she reported, "but I know what to do. I just softly say to myself, 'Jungle,' and the pain goes away. Practicing the image every day like I do keeps the trigger strong so I can use it whenever I really need it." It's always good to continue practicing an image if you're using its name to cue a particular phenomenon. This keeps up the pairing and reconditions your trigger's strength.

A sense of detachment from your body also allows you to feel detached from the situation your body finds itself in, such as a fearful or phobic one. You can therefore use dissociation to mentally or emotionally remove or detach yourself from any situation you find unpleasant, that would otherwise cause you anxiety or overwhelm you if you were to direct your attention to it. Claudine, 18, an actress who had come to Hollywood to study her craft, developed an incapacitating fear of flying over the past two years. "It started when I was 16," she explained. "'I was flying with my parents over the Mediterranean and lightning hit our plane. It scared me to death. I've been terrified to fly every since. I'm okay for about an hour, but I throw up every hour on the hour after that. It's awful. My brother is getting married in Paris in six weeks. I have to go back for the wedding, but I'm sure not looking forward to the flight."

In Claudine's case, I not only told her to practice the *Jungle Scene* regularly for the next six weeks, I instructed her to tape it and bring the tape on the plane with her so she could plug the recorder into her ear and listen to it during her flight. The dissociation that Claudine induced by experiencing this image enabled her to detach herself from the phobic situation of the plane. If she had shrunk out of physical existence there was certainly nothing to fear from an airplane. If your phobia is one where you can run through the image in the actual situation you fear, you may want to try doing so. It's easy to play an image through in your head when on an airplane, in a crowded theater, or in some other phobic situation where you have some control. However, if the phobia is one that may come upon you abruptly, such as a nonpoisonous snake suddenly crawling over your foot, or if it is one where you need your mind to be focusing on other things such as giving a speech or meeting new people, you may want to use a trigger word like "Jungle" to cue the dissociative state the moment you need it. Practicing the image regularly when you are relaxed and not afraid prepares you to trigger its effects on cue simply by saying the word you've associated with it.

Dissociation and out-of-body experiences are common with many drugs such as marijuana, hash, THC, PCP, LSD, mescaline, psylocybin, and downers, and you can use this phenomenon to substitute for the drug state if you are trying to get off a particular substance. Jake, a 22-year-old gang member, was sent to my by his father on recommendation of the court. He'd had several brushes with the law and had most recently been implicated in a ring of car thieves that reportedly ripped off the stereos and radios of over three hundred cars a week. Jake's father blamed his son's behavior on his heavy use of "angel dust," PCP. Jake justified his using it by saying, "The world is shit, man. The ghetto I live in is hell. You don't know what it's like. We've got roaches the size of footballs. It's hopeless. Nothing ever gets you out of there. Except dust. I just take a toot of that and I'm gone, baby. I'm somewhere else and it's fine. It's the only thing I've got going for me and you want to take that away?"

Fortunately, Jake had always been interested in hypnosis and altered states and was willing to let me teach him what I knew, although he made no commitment at that point to give up PCP. He proved a good subject and did very well with the *Jungle Scene*. "Where was I?" he asked the first time I gave him the image. "I lost you completely. I was outa here." Jake learned he could use dissociation, as easily and a lot more safely than PCP to detach himself from negative places and soar to greater sensory heights. "Scoring out there on the streets is getting pretty dangerous," he admitted. "Maybe I'll give this mental mumbo jumbo a try." Today Jake is clean. He doesn't need PCP anymore. He can use his mind to induce the same effects he wanted from the drug.

IMAGINING SHRINKING

You can use your imagining shrinking down to nothing for things other than producing dissociation. The *Jungle Scene* is excellent for weight control. Visualizing yourself shrinking, getting smaller and smaller, enables you to conceive of yourself as able to decrease in size. It's particularly good if you need motivation to stay on your diet. "What's the use?" asked Claire, a 56-year-old, 160-pound mother of six sons and two daughters, ages 22 to 36. "After eight children, what can I expect?" "You can expect to lose 35 pounds," I answered her. Claire had been thin in her youth, but started a gradual weight gain after the birth of her first child. While her pregnancies were certainly a valid excuse, she relied too heavily on using them as a reason to eat whatever and whenever she wanted. "I just can't imagine ever being thin again," she confessed. "A woman my age with my history—why try?"

Claire's last statement pinpointed her problem. She needed to imagine, to conceive of losing weight, before she could manifest it in reality. After she had practiced the *Jungle Scene* for a week her attitude changed. "I don't really see why I *have* to be this big," she said. "Maybe I could take off a few pounds." Claire got her desired weight loss, but first she had to conceive of herself as smaller. The

Jungle Scene accomplished that end. If you have a hard time believing you can weigh less, practice the *Jungle Scene* to change that maladaptive conception of yourself.

You will also find the *Jungle Scene* helpful for clearing up any skin problems you may have. Your fantasy of condensing to nothing is most effective for shrinking various types of lesions. Martin, a 36-year-old pediatrician, had a severe case of eczema covering his entire body that was especially bad on his hands and feet where his skin was inflamed, itching, and oozing from vesicular lesions, which became scaly, crusted, and hardened. Sometimes his itching was so intense, Martin would scratch till he was bloody, causing even more damage to his already distressed skin. To protect himself from this violent scratching, he was forced to wear gloves at all times, even at work which he found most embarrassing. He admitted being under stress. He was set to marry his girlfriend of three years and move to New York where she was waiting for him.

The thought of a new job, new home, and marriage was causing Martin stress so I taught Martin self-hypnosis and imagery to relax him. Then I had him practice the *Jungle Scene,* focusing particularly on his imagining his lesions shriveling as his body also diminished to nothing. In less than two weeks his eczema began to clear. You too can use the same techniques as Martin if you have a similar problem.

HEAT RECALL

Another way to make your body feel lighter is by imagining heat in various parts or all of your body. In reality, heat rises and cold falls. A balloon full of hot air goes up. When the air chills, the balloon comes down. A body you imagine hotter feels lighter, while imagining cold makes your body feel heavier. You not only feel lighter and warmer when you imagine heat in your body, you feel charged, energized. Heat *is* energy. Imagining heat gives you energy. Combining heat recall with dissociation allows you to mentally take off, to soar to new heights of awareness and experience.

With that heightened sense of energy and lightness you will gain a growing sense of motion, as if you are traveling to someplace wonderful and you just can't wait to get there. As your energy grows, so does your sense of movement and once again your perception of time and space continues to alter.

JUNGLE WITH HEAT TRANSFER SCENE

Lightening up your sense of mind and body not only causes your mood to elevate and spirit to rise, it has other practical healing applications as well which I'll tell you about after this image. You'll remember that one of the physical results of recalling heat in your body is a congestion of blood in the area you are focusing on. You can use your ability to mentally direct your circulation for many things, as you will see.

To help you master this increased control over your circulatory system I have modified the *Jungle Scene* to include a heat transfer. Just as you learned to transfer cold in the *Mountain Cabin II Scene,* you will now learn to transfer heat. Cold and heat transfers are two sides to the same coin. In transferring cold you are directing blood away from a body area; in transferring heat, you are directing blood to a part of your body. In either case you are mentally controlling your circulation. Please practice the following image three times a day for a week to familiarize yourself with the technique of the heat transfer.

JUNGLE WITH HEAT TRANSFER SCENE:

"You are in a sleeping bag. It's very early in the morning. The air is hot and humid. You can hear insects humming around you. You sit up. See that you are in the middle of a dense jungle, a tropical rain forest. Sunlight is just beginning to filter through the canopy of leaves above you, casting a lace-like pattern of light on the jungle floor. Birds are cawing. Monkeys are chattering.

"You get up. Begin making your way through the dense undergrowth, cutting your path with a machete. Beads of perspiration run down your face, armpits, the small of your back. Hair is matted to your forehead. Eyes sting from the salt in the perspiration. Getting warmer and warmer, hotter and hotter.

"Suddenly you come to a clearing, a grotto, a mineral hot spring. The grotto is composed of a white chalk-like substance resembling coral. It crunches beneath the weight of your feet. The smell of sulfur is in the air. Interspersed in this white chalk-like substance are pools of aqua-blue mineral water.

"Walk over to a pool of boiling water. Hold your right hand over the boiling water. Feel the hot, wet steam condense on the surface of your right hand. First the size of a pinpoint, then a dime, then a half dollar. Spreading like ripples on a pond. Getting hotter and hotter. When you feel that heat in your right hand, place your right hand upon your right cheek. (Really do this.) Now let the heat in your right hand drain into your right cheek. Cheek is becoming hot, flushed. The blood is rushing to the surface of the skin in your right cheek. When all the heat has drained from your right hand into your right cheek, place your right hand once again at your side. (Do this.) Now place your right hand again upon your right cheek. Let the heat in your cheek drain back into your hand. Hand is becoming hot, vibrant, pulsating, flushed. When all the heat has drained from your right cheek back into your right hand, place your right hand again at your side. (Do so.)

"Now you walk to another pool of water, warm but not boiling. Remove your clothes. Glide into the warm mineral water. Your muscles become soft and pliant as if in a sauna. Then you notice a curious thing. The pool is getting larger. First the size of a baseball diamond, then a football field, then a small lake. You look up. See that the trees are miles high into the sky. You realize that the pool has not been getting larger, you are getting smaller. You are shrinking, growing smaller and smaller. . . .

"A large, orange Monarch butterfly lights beside you. You crawl onto his back. He soars high up into the blue sky above the green jungle, dipping and soaring like a roller coaster. And you continue to shrink till finally there is nothing left at all."

REACTIONS AND USES .

After her first exposure to the above image, one woman responded, "I feel good. My hand felt really warm. It moved on its own." You may find, as this woman did, that recalling heat in your right hand actually makes it feel lighter and it seems to rise to your cheek of its own accord as if a hot air balloon was attached to it.

In addition to feeling heat and lightness in your right hand, you may also begin to feel that growing surge of energy I was telling you about. A young man in his teens reported, "That heat thing in my hand was great. I felt vibrating." You will quite often experience increased energy as a vibration. You may recall Anne's description of her experience after the *Garden Scene* where she felt a humming around her car as her energy soared and she felt charged by the heat of the pavement: "It was kind of sexual, but more electrical, like a surge of adrenaline. Then I noticed a rhythm to it as if it were somehow in pace with the car, like the car's life force." The feeling Anne is describing is a vibration and your recalling heat can cause the same sensation for you. It's wonderful. You'll feel like you can tackle the world, or as Anne said, "I was about to discover America!"

It's also interesting that the young man said, "I felt vibrating," not "My hand felt vibrating." Even though you may be recalling heat in a very circumscribed part of your body, the result may be a feeling of lightness, heat, and vibration throughout your entire body. Your recalling heat causes increased energy throughout your whole being.

The wonderful energy, lightness, and warmth you can experience with a heat transfer is excellent for banishing the blues and depression. Joyce reported her attitude was continuing to lighten up after practicing the last image. "I was out of this world. Time was eternal. My energy was incredible. I feel so much love now. I feel I could conquer the whole California real estate market." Anything that makes you feel better improves your functioning in all areas, whether it be work, relationships, or play.

ELIMINATING ANXIETY ATTACKS

Besides using heat recall to lighten your mood and energize your being, you can make use of its direct physical effect on your body, congestion of blood. You may have heard of the expression, "He got cold feet," to describe someone who chickened out of a venture or got too scared to go ahead with something. The expression has a basis in reality. People really do get cold feet, as well as cold, clammy hands, when they are uptight or having an anxiety attack.

You may remember a time when you dreaded shaking hands with someone you were worried about meeting, such as a potential employer, because your hands had suddenly grown so cold you didn't want your new acquaintance to know how nervous you were. When you are anxious, blood actually rushes from your extremities, leaving you with cold hands and feet. You can eliminate a case of nerves or anxiety simply by recalling heat in your hands and/or feet and directing your blood back.

Mel, a 56-year-old car salesman, came to me with the following problem: "I get so tense when it comes time to make a deal, my hands feel like ice. I like to close with a handshake, but when my customers get a grip that feels like an ice cube it puts them off. I think it makes them not trust me. They probably wonder why I'm so nervous and if I'm not trying to put something over on them." I asked Mel to practice the *Jungle with Heat Transfer Scene* for a week until he got the hang of it. At that point he was to use the trigger word "Heat," while focusing on his hands to direct blood there whenever he felt himself growing anxious with a client. Mel happily reports he now feels much more relaxed at work and has a warm handshake.

CURING MIGRAINES

You can also use your ability to mentally control your circulation in a rather ingenious fashion to eliminate the throbbing, pulsating pain due to the vasocongestion of a migraine headache. Research has found that you can actually end a headache by raising your hand temperature. If you imagine heat in your hands, blood will leave your cephalic or head region where it has overcongested and is causing pressure and pain, to be diverted to the area of focus, your hands.

Connie, a 46-year-old investment banker, complained of pounding headaches so severe they made her cry. "When I have one I think it'll never end," she explained. "My vision blurs, I'm nauseated, I can't eat, I miss work. I feel I'm going out of my mind. The worst ones last about three days. It was diagnosed as chronic tension. I set standards too high for myself. Plus my parents give me a lot of stress. I'm single and my social life is nil. I feel I have no control over my life. I think I'm a good person. I'm fair, honest, keep commitments, considerate, generous, faithful, educated, hard-working, ambitious without being cutthroat—but I'm too hard on myself when I fail."

"How about your hands?" I finally asked her. I think my question perplexed Connie, but she answered, "They're cold all the time." "Just as I thought," I smiled. "You've got so much blood pounding up there to give you a headache, there's not enough left to keep your hands warm. Most headaches are either muscular or vascular, caused by muscle tension or too much blood pressure in your head area. The pulsing, pounding sensations you describe lead me to believe your problem is vascular. The cure is getting that overabundance of blood to leave your head and neck. You do this by imagining your hands are hot. This heat recall will divert the blood from your head to your hands."

I asked Connie to practice the *Jungle with Heat Transfer Scene* as many times throughout the day as she could in order to keep her hands warm and the blood diverted from her head and neck. In a month her headaches began to ease up and in six months she was relatively free of them, reporting that when she did have a headache it was mild and she was able to dismiss it in a matter of hours by recalling heat in her hands.

NOURISHING SKIN AND DRYING LESIONS

You can also use a heat transfer to clear up a skin condition such as acne or psoriasis. In this case practice the *Jungle with Heat Transfer Scene* for a week, learning to transfer heat from your hand to your cheek and back again. Then, rather than transferring the heat from your hand to your cheek, transfer it from your hand to the areas of your body where your skin disorder is.

Grace, a 28-year-old cocktail hostess, complained of a recurring case of acne on her chin. "Maybe it's all that smoke and greasy food I'm always around at work that makes my skin act up," she said. "My face will be clear for a week or two. Then boom, pimple city on my chin. I can feel how oily my skin gets at these times."

First I asked Grace to practice the *Beach, Desert,* and *Farm* scenes to recall heat all over her body from the sun and the *Mountain Cabin Scene* to recall heat on her skin from fire. A month later, after she'd spent a week on each of these scenes, I suggested she practice the

Jungle with Heat Transfer Scene for a week, at which time she was to transfer heat from her hand to her chin whenever it started to feel oily, a telltale sign that she was about to suffer an outbreak of acne. This procedure worked and Grace is no longer bothered by facial skin eruptions. Mentally directing blood to the afflicted area served to nourish and heal the skin and dry up her acne.

CREATING SEXUAL AROUSAL

Your ability to transfer heat will serve you especially well if you wish to intensify your sexual feelings. You'll remember my saying that sexual arousal is partially a function of a congestion of blood in your genital area. Therefore, you can enhance your arousal by transferring heat from your hand to your genitals, once you've learned the hand-to-cheek transfer by practicing the *Jungle with Heat Transfer Scene* for a week.

Rebecca, a 30-year-old pet store operator, used a vibrator to masturbate and could also reach a climax through oral stimulation, but no man, including her present boyfriend, Chad, had ever been able to bring her to climax through intercourse. "I love sex," she said. "I'm easily aroused but something seems to be holding me back. I spent six years in analysis and figured out that I might be equating sexuality with letting go of my mother. Both my parents were tight and controlling. They never showed me or each other any physical affection. Somehow I don't think they'd approve of me having a climax, but what difference does that make? I don't think about them when I'm making love anyway. All I think is, 'Am I going to come?' "

Rebecca needed to be more grounded in the sexual sensory reality of the moment in order to block any fears or negative affirmations concerning her inability to climax. I asked her to practice a heat transfer to supply that grounding. She rehearsed the

Jungle with Heat Transfer Scene for a week, learning to direct blood to her hand and cheek. Then I suggested, "The next time you are making love to Chad and he is inside of you, I want you to use the trigger word, 'heat,' to induce heat in your right hand. When you feel that heat in your right hand, place your right hand as close to your clitoris as you can. Then let the heat in your hand drain into your genital area. When all the heat has drained from your hand to your genitals, remove your hand and hold the sexual heat as long as you can. Give yourself the affirmation, 'Every thrust he makes I grow hotter and hotter, hotter and hotter.' Continue repeating that affirmation, all the time concentrating on your sexual heat. You will feel yourself building to climax."

Rebecca was smiling when she reported back after her homework assignment. "At first I thought I was going to explode and I held back," she said. "It reminded me of the very first time I ever masturbated to climax. I guess I was about thirteen. I thought I was going to urinate. In fact, I did lose some urine the first time I had an orgasm. I suddenly realized I was associating letting go sexually with loss of bladder control and I gave myself permission to let go and experience the sensations of heat and sex. And I did it! I made the hurdle. I came. Chad was delighted. He says to thank you."

Nate, 56, a systems analyst, said he could be sexually potent with any woman except "a particular young lady." Unfortunately this was the woman with whom he was then in love. "I can't understand it," he said. "I have erections every day and every night. I wake up with them and I go to sleep with them. I was married twice. The first marriage lasted twenty-four years and sex was fine. We had two beautiful daughters. Then I was single for two years and I had a ball. I went to the South Seas. There were gorgeous women everywhere and sex was terrific. My second marriage lasted six months. We were in lust for half that time and when it wore off we realized we hated each other. But I was still potent as a bull.

"I think my trouble might have started with Enide. I call her the Dragon Lady. She was beautiful, but really pushy. I remember the first time we made love. I took her away for the weekend to a very expensive hotel. During dinner, the first night we got here, she said, 'We've got to get up to the room and see if you can make it with me.' Doesn't that seem like a strange thing to say? Why wouldn't I be able to make it with her? That one comment put me off balance and I lost my erection at the moment of penetration. She looked right at me and said, 'You got a problem.' I felt lower than dirt. My manhood had been tampered with.

"Now my present girl, Kitty, is just the opposite. She's sweet, childlike. We play kissy-huggy all day, but I don't get horny like I should. I feel a numbness down there. I can still masturbate okay, but . . . I don't know. Maybe it's the age difference. She's twenty-six. She's into things I should be through with. I keep asking myself, 'What does she want with me?' "

Nate's anxiety over his sexual failure with Enide and the age difference with Kitty was literally making him numb in his genitals. The feet and hands are not the only extremity blood leaves during an anxiety attack. Many a professional athlete can report the diminished size of the team's genitalia during the shower-up before the big game, hardly a boost to the male ego.

I asked Nate to practice the *Jungle with Heat Transfer Scene* for a week to gain control over his circulation. Then, as I had also instructed Rebecca, I told him to use "heat" as a trigger word to induce heat in his right hand during sex with Kitty. He was then to place his right hand on his penis and let the heat flow from his hand into his penis. I had already encouraged him to manipulate himself manually during sex to rid himself of his numbness and get the feeling back, the blood flowing, through his genitals. When all the heat had drained from his hand into his genitals he was to remove his hand and begin penetration, all the time focusing on the sexual heat.

"For a guy who can't stand up and chew gum at the same time,

I did pretty good," he reported. "I was able to insert and as long as I kept my mind on the heat I was okay. It's really just a matter of concentration, isn't it?" I was in complete agreement.

YOUR FUTURE

Using imagery-induced dissociation and heat recall to lighten up and transcend your common five-sense reality will become natural to you after you've worked at it awhile. That's what's so nice about it. Your paranormal reality will soon become your normal one, and your then paranormal one will be a reality greater than any you have yet to experience.

More and more you will come to see that reality is what you feel, what you experience. Everything in this book, whether it be about healing pain, eliminating an urge to smoke, or traveling out of your body, is really only dealing with what you feel. Your perception of time, space, and motion itself is a feeling.

If you see 24 frames of a picture pass before your eyes in the span of a second, you perceive the picture as moving. But, you say, the picture is not really moving at all. It is an illusion. True. The motion picture is a function of your limited perception, your inability to see 24 consecutive pictures in a one-second interval. Your limited ability to grasp space gives you an illusion of motion. You never really "know" motion at all. You only sense it.

In fact, your entire five-sense reality is illusion, a function of your limited perception. You force your senses upon the world and interpret them as reality, the true nature of things. However, as your perception expands, your limitations break, and you behold a greater reality.

Just as time is a psychological construct, a function of your consciousness, a thought process, so are space and motion. You can't see space. You can't see motion. You can only see objects in space, objects in motion.

Out of body, out of object—time, space, and motion cease to exist. You can be anywhere instantly or all places at once. Past, present, and future coexist. Dissociation combined with the energy of heat recall will take you toward independence of your five-sensory perception, i.e., independence of the illusions of time, space, and motion. There lies your truth. There lies your paradise.

EIGHT

Peace, Quiet,
and Playing
with Time

Now I'm going to show you how to
further develop your facility for psychologically controlling your
time sense. The results will be a broadening sense of peace, higher
spirits, and continually soaring energy. You may also experience a
surprising sense of motion. Senses of time, space, and motion are
inseparably linked. You cannot modify one without expecting
changes in the others.

TIME CONCENTRATION

In Chapter Six you were told how you could make good times last
longer by using time expansion. Since time itself is a psychological
construct, you have the power to not only lengthen it, but also make

it seem to pass more quickly. The phenomenon is called "time concentration." I'll teach you how to use this technique to make it seem that your bad times are speeding by. Using time expansion to make positive times last and time concentration to feel that negative times are zooming by will result in achievement of a vastly more positive reality.

You normally experience time concentration in everyday life when you are having a marvelous time. If you are at a great party with friends, time zips by. If you are feeling down with nothing to do, on the other hand, time drags. As discussed in Chapter Six, you want to be able to reverse this normal process, make good times "drag" and bad times "zip."

I'll explain how to apply time concentration to healing purposes following the image for inducing it. You'll be able to use this phenomenon to shorten any period of discomfort, such as a long air flight when you fear flying, an episode of pain or depression that runs in cycles, the interval between meals, cigarettes, alcohol, or drugs when you are withdrawing, and bouts of insomnia.

By practicing the *Clock Scene* you will learn to condense temporally any negative experience. Again, the key to time distortion is to imagine more or less time passing than is lapsing in reality. To expand time, you imagined that more time was going by than really was, such as the billion years of the *Space Scene*. To concentrate time, you will imagine that less time is passing than it takes to imagine it.

About 30 seconds lapse in the *Clock Scene*, but it will take approximately 5 minutes to imagine it. If the image seems completely real, apparently only 30 seconds will have passed instead of the actual 5 minutes necessary for the image, a tenfold concentration of time. The *Clock Scene*, like the past two images for time distortion, begins with your giving yourself affirmations for time alteration.

CLOCK SCENE:

"Ten minutes of actual time will seem like one minute to you. Time will go by very, very rapidly. It will seem like an instant. In less than an hour, you can accomplish an entire day's work and accomplish it more effectively than you would ordinarily.

"You are on the second floor of a house. It's almost midnight, early spring. In the room is a great bed with a canopy. On the bed is a Raggedy Ann doll and wooden toy soldiers. There is a bay window. Moonlight streams through the window, bathing the room in a silver glow.

"Go to the window. Look outside. See a city, a clock tower, a river like a ribbon of silver in the moonlight, a bridge, then rolling countryside. Now the clock begins to toll the hour of midnight. It strikes for the first time. See clouds pass over the moon.

"The clock chimes a second time. A breeze blows through the window, ruffling the curtains. On the third chime of the clock there is a scent of lilac from a hedge beneath your window. When the clock strikes for the fourth time you notice a taste of honey from tea and honey you had earlier that evening.

"On the fifth stroke of the clock you see a golden light outside your window, like sparklers, like gold dust. When the clock strikes a sixth time the golden light enters your room, washing the walls in orange.

"On the seventh chime you have a feeling of weightlessness. On the eighth stroke of the clock your feet leave the floor. When the clock strikes for the ninth time you float out the window.

"The tenth chime of the clock sounds very far away. You drift over the city, over the river, over the countryside. On the clock's eleventh stroke all sorts of happy childhood memories come to mind . . . circuses, lemonade, picnics, pots of gold, rainbows, sleigh-bells. . . . When the clock strikes midnight, you float straight up toward the stars."

REACTIONS AND USES

Mary, a 30-year-old housewife complaining of stress, fatigue, and poor memory and concentration, got what she described as "a quiet inside," from doing the *Clock Scene.* "There was also a sense of fast motion. And great spirits!" After practicing this image three times a day for a week Mary reported reading a 400-page book in only ninety minutes. This was a quantum leap forward for her in memory and concentration.

Stephanie, 32, a seamstress in the garment industry, reacted, "That's probably the best image I've done so far. It was so clear. I felt weightless. Did you see my hands coming up? Feet too? I was just getting lighter and lighter." I didn't see Stephanie's hands and feet actually rise off the couch, but to her it really felt as if they were. Her self-induced sensations were intensely vivid to her.

You too may discover that changing your time sense alters your space sense. This in turn changes your sense of body weight, i.e., your sense of the amount of pull the Earth's gravity has on you. Newton's Law of Gravitation states: "Any two bodies in the Universe attract each other with a force that is directly proportional to their masses and inversely proportional to the square of their distance apart." Mass is the amount of matter in your body. Since you cannot have matter out of space, you cannot have your body out of space. To exist without your body you must therefore rise above your illusion of space.

On a more practical side, Stephanie proclaimed the following benefits from time concentration: "My workday at the factory seemed much shorter. I had more energy in the evenings."

SHORTENING NEGATIVE EXPERIENCES

You can use time concentration to shorten any negative experience. I told Claudine to practice the *Clock Scene* for a week and then when she was on her plane to Paris, combine time control with her dissociation from the *Jungle Scene* by telling herself throughout the flight, "Time is going very, very rapidly. It seems like an instant." These affirmations had more power because she'd paired them with imagery-induced time concentration for a week. She reported, "It worked great. The whole flight seemed to last less than an hour."

Two years ago, Gladys, 77, had a bilateral mastectomy and later developed osteomyelitis of her sternum, an infectious inflammatory bone disease marked by local death and separation of tissue. Her husband, Ira, 80, a noted pianist, died of a heart attack six months later, leaving her depressed and with little money to live on. "I keep having black thoughts of being an old lady in a convalescent home with nothing to do all day," she said. "I hate being alone, but I had to quit my job as a day care supervisor, the pain in my chest gets so bad. I can't even work part-time. I have no children. I'm no longer useful. I can't bear to stay in my room. All I do is walk around the block. I need more social contact, but the people in my building are so old and non-stimulating. If I could just get rid of some of the pain I could join a theater group, make some friends away from the hellhole I live in. But I could never sit through a whole play the way I feel now."

Gladys's pain ran in cycles. She would feel fine for an hour or two. Then she'd have attacks like sharp stabbings that would last anywhere from 30 seconds to 5 minutes. I taught her glove anesthesia using the *Mountain Cabin II Scene* and asked her to transfer anesthesia from her hand to her sternum during an attack. She learned to induce time expansion with the *Space* and *Farm* scenes, at which point she was to give herself time expansion affirmations whenever she was pain-free to prolong the time between attacks. I also had her work on dissociation using the *Jungle Scene,* such that she imagined herself shrinking to nothingness during an attack, separating herself from a body in pain.

I then taught Gladys the *Clock Scene* so she could use time concentration to shorten her sense of the length of her pain attacks.

Whenever she felt an attack coming on, she was to affirm to herself, "Ten minutes seem like one. Time is going very, very rapidly. It seems like an instant."

It took a few months, but Gladys showed progress. "It's funny," she said. "When I use time concentration, the attacks not only seem shorter, they seem less severe. Time distortion seems somehow to take me out of my body and away from my pain." With her new supply of pain-control images, Gladys was able to join a theater group and a book club. She has two good friends and looks forward to cultivating more.

Carrie, 38, found it difficult to quit smoking amidst the stress of the public relations firm where she worked as a publicist. "The time between cigarettes seems like an eternity," she complained. "I'm not having any trouble stopping smoking at home, but at work—oh, brother!" After using the *Clock Scene* to practice inducing time concentration for a week and then giving herself time concentration affirmations throughout her workday, Carrie said, "I can't believe how much faster work seems to be going. I no longer need a cigarette to break up my day." You too can use time concentration to shorten the periods when you are edgy or have strong cravings if you are withdrawing from cigarettes. Practice the *Clock Scene* three times a day for a week. Then give yourself the affirmations for time concentration whenever nicotine withdrawal is making you tense or your urges to smoke are strong.

You can also use time concentration to substitute for the effects of certain drugs you may be trying to release your dependency on. Two drugs that are commonly associated with a feeling of time moving rapidly are cocaine and "speed," or "crystal." Any "upper" will usually result in a sensation of time speeding by.

"My life's a bore," explained Damien, a 23-year-old unemployed cocaine user now living at home with his parents since being fired from his last job as a chauffeur for being high and driving his employer into a tree. "I'm in a rut. Everything is the same ol' thing.

I never go out. I just sit home and watch TV. Sometimes my girl comes by, but I'm tired of her too. The only thing that puts a little spark in my life is coke—it speeds things up, gives me energy, makes things exciting."

I suggested that Damien practice the *Clock Scene* for a week. Then, the next time he felt especially bored, when time was really dragging, he was to give himself affirmations for time concentration to the effect that time was speeding by, just the opposite of what he would normally be telling himself during these slow times. "It really helped," he reported after two weeks of practice. "The time concentration wasn't as great as the coke, but it did teach me a lesson that I'm really responsible for my own boredom. When I was able to turn it around mentally with time concentration I realized I could live without coke. Excitement is a state of mind and I can generate it myself." You can create a sense of accelerating time and heightened adrenaline flow anytime you wish by inducing time concentration. Now let's look at another image you can do to induce time concentration and further heighten that energy.

BLUEBIRD SCENE

This image increases your sense of time concentration because even less time passes in it than in the *Clock Scene*, yet it takes the same amount of time. About 30 seconds lapse in the *Clock Scene*, providing a tenfold time concentration if it takes 5 minutes to imagine. In the following image, however, only about 5 seconds pass (the time it takes a bluebird to fly from a branch to your outstretched hand), a sixtyfold time concentration. I wouldn't really expect your sense of time to condense sixty times from practicing this image, but if time seems to go at all faster than the last image, you've done well and the *Bluebird Scene* is definitely worth the effort.

BLUEBIRD SCENE:

"Ten minutes of actual time will seem like one minute to you. Time will go by very, very rapidly. It will seem like an instant. In less than an hour you can accomplish an entire day's work and do it more effectively than you would ordinarily.

"It's a beautiful spring day. You are sitting on the bank of a river, under a willow tree. You are looking up at a branch on which is perched a bluebird. Your arms are outstretched. The bird leaves the branch flying toward you.

"Notice the sound of the water babbling over the rocks of the river bottom. The bird draws closer. A breeze blows through the woods, bringing to your nostrils the smell of a picnic lunch spread before you on a red and white checkered tablecloth. There's milk, French bread, cheese. The bird is getting closer.

"Look up the river. See a pink castle with high turrets. Flags wave from the turrets. Suddenly feel a tickle on your palm. A feather grazes it. The bird lands in your hand. Feel its weight. Feel its body heat.

"Gaze into the eyes of the bird. See yourself sitting on a riverbank, under a willow tree. The tree turns to glass, becomes transparent. There is a glittering, moss-like substance hanging from the glass branches. The bird closes his eyes. The scene is gone."

REACTIONS AND USES

Reactions I typically get to the *Bluebird Scene* are: "I can't believe how quick that went. How long was I there?" or "I lost all track of time. I feel so light. Why is that?" or "I feel so charged up. What energy! How come it went so fast?"

You can put the time concentration you achieve from practicing the *Bluebird Scene* to the same uses as the *Clock Scene*, condensing any negative experience. Cynthia, 55, the mother of three grown daughters, went into deep depression over financial matters when she and her husband, Sam, borrowed heavily on their restaurant to pay for the wedding of their youngest daughter, Candy. "Then everything went wrong," she explained. "A lawsuit from an employee, problems with the Health Department, building permit violations, an illness with my husband. The wedding was beautiful and I tried to get through it okay, but everyone knew I wasn't right.

"I saw several doctors and one of them put me on an antidepressant. It helped a little, at first, but my depression kept coming back. That was eight years ago. Financially, we're back on our feet. Candy is happily married. But that damned depression still has a grip on me. The slightest thing can set me off. Something as minor as missing a bus can send me into despair. It usually lasts about three days. Then bang, for no reason at all, I'm fine again."

I suggested that Cynthia practice both the *Clock* and *Bluebird* scenes to learn how to induce time concentration. She seemed especially fond of the bluebird, as I noticed a broad smile cross her face the moment I asked her to recall it, and I decided to have her focus on this image. Once she had practiced it a week I advised her to give herself the time concentration affirmations whenever she felt a bout of depression coming on, to speed up the cycle. After a month she said, "My depression never lasts more than a day now, and it isn't as bad. I think the worst thing about it was my fear it would never go away. I'm over that fear now. I know it'll go away because I know how to *make* it go away."

If you too, like Cynthia, suffer spells of the blues for no apparent reason, practicing the *Bluebird Scene* to induce time concentration will help them fade fast. Practice the image a week and then, whenever you feel yourself slipping into a bad mood, give yourself time concentration affirmations to speed your mood's cycle. Depression runs in cycles and there's no need for you to wait it out when there is a way you can end it much sooner.

Monty, a 42-year-old clothing merchant and father of Dick, 16, and Nancy, 12, was drinking a bottle of wine a day and realized he had a problem. "My wife hates it when I drink," he said. "I get belligerent. Me and her are good friends though and I want to stop. The stuff keeps me from sleeping and then I feel lousy all day at work, which only makes me want a drink more when I get home to relax me. It's a vicious circle. I think that's how I got started, the cocktail after work for relaxation. You know, that's the hardest drink to get rid of. If I could just go without drinking in that period between when I get home and we all sit down to dinner, I know I'd have it licked. I'm having trouble with my insurance policy because of an elevated liver function and my blood pressure is up. I'm worried about this quadruple bypass business I keep hearing about. A guy at work younger than me just had one."

I worked with Monty on the *Bluebird Scene,* teaching him to use time concentration to speed up his sense of the hour or two interval between his getting home from work and eating dinner. "Now I don't have *time* for a drink when I get home from work," he laughed. "At least I don't feel like I do." Monty proved to be right. When he stopped his drinks after work, he stopped drinking completely.

A use you can make of the *Bluebird Scene* that is not related to time control is to induce hunger if you wish to improve your appetite or if you have anorexia. Imagining yourself happily and hungrily eating the milk, bread, and cheese of this image will not only make you hungry for these foods, it will help you to conceive of actually enjoying eating them. If there are certain foods such as vegetables, yogurt, or cottage cheese that you feel you should be eating for better nutrition, weight loss or gain, substitute these foods for the picnic lunch in the *Bluebird Scene.* You'll be pleased to discover that you'll actually start liking these foods. But remember, your image is that you like these foods, not just that you eat them. Anything is possible in mind.

INCREASED ENERGY

One of the greatest benefits you will experience from practicing time concentration is heightened energy. After Mary practiced the *Bluebird Scene* three times a day for a week she reported, "My energy is limitless. I do booster shots when doing the housework . . . little time concentration sessions of less than a minute. My inductions are becoming shorter. I can get an effect in less than half a minute now where it used to take as much as ten."

Energy is not a kind of matter. It neither takes up space nor has weight, in the usual sense. Energy is manifested in things like electricity, light, sound, and heat. Energy is something that produces changes in matter. Energy, while not of your body, can change your body. It is in your world of the body, but it is not of your world of the body. Your body is its temple. It houses energy.

Your body, because it is of matter, which is of space, which is of time, which is of motion, which is of your illusion, is also illusion. Transcending the illusion of your body will lead to your reaching the greater reality that is your paradise.

You reach paradise not by the flesh that is matter, but by something that produces a change in matter, i.e., energy. Shortening time is in essence shortening an illusion. As your illusion of matter and its associated time, space, and motion fades, your sense of energy expands. You'll learn more about the nature of energy and how to create it with imagery in the following chapters. But first I'm going to teach you to strengthen your powers of imagery so you can get even greater positive results.

NINE

Strengthening Imagery

People sometimes complain that they have trouble imagining. Some of their senses aren't as vivid as others in their imagery or they may feel they are going in and out of it, not maintaining their concentration as long as they'd like. Sometimes unwanted material such as things they have to do or a past fear creeps into their imagery and distracts them. Or maybe your image isn't quite "real" enough to get just the effect you want. One man who was practicing glove anesthesia to alleviate the pain of a herniated disc said, "My hand starts to get tingling when I imagine sticking it into snow in the *Mountain Cabin II Scene* but my image of snow never seems to be quite strong enough to get my hand really numb." After he practiced the four strengthening images in this chapter he was able to resume his practice of glove anesthesia, making his recall of cold real enough to actually anesthetize his hand.

The purpose of the four images I'm going to introduce you to in this chapter is to give you a greater facility for imagery in general. You will find that after practicing them, you'll be able to do *any* image better. If you had difficulty with any of the images thus far, you'll be able to go back to them and find that they come much more easily for you.

Since I designed these four images primarily to strengthen your imagery powers in general, they were not meant to be used in the treatment of any particular specific problems. However, in the over fifteen years that have passed since their creation, I've discovered that these images can be applied individually to helping certain problems. I'll tell you what those are as I give you each image.

HEIGHTENING YOUR RECALL OF TOUCH

In order to strengthen your imagery powers you'll be focusing on your recall of the sensory components of touch and their subcomponents: pressure (light/heavy), temperature (hot/cold), liquidity (wet/dry). Of all your five senses, you concentrate most heavily on touch to strengthen your imagery because touch is the sense most related to the phenomena you have been inducing—relaxation, anesthesia, pressure, time expansion, dissociation, heat and time concentration. All these are phenomena you know most by your sense of touch. You cannot experience any of these phenomena through your senses of sight, hearing, taste, or smell. In order to better induce these phenomena, it will therefore help you to intensify your recall of touch. In the following imagery sequence you will focus on recalling the tactile sensory subcomponents of pressure, temperature, and liquidity in different combinations.

POOL SCENE

The *Pool Scene* asks you to concentrate on recalling the tactile subcomponents of liquidity and temperature in four combinations. Those subcomponent combinations are: wet/cold, wet/hot, dry/cold, and dry/hot.

Your ability to imagine combining simple component sensations into more complex assemblies is important. It allows you to create a feeling you've never experienced before by recalling a given number of simple sensations and putting them together to feel in a specific area of your body. For example, a woman who has never experienced an orgasm can "create" one by recalling the simple sensations of warmth, pressure, and pulsation and transferring them to her genital area where they combine to compose the complex sensation of the orgasm. You'll remember from your work with anesthesia and heat transfers that you can recall a sensation in a part of your body where you've experienced it before and then transfer that sensation to a place in your body where you've never before felt it.

POOL SCENE:

"You are sitting in a white ice-cream chair by an Olympic swimming pool in a sunken garden. It's one o'clock in the afternoon, mid-July, very, very hot. You are wearing a black bathing suit. At the far side of the pool are cabanas, Arabian tents in multicolored stripes. Beyond the cabanas are coconut palms. Parrots with brilliant plumage of purple, chartreuse, and turquoise perch in the palm fronds.

"You are sitting at a table out of the center of which is a great orange and blue striped umbrella. Before you on the table is an ice-cold glass of lemonade. Beads of moisture condense on the surface of the glass. Pick up the glass. Feel it *wet* and *cold* in your hand.

"Stand up. Your bare feet touch the *hot, dry* cement. Run to the edge of the pool where water has been splashed. Stand on the *hot, wet* cement. Bring the glass of lemonade to your lips. Drink. Feel the ice-cold lemonade run into your mouth, down your throat, into your stomach. Notice the contrast between the cold on the inside of your stomach from the lemonade and the heat exerted on the outside from the sun.

"Go lie in a lounge chair. Bask in the sun. You are getting thirsty again. Get up. Walk over to a Coke machine. Press your warm body against the *dry, cold* metal of the machine. It takes your breath away. Withdraw immediately. Put money into the machine. The Coke is dispensed. Drink. Feel the light, wet bubbles of the carbonation. Taste the Coke's sweetness.

"Leave the Coke machine. Go lie down in a grove of coconut palms. Drift to the sound of the wind in the palm fronds. . . ."

REACTIONS AND USES

People's reactions to the *Pool Scene* generally show that they have experienced the image in greater detail than they have done with prior images. This is especially true in reference to their recall of temperature and wetness or dryness. A woman in her forties reacted, "That place was so hot. I could hear the Coke drop . . . Crash! . . . the ice tinkle. . . . When I reached for the lemonade I saw two bracelets on my wrist I wore years ago. That lemonade was good! My hand still feels wet from holding the glass."

As your imagery becomes more vivid, the feelings you are able to induce with it become more extreme. A 29-year-old man reported the following reaction: "First I felt like I was sleeping. Then my hand was freezing . . . so weird. Like my body was moving. I lost a lot of body awareness. I can't feel my extremities." Your mind knows not the limitations of time, space, and motion. As you continue to develop your imagery, your senses of these three phenomena will continue to alter, even though that is neither your conscious purpose nor your direct mental focus.

Again, the primary use of this image is to bolster your powers of imagery in general, such that you are better equipped to induce the phenomena you've been working on producing thus far or produce a specific image so vivid it will manifest in reality. All the images in this book are designed to increase your ability for pleasure in all five senses by directing your attention to their positive aspects and lowering your positive sensory thresholds. I have, however, discovered that the practice of the *Pool Scene* is a particularly reinforcing experience because it involves your recalling especially pleasant activities, lounging around a beautiful pool drinking lemonade and Coca-Cola.

If you are subject to bouts of depression or even just the blahs, you'll find it helpful to practice the *Pool Scene* or similar imagery involving pleasant activities. It will help you to remember the joy you once experienced from the same or similar activities and motivate you to do them again.

Sheila, 26, gave up her job as a filing clerk when she married Jeff, 25, a plumbing supplies distributor. She hated her job and looked forward to spending her time building their marriage. A year later she was depressed. "I don't know what's the matter with me," she said. "The marriage is great. I love Jeff a lot. I just don't feel like doing anything anymore. I hate to say it, but I'm bored. Yet I don't want to go back to work."

"What do you do for excitement?" I asked, thinking I'd already discovered her problem. Sheila looked at me blankly, then said, "Nothing much. Mostly watch TV." I asked her to practice the *Pool Scene*. After a week she reported, "I'd forgotten how much I used to enjoy swimming, boating, diving, just basking by a pool." "Being married doesn't mean you're a prisoner." I smiled. "You can still do those things." A week later Sheila joined a gym and her depression lifted. Sometimes when you get in a rut you just need to jog your memory to remember the activities that used to make you happy. Then do them!

ARCTIC SCENE

In this image you'll learn to further intensify your imagining of the four combinations of the sensory subcomponents you focused on in your last image, the *Pool Scene*: wet/cold, wet/hot, dry/cold, and dry/hot. The image teaches you to recall the extremes of hot and cold. You start your snowy journey in the frigid climes of the polar icecap and conclude it in the steaming jungles of a prehistoric world.

ARCTIC SCENE:

"You are walking through mountains of ice and snow. It's forty degrees below zero. You are wearing a fur parka. You are at the polar icecap, the North Pole. The sky is a pale blue, the sun a faint yellow, the snow a dazzling, blinding white.

"You are approaching the mouth of a cave. All around the cavern's mouth are long, slender, glistening icicles. Take the glove off your right hand. Run your right hand up and down the *wet, cold*, slippery surface of the icicle.

"Go inside the cave. In the center of the cavern is a pool of deep, dark water. From a knapsack on your back you take a tin cup. Scoop up the water. Bring the *dry, cold* metal of the cup to your lips. Drink. Feel the ice-cold water run into your mouth, down your throat, and into your stomach.

"Stand. Go back to the mouth of the cave. Suddenly from above you hear a whirring, mechanical sound. Look up. See a helicopter. A wind is created from the motion of the rotor. The copter lands. Walk over to it. Place your bare right hand on the *dry, hot* metal where the engine is. Withdraw it immediately.

"Get inside the helicopter. Fasten your seat belt. The copter begins to ascend. You are engulfed in a silver mist. Before you, on your lap, is a tray. On the tray is a white plate with a sizzling, juicy T-bone steak. Next to it is a bowl of crisp, green salad. Begin eating. It tastes delicious. Notice the contrast between the pressure on the inside of your stomach from the food and the pressure exerted on the outside from the seat belt.

"The copter begins to descend. Look at the altitude gauge. You are 5,000 feet above sea level. You are going to land 2,000 feet above sea level. As the copter goes lower and lower, it gets warmer and warmer inside your compartment. At 4,000 feet above sea level it's 90 degrees inside your helicopter. The windows are steamed up. At 3,000 feet beads of perspiration run down your face, the small of your back. Hair is matted to your forehead. Eyes sting from the salt in the perspiration. At 2,000 feet above sea level it's 110 degrees inside your compartment. This is strange. You were to have landed at 2,000 feet above sea level, but the helicopter continues to descend . . . 1,000 feet . . . sea level . . . you land.

"Unfasten your seat belt. Get out of the helicopter. You find yourself in a forest primeval. There are towering redwoods, lush ferns. Walk over to a river of boiling water. Feel the *wet, hot* steam condense against your skin.

"Lie down beside the river. You drift . . . you float . . . you dream . . . in a world as it existed over a million years ago."

REACTIONS AND USES

Your ability to recall hot and cold will improve rapidly from your practicing the *Arctic Scene*. I often observe that my patients have sweaty hands when coming out of this image. You can actually raise your skin temperature to the point of perspiring by imagining yourself hot and sweating.

FURTHER BENEFITS OF YOUR BEING ABLE TO RECALL HOT AND COLD

Carl, a 26-year-old architect who withdrew socially because he had embarrassing sweating spells in public, imagined heat so well at the end of the *Arctic Scene* he voluntarily caused his palms to sweat in my office. "By learning to induce sweating," I told him, "you have developed control over it. What you can induce, you can eliminate." Once Carl realized he could in fact control his sweating, these involuntary spells ceased. If you have episodes when you perspire too much, try practice sessions where you work to induce sweating using the *Arctic Scene*. You'll find that when you have control sufficient to induce sweating you will also have control to reduce or prevent it.

Practice recalling extreme heat in the *Arctic Scene* prompted Stacy, 33, a dental hygienist experiencing "unexplainable" crying spells, to report that her emotions as well as her sense of body weight were lightening. "I'm really lightening up. My relation with my boyfriend is so much better. We're giggling, cuddling, enjoying each other." As your facility for recalling heat continues to improve, you'll go on feeling emotionally and physically lighter and your relationships will become better in addition.

Further practice led Stacy to state, "Imagining heat gives me such energy! And I feel so light. At work I imagine myself light and glide through the day by recalling a seagull's feather. And I can decrease perspiring by recalling cold." Here you see another way to reduce perspiring in public, by imagining walking through the mountains of ice and snow of the *Arctic Scene* whenever you feel your temperature rising in a social situation. When you are alone, you voluntarily induce sweating by recalling heat to show you have control over it. Then, when you are in the actual situation where you need to reduce sweating, you imagine yourself in the cold.

A CURE FOR CONVERSION HYSTERIA
OR PSYCHOLOGICAL PARALYSIS

In the course of your practicing these images you may accidentally come upon new and valuable ways to use them. This is what happened to me a few years ago when I was teaching Richard, 50, a security guard and ex-airline pilot, the *Arctic Scene* to improve his imagery skills for self-inducing relaxation. Richard's right arm and hand had been paralyzed for ten years and diagnosed as a case of conversion hysteria, paralysis of psychosomatic origin brought on by traumatic anxiety.

He had come to me to learn how to reduce his job stress with no intent to work on the paralysis which he had resigned himself to live with. In the middle of giving him the *Arctic Scene*, when he was to imagine his plane rapidly descending, the altitude gauge indicating a sharp drop, Richard suddenly made an upward grab with his "paralyzed" right hand. "All I knew is I had to save the plane"—he smiled when the image was over—"so I grabbed for the controls." Richard was so involved in the reality of his image that it overrode the reality of his hysterical paralysis. To this day he has full use of his right arm and hand.

THE NEGATIVE REINFORCEMENT
PARADIGM

I tell you this story about Richard not only to illustrate the serendipity you may encounter in your adventures with imagery, but also to give you an excellent paradigm for constructing your own *specific* images, whatever your problem may be.

Richard's case is a prime example of the negative reinforcement paradigm at work. A reinforcer, by definition, is anything that increases your probability of making a given response. A punisher is anything that decreases the probability of your making a certain response. Reinforcers and punishers are defined by their results. Nothing is inherently rewarding or punishing until it is observed what effect it has on you. A positive reinforcer is quite plainly anything you'll work to get, such as money, candy, or social recognition. A negative reinforcer is anything you'll work to get away from, such as an avalanche, gun at your temple, or barking dog. A negative reinforcer is not the same as a punisher because it increases, rather than decreases your probability of responding.

If we look at Richard's case we can say that the response we wish to increase the frequency of is his moving his right arm and hand. The negative reinforcer here is the plummeting airplane. His reward for moving his right hand is removal of the condition of the falling plane. He reaches for the controls and rights the aircraft.

Whenever you wish to be able to do something, you can create an image of your own in which your reward for accomplishing it is your removal from a bad situation. For example, if you fear flying, you may not only imagine yourself rapidly flying in a relaxed state, you may also envision a negative reinforcement paradigm that would run something like this: "You are on the thirtieth floor of a burning building (negative reinforcer). The flames grow ever closer. Suddenly outside you see a helicopter. It flies up to the window. You board the copter (response you wish to increase the frequency of). You joyfully fly away to safety."

Your reward for doing something you want to be able to do more, i.e., fly, is escape from a burning building. This type of paradigm is especially effective when you are down and nothing seems rewarding to you, when you don't care about candy or fame or money or anything. You'll never be so low you won't find escaping from a towering inferno reinforcing.

As you progress with imagery you'll find more and more practical applications you can put the images to. This progress runs in cycles. You can work for a long time before you notice any change and then suddenly, usually dramatically, you change levels. Old exercises become easy considering their prior difficulty and you experience new, unexpected imagery-induced phenomena. This is always an exciting time and you should remember these times when you are in a plateau or becoming impatient. It will take you a given amount of time and practice to reach a certain level of proficiency, and recognizing this, you only have to continue your exercises to reach the eventual, inevitable breakthrough.

LAKE SCENE

This image emphasizes your recall of four combinations of the tactile sensory subcomponents of temperature and pressure: hot/light, hot/heavy, cold/light, and cold/heavy. The greater your facility for recalling these combinations, the greater reality your image will have. The more real your image, the more intense the phenomena it induces will be and the greater impact it will have on your reality.

LAKE SCENE:

"You are walking down a gravel road. It's one o'clock in the afternoon, a beautiful summer day. Feel the heat of the sun against your back.

"On your right is a cottage. By the cottage is a garden of radishes, cabbages, turnips, parsley, and tomatoes. Next to the garden is an incinerator burning paper. *Hot, light* bits of paper ash blow in the wind, graze your skin.

"Now you come to an embankment. Descend a flight of stone steps leading down the hillside. Feel the cool pipe railing. The embankment is covered with birch trees and wildflowers, tiger lilies and columbine. Reach the base of the steps.

"A lake smooth as glass stretches before you. There's a dock and a boathouse. A white boat is tied to the dock. A dockboy is loading the boat. He brings out a red gasoline can which he places on the dock in the sun. Then he loads cushions, oars, a motor.

"You get into the boat. Feel it rock beneath the weight of your body. The dockboy picks up the gasoline can and hands it to you, placing it in your lap. Feel the *hot, heavy* pressure of the can. He gets into the boat, unties it, and shoves off with an oar. He takes the gasoline can from you. Feel the release of pressure. He starts the motor.

"You speed off across the lake. Feel the *cold, light* bits of lake spray against your skin. You are heading for the opposite shore. Tall rushes twelve feet high grow out from the coastline. The motor stops. There are canals among the reeds. Drift through the canals.

"You come to a clearing. The dockboy anchors the boat. Lie in the bottom of the boat, gently rocked by the waves. Now the dockboy pulls up the anchor. He hands it to you, placing it in your lap. Feel it *cold* and *heavy* in your lap. He starts the motor and takes the anchor from you. Feel the release of pressure.

"Shoot out through the rushes, heading back. See the dock loom ever larger as you approach the boathouse. The motor stops. Glide up against the dock. You get out of the boat. Walk down the dock, up the steps, down the gravel road, going home."

REACTIONS AND USES

The *Lake Scene* seemed so vivid to Jack, a 36-year-old stockbroker suffering from depression and job burnout, he said that he felt sunburned after concentrating on it. He later reported, "The detail of that image made it more real and put me more in the now. It made not just the image more vivid, but my external reality as well. Everything seems much more real now. My awareness is heightened. The sky is bluer. I notice things. The smell of flowers. I'm thinking less and feeling more. The job is starting to look new again."

The images in this chapter will ground and center you in the five-sensory world you live in. Your result from practicing them will be a heightened awareness of the beauty around you, free of the competing noise of negative thoughts. You will be in the moment, the eternal now of which the masters of the East speak so reverently.

FOCUSING ON THE SENSORY COMPONENTS OF THE SEXUAL MOMENT

Probably nowhere among the clinical problems I treat is this ability to be in the sensory now more important than in the area of sexual dysfunction. The competing noise of negative or unwanted thoughts is most often the reason for sex losing its punch or for sexual difficulties. When you fail to focus on the sexuality of the moment, sex loses its vitality.

Let's return to the case of Magrite to see how the results of your imagery can build, the consequences of each image providing a further step toward higher knowledge and experience. You saw how Magrite used relaxation and dissociation from the *Beach Scene* to reduce years of pent-up anxiety from the trauma of having been molested by her brother. I also told you how she used the *Mountain Cabin Scene* to recall heat in her genital area by imagining sitting in front of a fire. This recall caused her to direct blood to her genitals, the beginning of her achieving arousal and creating healthy sexual feelings.

You next learned that she used the *Garden Scene* to enhance her total sensuality, focusing especially on heightening her sensitivity to taste and smell. Smell has evolutionarily been the primary sense for stimulating sexual arousal and our modern culture has shamefully neglected it, actually inhibiting it with its emphasis on deodorants, antiperspirants, and perfumes that mask the highly arousing aroma of the body's natural sexual fragrance, the pheromones.

I also taught Magrite to prolong her positive moments of sexual pleasure using time expansion she induced from the *Space* and *Farm* scenes. She then developed deeper dissociation using the *Jungle Scene* to lower her sexual sensory thresholds and detach herself from any remaining negative thoughts her subconscious might be harboring about sex. Next, she practiced the *Jungle with Heat Transfer Scene* to focus on the recall of wet heat in her hand, transferring it to her genitals, directing more blood to that area, and intensifying her arousal.

All of these images helped Magrite to shape a new response, a feeling she had *never* had before, a sexual orgasm. By combining relaxation, dissociation, lowered sensory thresholds, and the recall of heat in her genitals, Magrite began to feel sexual.

The *Lake Scene* was the next step in her progression. I told her to concentrate especially on her recall of the *hot, heavy* gasoline can in her lap, and the resulting release of pressure when the dockboy removed it. Feelings of heat and pressure in the genitals are two main components of the experience of sexual arousal. Your ability to recall these sensations goes a long way to enhancing sexual sensitivity.

You can use the *Lake Scene* to heighten your own sexuality. It combines your recall of sexual heat which you have already learned to do in the *Mountain Cabin* and *Jungle with Heat Transfer* scenes with your ability to recall sexual pressure. Your recall of heat *and* pressure in your genitals will direct more blood there, and make you more aroused, than your recalling either one of these sensations alone. Whether you are a woman or a man, the images and procedures you can use to build your sexual feelings and shape a satisfying climax are the same.

OTHER USES

The *Lake Scene*'s focus on recall of pressure in the genital area also makes it a good image to practice if you need to develop bladder control. I used this image in conjunction with the *Desert Scene* with

Eric to help end his enuresis so he could stay overnight with friends and not be embarrassed by bedwetting. You will recall that you can lower your sensory threshold, heighten your sensitivity, to a particular sensation by directing your attention to it. When you become sufficiently sensitized to pressure in your bladder, the urge to urinate will be strong enough to waken you in time to get out of bed and go to the washroom.

The *Lake Scene*, like the *Pool Scene*, can help you to get out of a rut of depression or the blues. It involves a pleasant activity and can aid you in remembering the joy you experienced from other similar activities, thus motivating you to engage in them again.

Carla, 52, withdrew more and more after the death of her husband Bernie from lung cancer. He had left her well enough provided for so that she didn't have to work, but unfortunately this only allowed her to become socially more isolated. When I told her she needed to get out and do things in order to feel better, she refused. Practicing the *Lake Scene* got her to remember the joy she once experienced from boating. "I'd forgotten how much I used to enjoy the water," she said. "Even before I met Bernie."

Finally, your imagining heat on your skin from the sun in this image can be beneficial to you in clearing up a skin disorder such as acne or psoriasis, just as you used the *Beach, Desert,* and *Farm* scenes for this purpose.

THUNDERSHOWER SCENE

This image is the final one in your series of four images designed to heighten your recall of the components of touch and their respective subcomponents. You'll be concentrating on the tactile components of pressure and liquidity, and the following combinations of their sensory subcomponents: heavy/wet, heavy/dry, light/wet, and light/dry. Practice this image three times a day for a week to receive its full benefit.

THUNDERSHOWER SCENE:

"You are sitting in a lawn chair on a patio. It's mid-July, two o'clock in the afternoon. Around the patio is a white wooden fence. Flowers grow along the fence: sweet william, sweet peas, Canterbury bells, bells of Ireland. Beyond the fence is a green lawn. Two giant box elder trees grow on the lawn. Strung between the trees is a clothesline. White sheets billow from the line. Past the yard is a garden of tall stalks of blue delphiniums. Beyond the flowers is a vegetable garden with tomatoes, cucumbers, string beans, carrots, beets, radishes, squash, pumpkins, gourds, peas, green peppers, onions, and corn. Next is a row of silver poplar trees and a lake.

"Stand up. Strip down to a white bathing suit. Running the length of the lawn is a flat hose with fine holes shooting water into the air. You can see a rainbow in the water. Run through the water. Smell the wet grass. Feel it slippery beneath your bare feet. Feel the *light, wet* bits of spray against your body.

"Walk over to the clothesline. Gather the sheets, *light* and *dry* in your arms. Carry them up onto the patio. Place them on a table. Sit back in the lawn chair. Notice that storm clouds are building up in the west. A hush falls. It grows cool and dark. Put on a sweater.

"Suddenly there is a clap of thunder, a bolt of lightning. The sky rips open. Great deluge of water. Gusts of wind. Branches blowing. You are drenched. Sweater feels *heavy* and *wet*.

"Run into the house. Climb a flight of stairs. Go down a long hall to a master bedroom. A fire burns in the fireplace. There's a great bed with a canopy. Remove your wet clothes. Climb into bed under the *heavy, dry* quilts. Drift to the sound of the rain against the windowpane."

REACTIONS AND USES

"I didn't want it to end," said Jack the first time I gave him the *Thundershower Scene.* "The whole world suddenly seems so much more alive." After practicing the image for a week he reported, "I don't miss a thing. My awareness just keeps on growing. I'm full of grit and vinegar now. I can't believe I ever felt burned out. Work at the stock exchange is going great."

Jack also told me that he was getting a sense of time concentration from practicing the *Thundershower Scene*. This did not surprise me. Although this image was not designed specifically to give you this phenomenon, don't be surprised if you find yourself experiencing more and more time distortion as you continue to work with imagery. You are busting limitations everywhere and your awareness is growing. With this heightened awareness comes a change in your perception of time, space, and motion.

"I had a whole flood of childhood memories," Jack told me. "Time seemed to be racing by. It was like my whole life was zooming past me. Then pretty soon, a few days later, I was getting time expansion instead of time concentration. I found I was talking more slowly to my wife and friends. That amazed me. Usually after a harried day on the floor of the exchange I'm so wired, I rattle off my words so fast nobody can understand me. Even more incredible, the time expansion combined with dissociation. Without even trying, I found myself imagining I was standing outside of my body, observing myself in conversation. My speech slowed down even more. It's great. My wife couldn't believe it." The effects of your images will continue to combine, yielding hybrid techniques you can use in many ways to create new positive experiences for yourself.

Like the other images in this sequence designed to strengthen your power to imagine, you can use the *Thundershower Scene* to work on certain specific problems. Dennis, a 19-year-old college freshman suffering from constant acne over his entire face, chest, and back, imagined his body being heated by the blaze of the roaring fire of the master bedroom as he lay naked under the dry, heavy quilts of the canopied bed. His recall of both heat and pressure directed an increasing blood supply to the surface of his skin to nourish his cells and dry his lesions. If you use this image to focus on recalling heat and pressure in the region of your skin problem, you'll find it most effective in clearing up your condition.

Jim, a 32-year-old court reporter who had not been able to get a full night's sleep since his mother, a night duty nurse, would wake him at midnight for his dinner, used the *Thundershower Scene* to control his insomnia. Since the image ends with his drifting to the sound of the rain against the windowpane in a large, canopied bed with heavy quilts, he conjured the scene at bedtime and went directly from it into deep, restful sleep.

CANCER AND DISEASE

I'd like to conclude this chapter on strengthening imagery by talking to you about the use of imagery in treating cancer and disease. Many doctors and therapists send me patients to help them strengthen the specific disease-related imagery they're already working on. In other cases I work directly with the client, helping him to create and strengthen an image that is most appropriate for him.

The entire sequence of images I'm giving you in this book serves as an ancillary treatment for strengthening specific cancer-curing images. You'll remember my saying in Chapter Two that there are three kinds of images: images to produce phenomena, images to strengthen imagery, and specific images to solve specific problems. The images I gave you up to now were constructed to help you experience phenomena: relaxation, glove anesthesia, time expansion and concentration, and dissociation. The images in this chapter were created to help you strengthen your power to imagine. Throughout the text I've given you examples of specific images for specific problems, such as imagining slurping vomit through your cigarette to end your desire to smoke or boarding a helicopter to flee a burning building to decondition your fear of flying. The research you've read of involving imagery for the cure of cancer and other diseases concerns this third kind of imagery, specific imagery to treat a specific problem.

I want to make it clear that cancer and disease cure is where many people jump off the bandwagon in terms of what power they believe you have using imagery. They agree that you can certainly reduce stress and have more positive emotions using the appropriate imagery. Most are also in accord that you can eliminate or at least help many psychosomatic disorders such as high blood pressure, ulcers, migraine, asthma, acne, and psoriasis, with the right kind of positive imagery.

As for me, it has been my observation that faith and belief are wonderful things. Treatments that people believe in often work. Whenever anyone comes to me asking for this kind of treatment, I give it to them. There are too many intervening variables in a private practice, including additional therapies and premature dropouts, to give you any reliable figures or statistics on success rate. I leave this to the more pure researchers working in this field.

I can only say that sometimes what I witness is remarkable. A person's cancer stops growing or actually goes away. You can call this "spontaneous remission," saying that in a certain small percentage of cases evidence of the disease disappears for no apparent reason. The person in question would have gotten better whether he'd used imagery or not. This argument is certainly valid. There is to date no undisputed proof that imagery cures cancer. However, there has been recent laboratory evidence that positive imagery can raise your T killer lymphocyte count and bolster your immune system. That is an impressive beginning to the physical documentation of imagery's role in healing.

If you wish to develop imagery to work on healing diseases, including cancer, I'll tell you how to do it. I usually ask people to practice the *Beach, Mountain Cabin,* and *Garden* scenes about five times each in order to develop their facility with imagery before working on a specific image for eliminating their disease. At that point I ask them to alternate their specific image with the next image in the progression I'm giving you. For example, the day you start your disease-curing image you would alternate it with the

Mountain Cabin II Scene, the next scene in your series after the *Garden Scene,* which you would have already practiced. A week later, you can alternate your specific image with the *Desert Scene* for a week, and so on. Most people stick with the specific image they create once they've fashioned it to their liking, but you may change it as often as you desire. Interspersing the imagery progression with your specific disease-curing image provides a refreshing change and ensures your acquiring new imagery skills that will make your healing image increasingly more potent.

The specific image people use to treat their cancer is usually quite simple. You may ask a doctor or therapist to help you construct it or you may try making it up on your own. The basis is to imagine that a good force is killing your disease. You may envision this good force and your disease that it kills in any form you wish, although I encourage my patients to use forms they can imagine in all five senses.

You might, for example, imagine your wonderful killing agent as a beautiful fairy princess with a kiss the taste of honey and a gown the aroma of lilac. The cancer cells you wish to vanquish you may imagine as rotten hamburger. The beautiful princess waves her wand, and in a flash of white sparkling light the rotten meat is gone. Some people prefer to take a more aggressive approach, putting to use the anger they have at their disease. They may imagine themselves as the killer agent, miniaturized in their blood system, axing the cancer which they may see as a tangle of roots or tissues.

You may also preface your healing images with positive affirmations such as, "My body is healthy, vibrant, vital. My system is pure, clean, clear. I am strong. I am well." Remember to keep your affirmations positive, stating what you want, not what you don't want. I give these healing affirmations once the hypnotic relaxation is induced, immediately before the image. But you can put them anywhere you like, in the middle of your clearing procedure or even in your image if it suits you.

Explore. Do what feels best for you. If using all of your senses seems too difficult for this kind of imagery, don't worry about it. Marcy, 33, a hotel manager, one of my most successful cases, used a computer game as the foundation for her imagery. She saw white dots (good guys, white cells) eating black dots (bad guys, cancer cells). She did say that the white dots made a smacking, popping sound when they devoured the black dots, but she only used two senses in her imagery. Two were enough. Her cancer went into remission.

Three years ago, Laura, a 52-year-old airline reservationist, had a mastectomy. Five months ago a routine mammogram and chest X ray indicated a spot on her lung. She had surgery for lung cancer, an operation the doctors called 80 percent successful. They said they would know in seven months whether they had gotten all the cancer. "I keep asking myself what I did to get it," she said. "I guess I just can't handle stress. Randy, my teenage son, was sent to prison for wounding another boy in a gang war. He got out over two years ago, but I'm worried sick about him. My husband fights with him continually. Randy broke my husband's nose in one of their arguments. About eighteen months before my cancer diagnosis I was suicidal, filled with despair. I couldn't see any solution.

"Anyway, I've got to think of myself now. I need to feel I have some control over this, like I'm doing something. Randy and I are closer since my surgery. I think my worst time is around 4:30 in the morning. I wake up and just lie there in the dark worrying, with a depressed feeling. It's like there's no point in my making plans anymore for anything if I'm going to die. I think how fast time slipped by. All the things I still want to do, like take cooking classes and going to plays. I keep asking myself, 'Have I done in my life what I wanted to do? Have I accomplished anything?' I so want to see Randy straightened out, maybe go back to school. I keep blaming myself for getting sick. Why couldn't I have handled stress better? Everybody has problems."

Together, Laura and I created an image for the purpose of ensuring her lungs were free of cancer. Laura loved sunshine and I had her imagine that her good-killer force was sunshine and her cancer cells were shadows. Wherever the sunshine hit, the shadows were dispelled. "I just imagine my whole body permeated with healing sunshine and I feel so much better," she smiled. "I feel like I'm taking a positive responsibility for my illness now." An X ray seven months after her operation was clear. Laura showed no evidence of cancer.

It's true that Laura's happy results could be attributed completely to her surgery. At least, the imagery gave her a feeling of regaining control over herself, and dispelling her fears. At most, it saved her life.

You will learn to effect greater healing and physical control in the next chapter when you internalize the sensory subcomponents you recalled externally in the images of this chapter.

TEN

Focusing Concentration on Your Body's Internal Systems

□D eveloping your powers of imagery entails being able to recall sensations in, and thus control, the internal reality you call your body as well as the external reality you call your world. In time you will see there is no difference. Internal and external are one. Your perception of yourself as separate from the whole is illusion. You and the universe are one.

I will now give you ten images that will teach you to internalize the sensory subcomponents you recalled externally in the images of the last chapter. Your focus will be on four primary systems of your body: alimentary (digestive), circulatory, skeletal, and excretory.

You concentrate on recalling tactile subcomponents in these systems because touch is your sense closest to your actual experience of these bodily systems. You cannot see, hear, taste, or smell events transpiring within these physiological networks, but you can "feel" them.

While I expressly designed this series of images to strengthen your powers to imagine, wherever I discovered an image to have a specific application to healing and/or maximizing your other abilities as well, I'll explain it.

MANSION SCENE

Your first image in this series asks you to recall the tactile sensory subcomponents: hot/wet, hot/dry, cold/wet, and cold/dry internally in your digestive system. This involves your doing a sensory transfer. Once you've experienced a sensation in one part of your body, you have the ability to transfer it and experience it in any other part of your body. You learned to do this with the *Mountain Cabin II* and *Jungle* scenes, where you respectively recalled cold and heat in your hand, transferred it to your cheek, and then back to your hand again.

In the following sequence of images, you'll recall and transfer sensations to areas of your body where in many cases you've never experienced them before. Your acquisition of the ability to internalize previously primarily external sensations will give you greater control over your physiological functioning.

MANSION SCENE:

"You are walking down the busy, crowded street of Sunset Boulevard in Hollywood, California. It's hot, smoggy. Now you turn, walking up into the hills. Every step you take it gets quieter and quieter. Every step you take the air gets clearer and clearer.

"You come to a great iron gate. Beyond the gate is a gray stone mansion built in the thirties, the golden era of Hollywood. Open the gate. Hear it creak on its hinges. Find yourself in a field of dandelions gone to seed, great white puffs on slender stalks in the sunlight. Begin eating the dandelion seeds. Feel them *hot* and *dry* in your mouth, down your throat, in your stomach. *Hot* and *dry* in the center of your body.

"Now you leave the dandelions, going to another part of the garden. See a gazebo, yellowing with age, covered with red rambling roses. Sit down in the gazebo. Before you on a table is a glass of ice-cold limeade. Drink the limeade. Swallow an ice cube. Feel it *cold* and *wet*, in your mouth, down your throat, in your stomach. *Cold* and *wet* in the center of your body.

"Leave the gazebo. Go inside the house. Come to a great banquet hall. There's a massive oak table that seats thirty. A hunting mural is painted on the wall, fox hunters in red coats. Sit at the table. Before you is a bowl of hot, tangy vegetable soup. Eat the soup. Feel it *hot* and *wet*, in your mouth, down your throat, in your stomach. *Hot* and *wet* in the center of your body.

"Exit the banquet hall. Go out behind the house. There's a rock garden and a waterfall. Sit down on a stone bench under a willow tree. There materializes in your right hand a cherry snow cone of dry ice. Eat the cone. Taste the cherry. Feel the ice, *cold* and *dry*, in your mouth, down your throat, in your stomach. *Cold* and *dry* in the center of your body.

"Lie down beneath the willow tree. Drift to the sound of water falling on the rock."

REACTIONS AND USES

Focusing on your recall of sensory subcomponents in your various bodily systems will vastly heighten your concentration. This heightened concentration may take many forms including a sense of incredible energy to the point where you feel as though you could actually take off and soar into the sky. "I'm not coming out," said a woman in her mid-twenties who was working on stress reduction. "I had the most incredible desire to fly. I just wanted to fly, escape the world seriously."

John, 26, a professional golfer who had trouble shutting out the crowd and other players during a tournament to the point where he had outbursts of rage toward them, developed such a depth of concentration when I gave him the *Mansion Scene* that he was able to block out all extraneous stimuli, including the traffic noise coming from outside my office window. After he practiced the scene for a week he reported that the image gave him better emotional as well as physical control. "I now use my anger to cue relaxation on the golf course," he explained. "Whenever I begin to feel my temper rising, I simply say to myself, 'mansion,' and I find my concentration focuses immediately to the task at hand, getting that damned ball in the hole!"

EATING DISORDERS

The *Mansion Scene*'s focus on your digestive system makes it a good image to practice if you have trouble eating or are anorexic. Katie, an 18-year-old college freshman, was life-threateningly underweight from anorexia nervosa. "I guess it's all this emphasis on thin-is-beautiful that's causing my problem," she explained. "If losing ten pounds will improve my looks, losing twenty will be an even bigger improvement. I know that sounds stupid, but I really feel I look better no matter how much I lose, no matter what my friends may say to the contrary. When I see food, I immediately think of myself as fat, regardless of what I actually weigh at the time. And that really turns me off to eating."

I asked Katie to practice the *Mansion Scene* and really see herself enjoying drinking the limeade and eating the dandelion seeds, vegetable soup, and cherry snow cone. She was also to envision herself remaining at a normal weight while she ate, not ballooning way out of proportion as her fear of eating created her expectation to do. I requested that she concentrate on the *sensation* of her eating; the hotness, coldness, wetness, dryness of her experience, rather than the dire consequences she normally projected from it, i.e., becoming overweight.

By practicing the *Mansion Scene* Katie was able to get in the sensory moment when she ate in reality and thus regain a normal perspective on eating. Eating for Katie is now a positive sensory experience, not a cognitive projection of being fat. She is back to her normal weight and feels good about herself. If you have a need to view food more positively, you can use the *Mansion Scene* in much the same way as Katie did to ground yourself in the positive sensory reality of eating, free of your negative fears and projections.

SCUBA SCENE

The *Scuba Scene* further contributes to your gaining dominion over the internal world of your body. It introduces you to recalling the tactile sensory subcomponents of hot/wet, hot/dry, cold/wet, and cold/dry in your circulatory and skeletal systems.

SCUBA SCENE:

"You are perched on the edge of a boat in the Florida Keys, wearing diving gear. The sky is brilliant blue, the sun a fiery yellow, the water translucent aqua-blue. See a fringe of white sand and emerald palms across the water.

"Feel yourself falling forward, somersaulting head over heels down through the water. Pale amber sunlight filters down from above. As you go deeper and deeper, the water grows cooler and cooler. See brightly colored fish, salmon coral, pink sea anemones.

"Now you encounter an ice-blue net-like substance. Swim over to it. Touch it. It sends a current of electricity through your body to the very marrow of your bones. Bones feel *hot* and *dry*.

"Continue going ever deeper, getting cooler and cooler. You become encased in ice. Your blood feels *cold* and *wet*. Bones feel *cold* and *dry*. The ice in which you are encased rises to the surface of the water, floats to shore. It washes up on the hot, tropic sand.

"The ice melts in the sun. Your muscles thaw. See a bottle carried up on the shore by the waves. Go to it. It's a bottle of rum. Drink the rum. It heats your body, a sense of intoxication coming over you. Blood feels *hot* and *wet* coursing through your system.

"Colors around you begin to mesh and merge and melt . . . purple orchids, red hibiscus, emerald palms, blue sky, golden sun, white sand . . . you are engulfed in a sea of molten, swirling color."

REACTIONS AND USES

I frequently see goose bumps appear on people's skin while I am describing their body being encased in ice with cold, wet, blood and cold, dry bones. Also common is a slight flush during the portion of the image where you are asked to feel your blood hot and wet as the intoxication from the alcohol overcomes you.

You may also experience new kinesthetic sensations of motion. One man said, "I felt I was reeling during my underwater descent. I had that same reeling feeling at the end of the image when the colors were melting together." A woman had a similar sense of motion at the conclusion of this image: "I felt myself whirling and spinning in a state of complete euphoria."

ALCOHOLISM

You can use the *Scuba Scene*, which ends with your recall of intoxication and euphoria from drinking rum, to turn yourself off to alcohol if you wish. I used it on Monty to help turn him off to wine. In addition to asking Monty to use time concentration from his practicing the *Bluebird Scene* to shorten the period when he most wanted a drink, the time between his getting home from work and sitting down to dinner with his family, I also suggested a way he could use the *Scuba Scene* to develop a distaste for wine.

I asked Monty to imagine a bottle of wine rather than rum wash up on the hot, tropic sand. Then, instead of experiencing euphoria from drinking the wine, he was to experience nausea. I modified the image to read: "Begin drinking the wine. Your blood feels hot and wet. Every gulp you take, you feel a growing sense of nausea. The beautiful landscape around you begins to blur and fade. You have an urge to vomit. Throw the bottle back into the sea. Instantly the sparkling sand and sky and sea come back into focus. You feel wonderful. Take a deep breath of fresh salt air. Your mouth tastes fresh, like mint. From this point forth, whenever you say no to alcohol, you will experience this same incredible sense of health and liberation."

You can modify the *Scuba Scene* the same way I did for Monty to turn yourself off to drinking if you choose. Substitute your most commonly used alcoholic beverage for the rum in this scene. Then envision a bottle of it washing up on shore and your drinking it, getting more and more nauseated as the beautiful scene blurs and fades with every swallow. Then see yourself resist further drinking by throwing the bottle once more into the sea, at which point the beautiful scene comes back into focus. You take a deep breath of fresh air, and your mouth tastes great—all as your reward for avoiding or resisting liquor.

PICNIC SCENE

This image is your first exposure to your recalling tactile sensory subcomponents in your excretory system. You continue increasing your power to imagine by internalizing the subcomponents, cold/wet, cold/dry, hot/wet, and hot/dry in your excretory and skeletal systems.

PICNIC SCENE:

"You are walking down a gravel road in the country. It's a beautiful summer day. Leave the road to go down a ditch and crawl under a barbed-wire fence. Find yourself in a forested meadow region.

"A river flows through this area. Follow the river deeper and deeper into the woods. Come upon a spring bubbling cold, pure water from the earth. Drink the water. You have an urge to urinate. Go behind a bush. Expel the urine. It comes out *cold* and *wet* as the spring water went in.

"Move back down to the river. Remove your clothes. Wade into the water. It's cold. There's a swift current. Immerse yourself. Your blood chills, *cold* and *wet*. Bones chill to the marrow, *cold*, *dry* bones. Let the river carry you deeper and deeper into the forest.

"The river empties into a pond. There's a dock and a mill with a wheel. Hear the sound of the water gurgling over the mill wheel. Climb up onto the dock. See a bottle of tequila. Drink it, setting your system on fire. You have an urge to urinate. Expel the urine. It comes out *hot* and *wet* as you sensed the tequila going in.

"Leave the dock, following a path through the woods. Come out upon a pasture of grass, closely cropped like a golf green. Lie down in the sun. Your muscles melt into the earth. Bones bleach hot and dry in the summer sun."

REACTIONS AND USES

People usually find a lot of enjoyment in recalling new, strange sensations throughout their bodies. A woman who was working to develop her concentration as an actress smiled, "That hot and cold was a kick. I got chills. Brrr! . . ." An attorney developing her concentration for taking depositions reported, "I feel limp, like a strand of spaghetti boiled too long. I loved the ice-cold urinating. It was just plain fun."

GYMNASTICS

Cole, a 21-year-old gymnast, came to me complaining that his coach said his maneuvers were too stiff. "I think I freeze up on the bar," he said. "I can feel my body tightening. It's like my hinges need oiling. I hate it. I feel I age twenty years." I asked Cole to practice the *Picnic Scene*, concentrating especially on the feeling of hot, dry bones he was to create at the end of the image when he imagined his bones bleaching hot and dry in the sun. "Recalling heat in your bones will energize and limber you up," I told him. "Get your juices flowing."

After a week's practice, Cole reported, "What fun! I've never felt so loose. I feel like a bag of bones. I can't remember ever feeling so loose. The coach is impressed. He says I've now got 'fluid motion.' It's great!" Anytime you feel a stiffening in your joints or your body just doesn't move as smoothly as you'd like, you can use the *Picnic Scene* and your recall of hot bones to oil your machinery, and get back into the flow again.

SHANGRI-LA SCENE

This is the first image in which you recall internalized sensory subcomponents of pressure. The emphasis here is on control of your sense of pressure and liquidity in the digestive and skeletal systems. You recall the sensory subcomponents, light/dry, heavy/wet, light/wet, and heavy/dry, in order to gain greater control over your physiological functioning.

SHANGRI-LA SCENE:

"You are high in an open meadow. It's spring. In the distance you see mountains like the Alps or Himalayas. You wish to scale the mountaintops. Take a pump with a rubber air hose and place the hose in your mouth. Begin pumping yourself with air, growing lighter and lighter. Feel the *light*, *dry* air inflating your body. Your feet leave the ground. You float up like a balloon, drifting toward the mountain peaks.

"As you approach the snowy summits, the cold causes the air in your body to contract. You descend. Land on a narrow mountain ledge, sheer rock to your back. A blizzard is raging. Inch your way along the ledge. Come to a pass. Enter the pass.

"Instantly it's spring again. Find yourself in a peach orchard. Move through the orchard, past sparkling fountains. Come to a great stone temple. Climb the temple stairs. Enter a massive stone chamber. Before you on an ebony table is a plate piled high with pancakes and a pitcher of milk. Eat the pancakes, washing them down with the milk. They feel *heavy* and *wet* in the center of your body, weighing you down. You roll over like a turtle on its shell.

"Suddenly a gong sounds. A stone panel opens. An old man with a long, white beard appears. He carries a shimmering pink yeast drink. He gives it to you. Drink. Feel the *light*, *wet* bubbles. *Light* and *wet* throughout your body.

"You get up. Verily glide along the temple floor, down the steps, through the orchard, to a river. Float like an inner tube down the river and out the pass through which you entered. Suddenly feel a growing heaviness in your bones. Lie down on the mountain ledge. Muscles turn to dust, blowing in the wind. Bones petrify, *heavy* and *dry*, lying on the mountain ledge."

REACTIONS AND USES

Dramatic sensations of lightness and heaviness are what you can most often expect from the *Shangri-La Scene*. "I did better than I ever have," said Vince, who was working on how to deal with stress in his relationships. "I felt so light and then so heavy. It was a smashing image. I loved it!"

ANOREXIA

Katie was able to use the *Shangri-La Scene* in addition to the *Mansion Scene* to get over her anorexia. Like many anorexics, Katie said that she always felt full, as if she had just eaten. "I can go all day without a meal and still really believe I just ate," she said. "It's amazing. I actually feel stuffed." Katie needed to learn better reality contact so that she could accurately perceive an empty stomach as empty.

I asked her to practice the *Shangri-La Scene,* focusing especially on the sense of light, dry air in her stomach when she imagined pumping herself up like a balloon to float over the mountain peaks. "It worked," she reported. "At mealtime I imagine this sensation of lightness or emptiness in my stomach and I no longer feel full. I realize I need to eat, and I do." Whenever you wish to eat more or get rid of a stuffed feeling, you can use your recall of lightness in your stomach from the *Shangri-La Scene* to feel you have room for more.

CHALK CLIFF SCENE

The emphasis in this image is on internalization and control of your sense of pressure and liquidity in your circulatory and digestive systems. You proceed to master these systems by recalling the tactile sensory subcomponents: dry/heavy, wet/heavy, wet/light, and dry/light.

CHALK CLIFF SCENE:

"You are standing high on a cliff overlooking the sea. Smell and taste the salt in the air. Wind blows through your hair and undulates the grass around your knees. Behind you is a cottage with a thatched roof. A stone fence surrounds the cottage.

"A chalk-strewn path leads down the cliff. Start to walk down it. Pick up a lump of chalk. Eat it. Feel it *heavy* and *dry* in your mouth, down your throat, in your stomach. *Heavy* and *dry* in the center of your body.

"Keep eating the chalk lumps. As the chalk mixes with your blood, your blood feels *heavy* and *wet*, forcing its way through your system.

"The heaviness in your blood causes you to fall forward, somersaulting down the cliff path. The rapid motion of your body makes you take in air, filling your blood with bubbles. Blood feels *light* and *wet*. You bounce like a beach ball to the base of the cliff.

"Nearly a mile of sand stretches before the sea. The seascape is dotted with surrealistic, wind-hewn rock formations. Walk toward the water. Come upon an old ship wrecked on shore. Climb upon the deck. From a knapsack on your back take out a pack of soda crackers. Eat the crackers. Feel them *light* and *dry* in your mouth, down your throat, in your stomach. *Light* and *dry* in the center of your body.

"Lie down on the deck. Drift to the sound of the wind in the hull."

REACTIONS AND USES

The images in this series often seem especially strange to my patients. A common reaction is: "That was a strange one. Nothing seemed connected. I sure am sleepy." Sometimes the image may seem so bizarre that you'd rather escape into sleep than attempt to understand it. But don't worry if the image doesn't make sense to you. Only try to *feel* it.

These images dealing with your internalization of sensational components may also seem difficult to you, but please be on guard against dissatisfaction with the results. Be good to yourself. If you only experience one of the four component combinations in each new image, that's excellent. Once again I have to tell you that you'll master past images by practicing new images. Practicing the ten images in this chapter will make it much easier for you to do the earlier images to give you specific results and phenomena. Your powers of imagery are growing. Don't worry about getting the images in this chapter perfect. Just practice each image about ten times before going on to a new one. Positive results will be forthcoming.

I want to give you this pep talk now, here in the middle of this set of images, because it is at this point I most often meet with discouragement among my students. I hope you are brimming with energy, eager to move on, and don't need it, but if you are finding some of this imagery to be harder than it was before, you're right, it is.

In the beginning, your recall of an image produced deep relaxation because all aspects of the image were pleasant. In your present series of images, some of the sensory components may seem strange at first and not directly produce relaxation. For example, the thought of hot, heavy blood forcing its way through your veins and arteries as you somersault head over heels down a chalk cliff may not trigger relaxation, even though it embodies a combination of sensory subcomponents that is important for you to recall if you are to master the sense of your circulatory system. For this reason, some of these images may seem more like work than the earlier ones.

I've heard people say that they used to feel atop cloud nine after inducing an image. At this stage they may no longer be experiencing such an afterglow, because the present images are no longer intended to create a euphoric state, but rather to serve you in your mastery of the creation and transfer of given sensory subcomponents to produce an even greater sense of euphoria than you have ever experienced. Since you will then have new tools available for your experiencing, your imagery results will be ecstatic. So please bear with me—you are on the brink of something glorious.

LOWERING YOUR BLOOD PRESSURE

Ernie, a 62-year-old tax attorney with a long history of high blood pressure, complained of the medication he was taking to keep it under control. "That heart medicine puts me to sleep," he said. "I sit down to watch TV with my wife and I'm out like a light. She says I'm terrible company, like I don't hear what she says half the time. When my kids come to visit they say I'm like a different person, in another world. I really want off of this stuff."

I asked Ernie to practice the *Chalk Cliff Scene*, focusing particularly on the sensory subcomponent of lightness in his bloodstream when he imagines his blood lightening with bubbles as he takes in air somersaulting down the chalk cliff. "I have an empty, hollow feeling, like tubing," he said, "when I practice that image." With continued practice over nearly four months, Ernie gradually was able to eliminate the medication that was making him drowsy and still maintain his blood pressure within a normal range. You also may find that you are able to reduce your blood pressure level by recalling a sense of lightness in your circulatory system as called for in the *Chalk Cliff Scene*.

VOLCANO SCENE

In this image you recall the sensory subcomponents of heavy/wet, light/dry, heavy/dry, and light/wet in your excretory system. It is the first image where you recall solid excrement and gas in this system. Strange as it may sound, this image can be a lot of fun and contribute to your gaining dominion over your body, even if you have no particular problems relating directly to this physical system.

VOLCANO SCENE:

"You are standing by the mouth of an inactive volcano, peering down into the depths. The landscape is bleak and barren. Leafless, gnarled trees are silhouetted in black against a silver sky. It's 60 degrees above zero.

"Feel yourself falling, down into the depths of the volcano. Land on a sponge-like substance. Bounce up and down as if on a trampoline. You have landed in a bed of giant mushrooms. The walls around you are sheer, straight up and down. They emit an ultraviolet light, like black light. Begin eating a mushroom. It changes the chemical composition of the fluids in your body, turning them to deuterium, heavy water. You have an urge to urinate. The urine comes out *heavy* and *wet*.

"The walls begin to waver, turning brilliant colors of orange, magenta, chartreuse, and purple. Leave the mushroom bed. Come into a field of alfalfa. The sky above is molten, swirling lava, flaming scarlet. Eat the alfalfa sprouts. They form a gaseous silage within your stomach.

"Reach a lake. Remove your clothes. Float on your back, propelling yourself across the water by expelling the gas from your anus. Feel it *light* and *dry* exiting your body.

"You reach the opposite shore. Defecate the alfalfa. It comes out in *heavy*, *dry* pellets. Pass through a fringe of palms. Find yourself in a crystal garden.

"Pass through giant crystals of diamonds, rubies, emeralds, and sapphires, shooting beams of colored light crisscrossing in the sky. Come upon a waterfall, water falling over amethyst crystals. The liquid is very light, volatile. Drink it. You have an urge to urinate. It comes out *light* and *wet*, a purple mist, as if from an atomizer. You are engulfed in purple."

REACTIONS AND USES

Most people react to this image with humor. In spite of the heavy psychedelic effects, they find it extremely funny. Paige, a 32-year-old importer of Oriental antiques, came out of this image laughing. "It was so neat. I can't get over it . . . so full of things."

ENURESIS AND ENCOPRESIS

Max, 12, suffered intense humiliation in boarding school when he would bed-wet and on occasion lose fecal control as well, a condition known as encopresis. "Doing number two in your bed is even worse than number one," he confided with embarrassment. "It's harder to cover up and easier to detect. The guys really made fun of me the first time it happened. Now they all call me 'Stinky.' I begged my parents to take me out of that place, but they won't. They both travel and there's no one at home to take care of me."

I suggested that Max practice the *Volcano Scene*, concentrating particularly on his recall of bladder and rectal pressure that the image calls for. The first time that I gave him this image, he responded with laughter. "That was wild." He grinned. "It sure does give me a new idea of my eliminatory processes and a feeling of control."

By directing his attention to this physical pressure in imagery Max became more aware of it in reality. He was thus able to lower his sensory threshold to bladder and rectal pressure sufficiently to wake him up before he would urinate or evacuate in his bed. "I not only got over my problem," he said, "I feel a whole lot better about myself and I like my friends more." I hope that you too will experience how gaining more self-control makes you love yourself more and thus love others more as well.

CANTINA SCENE

In this image you internalize your recall of the tactile sensory subcomponents, heavy/hot, heavy/cold, light/cold, and light/hot, in your digestive system. This is also the only image in this chapter that you can use to produce a specific phenomenon in addition to mastering the recall of internal sensory components. The phenomenon to which I'm referring is sexual arousal. You can use the *Cantina Scene* to create sex energy.

CANTINA SCENE:

"You are riding horseback across the desert. Tall saguaro cacti are silhouetted in black against the flaming sky of a setting sun. In the distance you see flickering yellow lights of a small border town nestled at the foot of a purple mountain range.

"Ride into town. Hear the faint sound of guitar music. Come to a cantina. Dismount. Tie up your horse. Go inside. There's loud music and much laughing. Sit down at a table. Order a plate of tamales. They are served. Eat them. They feel *heavy* and *hot* in the pit of your stomach. Taste the red peppers.

"The waiter brings you a glass of 7-Up. Drink. Swallow an ice cube, *heavy* and *cold* in your mouth, down your throat, in your stomach. *Heavy* and *cold* in the center of your body.

"Keep drinking the 7-Up. Feel the bubbles, *light* and *cold,* in your mouth, down your throat, in your stomach. *Light, cold* bubbles in the center of your body.

"Next the waiter brings a glass of Alka-Seltzer in hot water. Drink. Feel the carbonation, *light* and *hot,* in your mouth, down your throat, in your stomach. *Light* and *hot* in the center of your body.

"The music grows louder. A striking young man/woman (choose whichever sex you are attracted to) with shining hair and flashing eyes steps out into the center of the dance floor. He/she looks directly at you, never for an instant taking his/her eyes off you. You are riveted to the dancer. There is a flow of sexual electricity between you. The music grows still louder, picking up tempo, the beat becoming stronger.

"He/she approaches you. He/she runs his/her fingers across your brow, around your neck, down your shoulders and arms to your legs. Feel his/her warm hand between your legs massaging your thighs. Feel a building heat, congestion, pressure, pulsation, between your legs. Your crotch and thighs are aching . . . ready to explode . . . pressure continues to build . . . constant dull throbbing . . . He/she takes you by the hand and leads you out of the cantina into the warm night air. Cross the road. Enter a livery stable. Undress each other. Stand naked together. Embrace. Feel the heat of his/her flesh. Fall into the honey scented hay. Taste the wet sweetness of his/her mouth on yours.

(Do this paragraph if you've chosen a male partner. If you've selected a woman, finish this image with the next paragraph.) "Feel him inside of you. Hard and hot and urgent. Every thrust of his body you feel a growing heat, growing pressure, growing pulsation, growing throbbing. Hotter and hotter. Harder and harder. You climax! . . . Feel a total, utter, absolute release as you sink into the warm shelter of his arms. The faint sound of guitars . . . whispering desert breeze . . . a groggy sensation steals over you as you pass into deep, deep sleep."

(Do this paragraph if you've chosen a female partner) "Feel a growing heat, growing pressure, growing throbbing, between your legs as you penetrate her body. Every movement you make you feel yourself growing closer and closer and closer to orgasm. Hotter and hotter. Harder and harder. You explode! You climax! . . . Feel a total, utter, absolute release as you sink into the warm shelter of her arms. The faint sound of guitars . . . whispering desert breeze . . . a groggy sensation steals over you as you pass into deep, deep sleep."

REACTIONS AND USES

Women, especially, report being sexually aroused by this image, stating they could climax if they so desired. In fact, in several seminars I have conducted, women have reached an orgasm using the *Cantina Scene.* While most men feel aroused by this image and several have recounted achieving erections by practicing it, no man has ever told me he climaxed from the above image, without his touching his genitals, as I've seen and heard women tell they could do. I am certain, however, that men as well as women can climax from erotic imagery as evidenced by the male's nocturnal emissions or "wet dreams," orgasms brought on solely by the vivid imagery of a dream.

RAISING YOUR SEX ENERGY

The *Cantina Scene* was Magrite's final image before she was able to reach a climax with a lover. "That was the best I've done," she said the first time I gave her this image. "I easily could have climaxed." She was then able to combine the relaxation, dissociation, lowered sensory thresholds, and her recall of heat and pressure in her genitals, that she had achieved through practicing the *Beach, Mountain Cabin, Garden, Space, Farm, Jungle, Jungle with Heat Transfer,* and *Lake* scenes with the sexual arousal she derived from practicing the *Cantina Scene* to reach a total sexual response.

You may find that any or all of the images mentioned are sufficient to give you the sexual response that you seek. Experiment. Use the combinations of images that work best for you.

Tom, a 31-year-old aerospace engineer, had dated Audrey for three years without being able to bring her to climax with him inside her because he lost his erection almost immediately after penetration. I told Tom to practice the *Cantina Scene* three times a day for a week. Then, the next time he was making love to Audrey, he was to recall the sexual feelings he had been able to generate by recalling this image. He wasn't to recall the scene itself, just the feeling of arousal he'd been able to conjure with it. All he needed to do was use the trigger word, "cantina," while he was sexually involved with Audrey. Tom was thus able to maintain his sexual arousal and satisfy both himself and his partner through sexual intercourse.

While raising your sex energy is excellent for enhancing your sexual performance with your partner, it serves other functions as well. The fact remains that energy is energy, whether it be sexual or not, and you can use energy to do work. The work I have in mind is raising your consciousness, increasing your knowledge, and propelling you ever closer to the next dimension that is your paradise. Sex energy can do all that, and what's more it feels good, not necessarily arousing, but definitely positive, charged, and vital.

So you now have two direct ways of raising energy with imagery: Recalling heat and recalling anything that arouses you sexually. Heat is already present in your *Cantina Scene* as a sensory subcomponent to start your energy rising, a primer for the release of sexual energy that is to follow.

HAYLOFT SCENE

In the *Hayloft Scene* you recall within your circulatory system combinations of the tactile sensory subcomponents of temperature and pressure. These combinations are: hot/light, cold/light, cold/heavy, and hot/heavy. This further increases your powers of imagery by giving you dominion over your circulatory system.

HAYLOFT SCENE:
"You are sitting in the loft of a barn. The sun is setting. The grain is aglow with a burnished orange gleam from the oblique rays of the sun. Hear a bell tolling Angelus. A shepherd winds his way homeward over a distant hill, bringing in his flock.

"Beside you on a bale of hay is a bottle of corn liquor. Drink it. Intoxication rushes over you, setting your blood on fire. As you continue to drink, the alcohol thins your blood and it becomes lighter and lighter; *hot, light* blood.

"Leave the loft, crawling down a ladder to the ground floor. See a large, massive door. Open it. Enter an enormous walk-in freezer. Hunks of meat hang from hooks in the ceiling. The frigid air cools your blood; *cold, light* blood.

"Minutes pass. Your blood grows colder and colder, turning to slush in your system; *cold, heavy* blood.

"Exit the freezer. Go out behind the barn. Behold a giant barbecue pit. The smell of barbecued beef permeates the air. Walk into the pit, passing among piles of red-hot coals till you reach the center.

"Stand motionless, getting hotter and hotter. Beads of perspiration run down your face, the small of your back. As more and more water evaporates from your system your blood gets thicker and thicker; *hot, heavy blood.*

"Finally, you ignite. You become fire."

REACTIONS AND USES

People usually have an easier time internalizing heat and heaviness than cold and lightness. This makes sense as you probably recall experiences when your blood felt hot, as when you were flushed or running a fever, or when your blood felt heavy or under pressure, such as when you felt throbbing sensations in your body. However, your blood has most likely never felt cold or light. Getting the sensation of cold and/or light blood involves your simply intensifying a sense of warm blood to hot blood or pulsation to heavy blood.

The most common reactions to these images for recalling sensations in your internal systems are not so much a commentary on the feeling of the sensory subcomponents called for as the depth of the altered state they produce. Common comments are: "I went under really deep, didn't I?" "Kind of strange. I felt like a kernel within a shell . . . strange." "I don't want to come out. I don't ever want to come out. I have this weird feeling that I see parts of the image before it's given."

As you continue to develop mind control over your body through imagery it becomes increasingly apparent to you just how much your physical being truly is a product and extension of your imagination. With this dawning awareness comes ever greater control. You emotionally realize that you truly are a kernel within a shell, a soul, spirit, or mind within a body that encases your understanding. As your understanding grows it breaks the casing that confines it, you outgrow your need for the body.

With this spiritual growth comes the cracking of not only the illusion of your body, but of the illusion of time as well. Present and future mix, possibly infrequently and only in flashes at first, but you swear you knew things were going to happen before they did. Usually the event you "foresee" is very close in time to your moment of prediction, sometimes only a matter of seconds. These precognitive experiences most often begin when your mind is clear, such as when you are doing an image. People often report at this stage in their imagery progression that they know an element of a particular image before I give it to them.

SWEATS AND SOCIAL PHOBIA

On a more earthly note, the dissociation you can invoke imagining yourself igniting to become fire in the *Hayloft Scene* makes it an excellent image for treating phobias. You are not only out of body at the end of this image, you have transmuted yourself into a different energy configuration altogether, fire.

A gay, world-famous 27-year-old actor I'll call T. came to me to be treated for an incapacitating social phobia. "I break into sweats," he said. "I get literally, dripping, wringing wet. It's terrifying. It's especially humiliating if I break out on the set, during filming. In a love scene I want to die if it happens. Although it can happen anytime there's people around—at a dinner party, doing publicity, on a talk show, an interview, anywhere. I guess the bottom line is

I'm afraid people will find out I'm gay. I do everything I can to conceal it. It's the worst thing you can call an actor, you know. The public wants their heroes to be macho, John Wayne and all that bull. I continually worry that an inflection, a mannerism, just a look, will give me away.

"I'm really so tired of having to be what I'm not. It's not like I chose to be gay, any more than I chose when puberty set in. One day I was a happy, adjusted kid with a family who loved me and the next my hormones kicked in and I was a 'faggot,' hated by everyone. How can people hate you for something you have no control over? My parents keep saying, 'You could change if you tried.' Could the blacks become white if they tried? Could the women become men? It's genetic. It's *not* something you choose."

First of all, I agreed with T. "You should stop punishing yourself for something you have no control over," I said. "Recent research shows a biological basis for homosexuality, and for years we've been able to breed homosexuality in animals through artificial insemination, a fact that also points to sexual preference as having a biological component. The fact that 10 percent of the population continues to be gay throughout time again indicates a genetic selection operating."

I then told T., "Being gay is good. Sweating over it isn't." I asked him to practice the *Hayloft Scene*, focusing especially on recalling sensory combinations of hot/heavy and cold/light in his circulatory system. T. was able to voluntarily induce sweating by imagining the blood in his system as hot and heavy. You will remember that recalling heat and/or pressure causes blood to congest in the area you are focusing on with resulting flushing and sweating. "If you can deliberately induce hot flashes and sweating spells," I told T., "you can also eliminate them." Next, I asked T. to imagine that his blood was cold and light whenever he wished to eliminate a sweating spell. This would cause his blood to divert from the surface of his skin, alleviating the flush that made him sweat.

Finally, I advised him that if these two techniques failed him, he was to dissociate himself from the feared social situation by imagining himself igniting to become fire. If he ceased to exist as T., there was certainly nothing for him to be phobic or embarrassed about. "But fire's hot," he said. "Won't I sweat even more?" "You'll sweat if you imagine fire in your veins," I replied. "But you won't sweat if you *are* fire. Fire doesn't sweat. Only you sweat." In a few weeks T. was happy to have his sweating spells under control. If you have unwanted periods of embarrassed flushes or sweating spells, you can curb them using the *Hayloft Scene* just as T. did.

SAND PIT SCENE

You continue developing your power to imagine and control your sense of your body by recalling tactile subcomponent combinations in your excretory and digestive systems. These combinations are: cold/light, hot/heavy, cold/heavy, and hot/light.

SAND PIT SCENE:
"You are walking through a forest of white birch trees. It's early spring. The trees are leafless, their brilliant white bark gleaming in the sun against a deep blue sky. Patches of snow are still on the ground. It's 65 degrees above zero.

"Come to a clearing, a sand pit. Start to cross the sand. The sky darkens to silver gray. It begins to sleet, fine bits of ice falling from the heavens. Look up. Open your mouth. The sleet goes in your mouth and out every other opening of your body; *cold, light* bits of ice through every other opening of your body.

"Finish crossing the sand pit. Enter a forest of maple trees. Tent stakes, like troughs, are driven into the tree trunks. Pails hang at the ends of the stakes collecting maple sap.

"Go deeper into the woods. Come to a great caldron of maple sap boiling down to maple syrup. The sweet smell of maple syrup permeates the spring air. Take a dipper and scoop up some maple syrup. Taste its bitey sweetness. You have an urge to urinate. Expel the urine as *hot* and *heavy* as the syrup went in. Feel the heat and pressure forcing its way through your urinary tract.

"The sky grows darker. It begins to hail. Look up. Open your mouth. The balls of ice, *cold* and *heavy*, go into your mouth and out every other opening of your body.

"Move closer to the cauldron and fire over which it boils. The hail in your stomach melts, turning to steam. The steam, *hot* and *light*, exits every opening of your body.

"Leave the cauldron, moving ever deeper into the woods. Night is falling. A hush falls over the forest. Come to a clearing which was a plowed field in summer, but is still frozen over from the winter. Lie down in the warm insulation of a snowbank. Gaze at the glint of moonlight on the ice."

A MUTUAL REACTION

Since her mastery of glove anesthesia by using the *Mountain Cabin II Scene*, Anne's headaches had stopped and she had no more menstrual pain. Her vaginal warts, which numbered over 160 when I first saw her, had gradually diminished over the course of our sessions together and had at this point cleared up completely. I had never given Anne an affirmation related to the warts and attributed her success in ridding herself of them primarily to the deep relaxation she was able to induce through all the images in the progression that I've given you.

As I mentioned earlier, stress reduction and profound relaxation alone can eliminate many a problem. In fact, Anne told me that very day that her endocrinologist said she might be able to relax herself right out of her diabetes. She reported digging ditches in her garden with no insulin reaction and her doctor had reduced her insulin dosage. Also, her energy level was phenomenal, light years from the chronic fatigue she had complained of the first day she entered my office. Her progress was altogether breathtaking and I marveled at her accomplishments, thinking that if she could do this well with the imagery techniques, so might my other patients. Anne continued seeing me after she became problem-free in order to keep on growing. She was feeling so good from practicing her imagery and experiencing such wonderful new sensations she asked if she could continue coming to master the imagery progression. I was delighted at her progress and happily consented. I'd let her be the judge of when she'd had enough.

"Do you hear a ringing?" Anne asked, opening her eyes after I had given her the *Sand Pit Scene*. Anne's question startled me. I did hear a humming, ringing sound. "It gives me such a sense of peace and tranquility," she said. "I haven't felt this relaxed in weeks." My thoughts were elsewhere. I was thinking back to the image, trying to figure out why we should both be hearing a humming. I found this experience eerily exciting. Then I had it. The image describes a hush coming over the forest at the end. During profound silence you often experience a ringing in your ears. I always go into the image with my patients and evidently this time Anne and I had both done exceptionally well. We'd created an image so vivid, we were both still feeling its effects. I told her my hypothesis and she smiled. "The hum of silence, huh?" she said. "I hope we get more of that. It feels divine."

Our reactions were totally exhilarating and unexpected on my part. Unpredictable sensations often occur using this imaginal sequence. In my experience they have always been of a positive, pleasurable nature and extremely exciting to both me and my subject. You too can expect the unexpected.

THE PEE SHY SYNDROME

Sam, 42, was thinking of quitting his job with a major corporate accounting firm because he had what is called the "Pee Shy

Syndrome." He was not able to urinate in a restroom if someone else was present. This surprisingly common condition forced him to make many trips to the restroom and he was constantly fearful and embarrassed. "It started when I was a kid, about twelve," he said. "It was the middle of the game at Dodger Stadium and there was a line a mile long to use the urinals. I must have waited ten minutes, but by the time my turn came I just froze up. I couldn't go a drop. All I could think of was all those guys behind me waiting for me to finish. It was hell. I had to leave the urinal with my bladder nearly bursting. I don't know how I ever got through the rest of that game.

"It's really a pain at work. If there's someone in the washroom when I get there, I have to go back to my office and try again later. I wonder what the rest of the staff thinks of me, always traipsing off to the restroom. If someone comes in when I first get up to the latrine it's okay if I've already started. Otherwise it's really embarrassing. Sometimes I try to wait for them to leave, but I know they think I'm strange standing at the urinal so long. Sometimes I just try to urinate in the commode and that can be easier, but there are times I can't even do that."

I asked Sam to practice the *Sand Pit Scene* to desensitize him to the idea of elimination through his urinary tract. Once he could conceive of easily urinating sleet, hail, syrup, and steam, eliminating water with a dash of uric acid seemed simple. "It's a piece of cake," he reported. "Whenever I go to a public urinal I just recall the part of the image where I'm peeing hail and the task at hand seems easy by comparison. It also takes my attention off the thought that someone might be watching me."

MINE SHAFT SCENE

This is your last image in your series dealing with your recall of tactile sensory subcomponents in the four systems of your body. With its completion you will have recalled every sensory subcomponent of touch in every physical system of your body in every possible combination. Here you recall combinations of sensory subcomponents of temperature and pressure in your skeletal system. The combinations are: hot/heavy, hot/light, cold/light, and cold/ heavy.

MINE SHAFT SCENE:

"You are standing at the entrance of an abandoned mine shaft. Enter. There's a long, steeply declining tunnel with a rail in it. A gold, metallic substance glitters from the tunnel walls. An old boxcar sets on the rail. Get into the boxcar. It begins to move slowly forward, squeaking on its rusty bearings, gradually picking up momentum, going faster and faster. You are roaring down the tunnel. Suddenly the boxcar stops. You are thrown out of the car into a vat of liquid gold. The gold soaks into your body and permeates you to the marrow of your bones. Bones feel *hot* and *heavy*.

"A blast of hot air comes from above, hollowing out your bones, whistling like a hot wind through aluminum tubing. Bones feel *hot* and *light*.

"Now the air blast turns cool, frigid, freezing. Bones feel *cold* and *light*. A glass elevator descends from above. Get into the elevator. It speeds upward. Streaks of brilliantly colored light pass you by—chartreuse, turquoise, hot pink, lavender, citrine. The elevator stops.

"Exit the elevator. See mountains and spires of colored ice, all shades of the rainbow. Wander through the peaks of rainbow-colored ice. Come to a round, brown tundra region. Walk out onto the tundra. It gives beneath your weight like caramel. The caramel fills the hollows of your bones. Bones are *cold* and *heavy*.

"Suddenly the tundra begins to turn, revolving very slowly at first, gradually picking up momentum, revolving like a turntable on a record player. Going round and round and round and round, the tundra is spinning. It spins the caramel into cotton candy. You are engulfed in a sea of cotton caramel candy."

REACTIONS AND USES

The states you are able to induce as you progress through these images become more and more positive. "I feel euphoric," said a woman immediately upon coming out of the *Mine Shaft Scene*. "I have a very, very thorough sense of well-being. I felt like I was stuffed with a heating blanket." As ever, your recall of heat will elevate your mood and energy. "Numb and weird is how I feel," sighed a middle-aged man when I asked him to relay his experience. "I opened my eyes and it was like my body wasn't there . . . all numb . . . everything real slow. The bed vibrates when I go under. Sometimes I get real dizzy." If you experience feelings of vibration, it's great—your energy is rising.

HEROIN ADDICTION

The "weird" feelings you may have experienced in practicing the *Mine Shaft Scene* can be applied to the treatment of heroin addiction. The surges of hot and cold, lightness and heaviness, shooting through the very marrow of your skeletal system is similar to the "rush" experienced from heroin.

"I went on the stuff when I learned my sister was dying of AIDS," said Didi, a 19-year-old heroin addict. "How can people be so hateful?" she asked, starting to cry. "My mom lost her job as a teacher when the community found out Becky had AIDS. We're Mormons, from Utah. They made life miserable for my whole family."

Didi was able to get off heroin by substituting the imagery-induced rush of the *Mine Shaft Scene* for drug use. "That heroin flow of hot pressure through my body, to the very core of my bones, was the closest thing to Heaven I'd ever known. Now I can come close to duplicating it by zeroing in on the hot/heavy sensation of my bones permeated with simmering liquid gold in the image. It's not exactly the same thing, but it sure takes the edge off and I feel wonderful afterward . . . kind of like drifting in a warm cloud."

It says a lot for a state that it is positive enough to serve as a suitable substitute for a drug. Soon you will see that imagery-induced states can take you further than any drug ever could, safely and unalterably. Prepare yourself to take a journey out of time and out of body. Paradise is waiting for you.

ELEVEN

Out of Time
and Out
of Body

□Did you ever wish you could experience the world as a child again, wake up to each new day filled with awe and the wonder of what was in store? A reality where everything is new and fresh, unblemished by negative experience or personal failure. Wouldn't it be great to be filled with the vigor and enthusiasm of youth, to never worry that things might not work out, because so far, things always have? How marvelous to be free of that plodding sense of routine where every day is just like the next because you've gone through the same motions so long you can't differentiate one time from another.

Remember how good the grass once smelled? How blue was the sky? How fresh was the air? Remember the taste of sun-ripened watermelon and Mom's blueberry pie? Do you recall how much you loved to run and jump and skip and tumble—wanting to be everyplace at the same time? The days weren't long enough for all the wonderful things you wanted to do. There was so much to experience, so many places to go, so many friends to make. The world was beautiful then, full of magic and promise. Has it really changed that much? Or have you?

AGE REGRESSION

It's still the same world, just as wonderful and exciting as ever. But perhaps your perception of it has changed. Maybe you view it in a different light, colored by the brush of your past experiences. Maybe these experiences weren't all so positive. Perhaps many of them were downright painful. Reality then begins to lose its luster. Life closes in. You see limitation where there was once only freedom, hurt and failure instead of adventure, a dull predictable existence where once was a realm of unending possibilities.

How would you like to get that wondrous childlike perception back again? To see beauty in everything, adventure in every moment, joy in every endeavor? You can with the phenomenon of age regression. It's only a state of mind, you know, this thing we nostalgically refer to as the "good old days." You control your state of mind. If you don't, who does? If you're tired of the way the world looks to you today, why not change the way you look at it? Why not step out of time and see it the way you did as a child, or the way you did when you were happiest?

"Age regression" means just that—regressing in age, in time, returning to a previous level of your reality. Since every sensation you've ever experienced is recorded, you have the power to reexperience anything stored in your cortex—not only a specific event, but your then mode of perception. You can therefore experience to-day just as if you were two, or ten, or twelve. You needn't live in the past, only perceive the present with your past mode of reception.

I will now teach you age regression, not so you can recall and work out some past trauma or remember where you hid your extra house key, but so that you can retrieve a past way of perception, a fresher mode of experiencing your world.

AUTUMN SCENE

This image has been designed expressly to help you create the phenomenon of age regression. All recall is in fact a form of age regression. For example, you induce a feeling of warmth by regressing to a time when you were actually experiencing warmth and then relive it. With the *Autumn Scene*, however, you will achieve an emotional as well as sensory regression. You will feel the joy of childhood again!

The *Autumn Scene* incorporates activities you would probably have engaged in as a child. It emphasizes your recall of kinesthetic sensations like running, jumping, diving, and springing. Your recall of these experiences will trigger other childhood associations and thoughts. As you begin thinking the same thoughts you did as a child, you'll cue the feelings associated with these thoughts and "feel" like a child again.

You can use the *Autumn Scene* to bring back any positive feeling from any time period you wish. Simply tell yourself that you are going back in time to the period you felt the feelings you wish to retrieve. I only use twelve as an example age. It's an eventful year for most people, around the dawn of puberty and transition into adolescence. It may therefore be a good place for you to start, but feel free to regress to any age you desire to bring back.

AUTUMN SCENE:

"You are going back in time . . . back a second . . . a minute . . . an hour . . . a day . . . a week . . . a month . . . a year . . . a decade . . . back to the age of twelve. You are twelve years old, standing on the edge of a forest. It's a beautiful, positive day in the late fall. The leaves of the oak trees around you are orange and crimson and gold. You are standing before a field of pumpkins, bright orange from a recent frost.

"Think the thoughts you were thinking at twelve. Who are your friends? What grade are you in? What classes are you taking? Who is your teacher? What do you do for fun? What do you want to be when you grow up? How do you think, and feel, and see yourself at the age of twelve?

"Walk out into the pumpkin patch. Pass on to a field of corn that's been harvested, stacked in shocks like tepees. Next you come to a great golden haystack. Climb the haystack. Begin jumping up and down, higher and higher. Now you go way up into the blue sky and land at the base of the stack in a cloud of golden dust.

"Leave the haystack. Come to a chain of granite quarries, great holes in the earth filled with water. Stand high on a ledge above a quarry. Remove your clothes. Dive head first. Feel your body sailing through the air. Hit the water and shoot down through the liquid. Bring your chin up. You surface. Take a big, deep breath of fresh air. Swim to the shore. Breast yourself up on the rock.

"Move to another quarry. See a diving raft in the middle of it. Get a running start. Jump, bringing your knees to your chest in a cannonball dive, landing feet first with a great splash in the water.

"Swim to the raft. Climb up onto it. Now get onto the springboard. Walk to the end of the board. Feel the coarse burlap beneath your bare feet. Begin springing on the end of the board, going higher and higher with each spring. Go way up into the air. Tuck your knees to your chest. Bring your chin to your chest. You somersault in midair. Land in the water.

"Swim to shore. Lie in the sun on the warm rock. Feel young, alive, vital; filled with the energy, the enthusiasm of youth."

REACTIONS

People most often react to the *Autumn Scene* with a wonderful, detailed recall of the feelings of youth, energy, and love of life. "I'd forgotten how beautiful the world used to be," said a retired merchant in his mid-seventies. "It's great to know I can still feel that way again." A woman who just turned forty evidenced childlike laughter through much of her image. "The little details were incredible," she stated. "I remembered things about myself at the age of twelve I haven't thought of in years. How concerned I was over my developing breasts, how proud I was of my early maturing figure . . . the exuberance of preadolescence. I was very happy at this time in my life. I was really glad to get that feeling back."

RETURN TO A MORE POSITIVE OUTLOOK

Most commonly, age regression has been used therapeutically to uncover traumatic or repressed data in a person's past to help understand his present. It has also been widely used in forensic psychology to recall the details of crimes and accidents. I've used it to aid people in remembering details of events such as an auto crash or a murder, so they can uncover what really happened. Dr. Kroger used age regression in many famous criminal cases including the Chauchilla case for which he was written up in *Time* magazine. He used regression to aid in the recall of a license plate number and to save a buried busload of children. While you can certainly use regression for these purposes, I believe its most valuable asset is in returning you to a fresher, more youthful mode of perception.

Age regression makes you feel younger. It gives you a more youthful perspective on life. You see things unjaundiced, unjaded, with positive expectations. You feel motivated, like trying new and different things. It seems easy to start anew, from scratch. Once-beautiful elements of your life that have become tainted with negative experience look good again. Your experiencing of age regression is a poignant illustration of the degree to which the world's beauty and ugliness is a function of your own perception. It is an impetus for changing and evaluating your present values and outlook on life.

Jane, a 35-year-old housewife with a daughter, Robin, 15, was so depressed in her marriage to Henry, a 36-year-old pilot, she couldn't muster the energy to either work at making it better or create a new life without her husband. After working a week on the *Autumn Scene* she said, "That image unleashed a deluge of positive feelings and emotions that I'd long forgotten. I was beginning to think that sad is the only emotion there is. I've let Henry have his way, bit by bit, year by year, until I don't know who I am anymore. I feel like a nobody, totally inadequate, incapable of doing anything on my own. I forgot how good I once felt about myself. When I was seventeen I thought I could conquer the world. I was going to be a famous attorney. Maybe even the first woman Supreme Court judge. I was so sure of myself then. I can't believe I sold myself so short."

Jane used the *Autumn Scene* to get back a positive part of herself that she had lost eighteen years ago. She continued conjuring the image till she had retrieved enough of her prior positive self to feel sufficiently strong and independent to end her bad marriage and start a new life.

RETURN TO A BETTER LEVEL OF FUNCTIONING

You can use age regression to retrieve not only a better attitude, but also a superior performance. Madeline, a single, 24-year-old nurse, was raped returning to her car after finishing night duty. "I always loved sex before," she said. "Now I can't stand it if a man even touches me. I wish I could feel the way I used to." Madeline told me that she was at her sexual best when she was about eighteen. I asked her to practice the *Autumn Scene*, regressing to eighteen rather than twelve. She was to think the thoughts she was thinking then, revive the associated feelings. After practicing a week she reported, "It's coming back. Those sexual feelings that I thought were dead are returning. I'm beginning to feel the way I did at eighteen again."

You can use the *Autumn Scene* to retrieve the way you felt and acted before you developed any debilitating condition. You may want to recall your state of mind before you suffered a depression, developed a phobia, incurred a pain, started to stutter, needed drugs, cigarettes, alcohol, or too much food, couldn't sleep, lost your energy and/or concentration, burned out, became anxious, got high blood pressure, or became anorexic. When you are able to rejuvenate that past positive state of mind, the associated healthy behavior is likely to return with it. Your walk, your talk, even the glow in your face, will reveal your return to youthful vigor.

OUT OF BODY: DEEPER DISSOCIATION

You traveled out of time using age regression to retrieve a past healthier state of mind. Now, in your next four images, you are going to imagine stepping out of your body to achieve even more profound states of relaxation and sensuality than you have before.

THIS ROOM SCENE

I want you to help me create your first exercise in deep dissociation. You will be imagining that you are in whatever room you really are while doing the exercise. Your reality and imagery thus begin to merge.

THIS ROOM SCENE:

"Imagine that you are standing in the room where you are actually practicing this exercise. You are looking directly above where you are lying in reality. Imagine the room clearly in all five senses. Now turn around. Take in the rest of the room. Turn back around. Look down and see yourself lying where you are actually practicing this exercise. You look the total picture of repose. Your lids are closed, hands rest calmly at your sides, breathing is slow, deep, and regular. Now you turn back around. Imagine yourself leaving the room where you are actually practicing this exercise.

"Go outside. Enter another building. Walk down a hall. Enter a room that is all white. White walls, white ceiling, white floor. Move to the window. Look out the window and into the window of the room you just left. See yourself lying in the same position with the same peaceful expression as the last time you looked. Turn around. Gaze into the whiteness of the wall."

THAT LOVING FEELING

Most people report feeling "disembodied" from practicing the *This Room Scene*, along with an incredible sense of euphoria, peace, relaxation, and love. "I feel disembodied," said Allan, a 38-year-old data processor suffering from nervous exhaustion and trouble relating to peers at work. "It's fantastic . . . higher than I've ever felt before."

Allan later told me that this fantastic feeling he was able to achieve from the *This Room Scene* had practical value in increasing his coping abilities with other people. "Feeling good improves all other aspects of my life as well." He smiled. "I like people when I feel good. I'm nicer to them and they're nicer to me. It's easier to be loving, to love, when you feel good." Deep dissociation will definitely help you to feel more loving and more lovable as well. It gives you a sense of profound relaxation. This relaxation makes you more sensitive to all positive stimuli. Love is the most positive emotion you know. Deep dissociation thus makes you more sensitive to love and gives you that loving feeling.

Patients addicted to Quaaludes often claim that this drug makes them feel more loving, as if they could embrace everyone and everything in the universe. They feel greater love, empathy, compassion, intimacy, closeness, to all creation. You can achieve the same higher feelings by cultivating deep dissociation, which is why I ask people addicted to Quaaludes and similar drugs to practice the *This Room Scene* and the other three images for deep dissociation I give you in this chapter. These scenes serve as a far better and safer substitute for producing euphoric feelings than any drug could.

ATHENS SCENE

I give you this image to further intensify your sense of deep dissociation. You not only imagine going partially out of body in this scene, you travel out of time as well, regressing farther back than you have in imagery so far. You imagine going back in time four thousand years. Being out of time *and* out of body gives you ever greater dissociation and detachment from your present, common five-sensory reality.

As Albert Einstein showed, time and space are the same dimension. If you move fast enough through space, faster than the speed of light, you go back in time. Increasing your sense of motion reverses your sense of time. Your mind is not limited by time, space, and motion. You can project your awareness anywhere at any time. Past, present, and future coexist. It is a question of where you direct your attention. Whether you accept these statements or not, you are to *feel as if* you have regressed four thousand years in time, dissociating yourself from the present.

This is the first image where I would actually touch you if you came to see me in my office. While you are imagining another person making designs on your skin with his finger, I would really finger-trace these figures on your skin myself. I would then suggest that when you practice the *Athens Scene* on your own, you run your own finger over your skin while imagining it is the person in your image who is producing the tactile stimulation. You are, in essence, dissociating your finger from the.rest of your body. The sensation you would normally feel in your fingertip from tracing it over your skin is not your feeling, but that of the person you imagine making the tracing. You have projected your feeling into that of another being, a being you created imaginally.

ATHENS SCENE:

"You are going back in time. Back a second . . . a minute . . . an hour . . . a day . . . a week . . . a month . . . a year . . . a decade . . . a century . . . a thousand years . . . back to the year 2000 B.C.

"You are lying on a stone slab in an underground chamber. Smell smoke from the torches that burn on the walls. Hear the sound of dripping limewater.

"Suddenly there comes to your ears the sound of approaching footsteps, moving down one of the many halls that lead into your chamber. A young man/woman (sex you are attracted to) comes to your side.

"With his/her right index finger he/she traces a circle on each of your temples. (Run your own index finger in these motions on your body while imagining it is being done by the person you have created in your image.) Then he/she runs his/her finger from temple to temple across your forehead. He/she makes a circular motion on each of your cheeks. He/she runs his/her finger the length of each of your arms from your fingertips to your shoulders. Finally, he/she traces a figure 8 on the back of each of your wrists.

"He/she leaves your chamber. Hear the receding footfalls, leaving you alone with the smell of burning torches and sound of dripping limewater."

SENSORY EXPANSION: HEIGHTENED SENSUALITY

While the *Athens Scene* further intensifies your sense of separation of mind and body, strangely enough, this sense of disembodiment can lead you to extremely sensual experiences due to the fact that the deeper the dissociative relaxation you produce, the more your sensory thresholds lower, and the more sensitive you become in all five sense modalities. I often hear reports that the tactile tracings feel so vivid they seem like separate entities, floating in space a little above the skin. You may still be able to sense these energy forms when the image is over and your eyes are open.

Nicole, a 29-year-old travel agent, living with Sean, 30, for three years, told me that while she was very much in love she was afraid to marry because she didn't trust her sexual feelings. "I wax hot and cold like the moon," she complained. "Sean says it drives him crazy. He never knows how I'll react, whether I'll want to have sex with him or not. The problem is, neither do I." Nicole was able to use the *Athens Scene* to induce dissociation and its accompanying sense of heightened sensuality to gain control over her responsiveness to Sean and "tune in" sexually to him at will. Whenever she wished to make love to him she'd silently give herself the trigger word, "Athens," and it would cue the sensuality she had previously practiced the image to induce.

SENSORY EXPANSION: TELEPATHY

The heightened sensuality and lowered sensory thresholds you experience from deep dissociation are in actuality sensory expansion. The range of experience you are capable of feeling is increasing. You are widening the band width of the psychophysical data you can receive and process. You as a receiving, perceiving being are growing. A physical process you may now be able to receive that previously your awareness was too limited to tune into is the thoughts and images of others.

Anne lay very still after I gave her the *Athens Scene*. Then her eyes fluttered open and she said, "I don't think I'm back yet . . . there's no way to verbalize that . . . it's a long way to come back to."

Without thinking I asked, "Why did you make it Egypt when it was supposed to be Athens? And why did you put all that gold and treasure there and make it a tomb?"

Anne was still lying immobile on her back, piercing the ceiling with her eyes as if looking far, far beyond. A strange, enigmatic smile illuminated her face. She seemed to radiate. The air in the room felt silky, palpable, a strange kind of light electric fluid that had the slightest cast of white to it.

"I was an Egyptian priestess," she breathed with that same ethereal smile, "lying in my tomb surrounded by my treasure. I know I lived that life before."

It wasn't till then that I realized I'd seen the contents of her image without her telling me. It felt so natural to me at the moment, I took the experience as a matter of course. Anne didn't even comment on it. She was still caught up in her revelation of a past life.

I didn't take her claim to reincarnation seriously, but I was impressed by the apparent telepathy transpiring between the two of us. How did I know she had placed herself in Egypt rather than Athens? I was further confused by the fact that the image I intended to give her next time was of Egypt, not the interior of a tomb, but the roof of one. I had conceived the *Egypt Scene* just prior to her session. Was I getting thoughts of the *Egypt Scene* while I was giving her the *Athens Scene* and was she telepathically picking up on it? Or was she precognitive? Did she know beforehand the next image I was going to give her?

The only thing I was sure of at that time was the energy present during her experience. It was riveting. She was positively charged beyond anything I had ever witnessed. I could *feel* the energy in the silken quality of the air. I could see it in her eyes.

Clairvoyance, the professed power of discerning objects not present to the senses, and precognition, clairvoyance relating to an event or state not yet experienced, were out of my realm of experience at that time. They are not, however, out of the realm of the phenomena you can expect with sensory expansion. Clairvoyance and precognition are a natural byproduct, exactly what you would expect from extending your range of perception beyond your common five-sensory world—discernment of objects not present to your ordinary sensorium and breaking down of the illusion of time, space, and motion, a reality where past, present, and future merge. In such an expanded reality, the term "precognition" is meaningless. You cannot know beforehand when you know all things now, when the moment is eternal and everlasting.

EGYPT SCENE

I'm giving you this image to help you reach an even deeper state of dissociation. If I were giving you the *Egypt Scene* in my office, I'd make designs on your body with my finger while asking you to imagine that your resulting sensations belong to someone else. I'd then ask you to practice by doing what I'm now going to ask you to do from the start, since I won't be available to you in person for the first phase of this exercise. When you practice the *Egypt Scene*, run your own finger over the appropriate areas of your body and imagine that you are tracing your finger on someone else's body.

Not only are you detaching yourself from your own feelings, you are imputing them to someone else. You are to feel *as if* the sensations produced by the finger-tracings on your own body are the sensations of another person. This will lead you to a great empathy and compassion for other people, at an emotional as well as sensory level.

If you can give your feelings to someone else, you can take theirs from them. You can feel *as if* you are taking or giving to the feelings of all people and combine them into an ultimate experience, a universal experience.

EGYPT SCENE:

"You are going back in time. Back a second . . . a minute . . . an hour . . . a day . . . a week . . . a month . . . a year . . . a decade . . . a century . . . a thousand years . . . back to the year 2000 B.C.

"You are walking along a river lined by date palms. Long, sleek barges glide by the tall, slender rushes of the river. The air is dry and warm, the water dark blue, the sky a light azure.

"Leave the river, walking out into a vast expanse of desert, fine, white sand as far as your eye can see. Seconds pass . . . minutes . . . hours. A pyramidal structure towers on the horizon. Approach the pyramid. More time passes. Reach the base.

"Begin climbing the pyramid's steps toward its apex, going higher and higher into the desert sky. Minutes pass. Reach the top. It is flat with a large stone block in its center.

"Lie down on the block. Stare at the intense blueness of the sky. Hear footsteps approaching from the other side, drawing ever closer. A young man/woman (whichever sex you are attracted to) comes to you. He/she lies down on his/her back beside you.

"You sit up and kneel over him/her, placing your knees at either side of his/her thighs. You are directly over him/her, looking down upon him/her, staring into the clearness of his/her eyes. Trace a circle with your right index finger on each of his/her temples. (Move your own index finger through these motions on your body while imagining you are doing it to the person you have created in your image.) Then move your finger from temple to temple across his/her forehead. Make a circular motion on each of his/her cheeks. Run your finger the length of each of his/her arms from his/her fingertips to the shoulders. Finally, trace a figure 8 on the back of each of his/her wrists.

"Lie down upon him/her with an embrace. Your breathing becomes as one. Your heartbeats become as one. Your bodies become as one . . . floating into the mellow blueness."

HEAVINESS AND INERTIA

A most common reaction immediately upon coming out of the *Egypt Scene* is a great sense of heaviness and inertia. After the lightness of deep dissociation your body can feel like lead. This is an encouraging sign. It shows that you've done an excellent job "lightening up" for you to feel such a contrast. "I must weigh six thousand pounds easy," said one woman as soon as she'd finished this scene. "I've never had such inertia," sighed a man in his twenties. "I feel so heavy. It feels like I can't get off the couch."

A SUBSTITUTE FOR "DOWNERS"

Trent, 22, unemployed and living at home, was brought into therapy by his mother, a single parent working hard to survive as a legal secretary since her separation from Trent's father. Trent was hooked on relaxants or "downers" and had been at fault in two auto accidents where he nearly killed himself and the other drivers. "I do drugs to take the edge off," he said, "to stop worrying my mom and dad are no longer together, to forget and feel good."

I taught Trent to take the edge off by inducing deep dissociation with the *Egypt Scene* instead of abusing drugs. "It really mellows me out," he said. "Whenever I get that panicky feeling I do the image and it relaxes me. Then there's no point in taking a downer. I'm already there."

AN ALTERNATE REALITY

"Why did you leave my place so suddenly the other night?" Anne asked me in the next session she had after I gave her the *Egypt Scene*.

I looked at her blankly. I'd never seen her out of my office.

"You did stop by?" she asked, noting the confused look on my face.

I shook my head, "No, what made you think that?"

"I was at home," she said, "in the den practicing dissociation by imagining that I was outside my body in the room where I was actually lying, like I did with the *This Room Scene*. Then I heard a jangling of keys and was certain that you had entered the room. You said to me, 'That's wonderful. That's fantastic. You've finally got it. Keep on. I'll see you soon.' Then I heard the keys jangle a second time and I came out of my image.

"I looked for you 30 to 45 minutes afterward. I was sure you'd really been there. I checked all around the house and yard. The experience was so real. I told David about my experience and he admitted that he entered the room while I was in my image and that he accidentally jangled his keys. But he says he only made noise with them once. I distinctly heard them on two separate occasions, once when you came into the room and once when you left. I just know you were there. Weren't you really?"

Anne's image had induced an audio hallucination so vivid she couldn't distinguish it from reality. Her power to imagine was growing rapidly. Her imagery was impinging on reality. The two were merging.

Eastern philosophies speak of four levels of consciousness that you pass through in order to attain nirvana, paradise, or the "universal one." In the first level there is an alteration of your common reality, including color and form distortion. Pronounced states of dissociation appear in the second and you feel you are outside of your body looking at yourself. Your dissociated self travels and explores the next dimensional world in the third phase. In the fourth and final phase of consciousness raising you become one with the cosmic forces and no longer return to your body.

Positive and negative hallucinations are an alteration of five-sensory reality. Anne's audio hallucination of my voice while she was in a state of deep dissociation was an alteration of her "normal" reality.

Now we call the sort of auditory perception that Anne had a hallucination because it wasn't "real." My voice and I weren't really there. They existed only in her mind. But what about Anne's first audio hallucination, the one she experienced after the *Sand Pit Scene* when she heard a humming sound? Did that exist only in her mind too? No, it didn't exist only in her mind, it existed in my mind as well. We both heard it. Is an event "real" if two people experience it? Or is it just a "joint hallucination" or *folie à deux*?

How many people have to experience something before it's really "real"? A hundred? A million? A billion? What if six billion people sense a world that isn't "really" there? All reality would then be a mass hallucination, a function of billions of minds entertaining the same common five-sensory hallucination, the ultimate form of democracy. In this case can we argue that the world is still not "real"? How do we determine reality except by *consensual validation*? The majority rules, perceptually as well as politically.

But who creates this hallucination called "reality"? *You* do. The power to create is within you. You project reality outward. It cannot exist independently of your consciousness. And your consciousness cannot die, nor can this thing we call reality. In the true spirit of solipsism, the self can know nothing but its own modifications and the self is the only existent thing. Your ascent to paradise is thus a modification of your own consciousness.

If you like it here in the earthbound democracy of a five-sensory reality, there's nothing you need to change in mind. If you prefer something better, you'd best set about altering the present spiritual quagmire you call your "reality." Continuing to develop your images is a good place to start.

SOUND STAGE SCENE

This is the last image in the series of four I've developed to help you increase your powers to achieve a state of deep dissociation. It asks you to recall the first half of the image during the last half. The first half you are to experience as "reality," while the second half is a recall of that "reality." The only thing that makes either half "real" is your decision to make it so. This image within an image provides you with an emotional understanding of the arbitrariness of "reality." "Reality" is truly what you make it.

This is the first image where you are asked to actually walk while imagining it. You can do anything in a hypnotic state and do it better because you are more focused. The *Sound Stage Scene* will help you get used to the idea of functioning in a hypnotic state. It's time for you to merge realities, combine a better state of consciousness with physical navigation in this reality.

SOUND STAGE SCENE:

"You are lying on your back in a large box of plush, red velvet. Above you is a brilliant blue sky.

"Sit up. (Actually sit up, keeping your eyes closed.) See that you are perched high on a mountaintop, so far up that you can see the curvature of the earth. You get out of the box. (Stand up beside the couch.) Before you is a clear stream babbling over a stony bottom.

A grove of palms is on the other side. Put your right foot on a rock in the stream. (Step forward with your right foot.) Feel the hard, wet, slippery surface of the rock beneath your foot. Feel the icy water splashing against your leg. Shift your weight to this foot and bring your left foot forward, placing it on another rock in front of your right foot. (Place your left foot in front of your right one.) You now place your right foot onto shore and bring your left foot up even with it. (Step forward with your right foot and bring your left foot even with it.)

"The setting sun turns the sky to blazing crimson, silhouetting the palms before you in black. Suddenly a white light blinks on and the palm trees roll away. You see that you are in the middle of a Hollywood sound stage. Turn around. The mountain and river are gone. See instead an old mattress. Walk over and lie down upon the mattress. (Actually turn around, take three steps forward, and lie back down upon your couch.)

"Look up at a monitor. On the screen is an image of a box perched on a mountaintop. See yourself sit up, get out of the box, and cross a river. See yourself silhouetted in black against a flaming sunset. A white light comes on, palm trees roll away, and you turn around to walk over to a mattress, lie down, and look up at a monitor on which is the image of a box perched on a mountaintop. See yourself see yourself get out of the box. . . ."

REACTIONS

You will likely find, as many people do, that imagining the first half of the image replayed on film during the last half makes the first half seem more real by comparison. It also increases your sense of dissociation during the second half of the image because the self you are imagining is detached from the experience it is viewing on the monitor.

TRANSCENDING STRESS

This final image on deep dissociation will alter your emotional state even more for the better. Steve, a 31-year-old pattern cutter for a high fashion house, said he just couldn't take his job anymore because of the woman he worked for. "Nothing I do is ever right for that bitch," he complained. "She's at me morning, noon, and night. 'Do this. Do that.' She can't just ask me to do one thing at a time. One demand is no sooner out of her mouth than she's thought of three more. Sometimes she's sweet as a lamb and a minute later she's Godzilla. There's no figuring her out. Everyone there is a nervous wreck. We never know who she's going to pick on next. One day I'm the fair-haired boy. The day after I've got the plague. Her mood has nothing to do with whether I do my job well or not. She's just plain impossible."

"It's amazing," Steve said after practicing the *Sound Stage Scene* for a week. "Instead of hating my boss when she yells at me and makes impossible demands, I now feel sorry for her. I think what stress she must be under and realize her outbursts have nothing to do with me personally. That image really made me feel more compassionate. The job doesn't bother me anymore. I've learned to rise above it. In fact, I'm starting to enjoy it."

I hope that by now you too are in touch with more positive aspects of your consciousness. You will see that paradise is right here all the time if you can raise your awareness sufficiently to attain it.

TWELVE

Paradise and
the Negative
Hallucination

□You can use the phenomenon of the
negative hallucination to raise your awareness sufficiently to glimpse
paradise. In this final chapter I'll show you how you can eliminate the
illusion of your five-sensory world and process that which lies beyond.

THE NEGATIVE HALLUCINATION

As we discussed earlier, a positive hallucination is the phenomenon
of your experiencing something in one or more of your senses that is

not there. A negative hallucination is the converse, your not experiencing something in one or more of your senses that *is* there. Again, positive and negative hallucinations occur in your normal, everyday life. Positive ones are especially common when you are expecting something. If you're waiting for a friend to come by, you'll swear you hear footsteps outside the door or see headlights against the window. These are typical examples of positive audio and visual hallucinations. On the other hand, you may be reading a story and not hear someone next to you speak, or be looking at a pen and not see it right in front of you. These are examples of negative audio and visual hallucinations, but they can occur in any or all of your five senses.

You can use the negative hallucination to benefit you in healing. Pain control, for example, is in essence your mastering a negative tactile hallucination, tuning out a signal in your sense modality of touch that actually does exist. Your tuning out an urge to smoke, eat, drink, or do drugs is another example of the clinical use of the negative hallucination. Visually shutting out an audience to eliminate performance anxiety and auditorily shutting out noise to increase concentration are further uses of this truly positive phenomenon called the negative hallucination.

Your learning to positively and negatively hallucinate will enable you to control your entire personal reality, from being pain free to attaining a state of joy or ecstasy. Since the world comes to you through your senses, being able to control what you receive (tune in and tune out) in each sense modality leads to your being able to control your world.

All your images thus far have actually been lessons teaching you how to positively hallucinate—sense a world in five senses that does not "really" exist. I'll now show you how *leaving senses out* of your imagery can lead you to the mastery of reality as well as putting senses in. When you can create (positively hallucinate) all positive in all five of your senses, and tune out (negatively hallucinate) all negative, you'll be well on your way to paradise, if not already there.

DEVELOPING A FINE DISCRIMINATION

It is not sufficient for your mastery of the negative hallucination that you merely have the power to globally shut out a given sense or senses from your reality. The ability to simply shut out all sight or all sound or all touch doesn't really enable you to work well *within* your five-sensory reality.

For example, if you have pain in your left foot, you want to be able to negatively hallucinate that particular pain, not *all* touch. If you're giving a public speech and want to visually shut out your audience, you still need to be able to see the notecards before you on the podium. You really want the power to *selectively* negatively hallucinate. This requires your developing a finer sensory discrimination.

Aristotle divided reality into four elements: fire, water, earth, and air. What was good enough for the Greeks will be good enough for our purposes here. You will begin your mastery of the negative hallucination by negatively hallucinating *one element at a time, in one sense at a time*. You start with fire.

MIRRORS SCENE

In this image you are asked to imagine fire in its pure sensory form, experiencing it only through your senses of sight and touch. Fire itself has no sound, smell, or taste independent of the substance it is burning. The crackling sounds and associated smell and taste of smoke and vapors comes from that which is burning, not from the fire itself. The *Mirrors Scene* helps you get a clear sensory impression of fire before you begin selectively negatively hallucinating it in the two images that follow.

MIRRORS SCENE:

"It's a warm summer night. You are standing on a rain-soaked street, looking at the black pavement. Brilliant neon lights reflect on the shiny black surface. Smell of asphalt.

"Begin walking. Pass a theater. Smell popcorn. Buy a bag. Start eating the popcorn, hearing it crunch, dry in your mouth, covered with rich, creamy butter. Leave the theater. Come to a caramel apple stand. Sweet smell of caramel wafts through the air. Buy an apple. Bite into the crisp, juicy fruit covered with sweet caramel. It melts in your mouth.

"Continue your walk till you come to a park. Smell of wet grass. Moonlight glistens on the raindrops clinging to the blades of the park lawn. Smell the kerosene from globed lights lit by an old lamplighter with long white beard. Find a bandstand in the park's center. Sit on a bench. Hear the sound of a horse's hooves over cobblestones. A horse-driven carriage passes by you, disappearing around a hedge of lilacs.

"Get up. Begin walking again. Smell salt in the air as you come to the ocean. Walk along a boardwalk, passing a shooting gallery. Hear the metallic sound of pinball machines.

"Find yourself at last in front of a fun house, a hall of mirrors. Enter the maze of mirrors, wandering among the cold, hard, slippery surfaces of multi-reflected light and images . . . room after room of mirrored walls.

"Come to the final room. In the center is a silver cube from which a flame is burning. The fire is reflected in the mirrors, surrounding you with flickering light of great brilliance and intensity. Sniff the fire. It has no smell. Hold your tongue near the flame. It has no taste. It makes no sound. The room is permeated by silence. You cannot even hear your own breathing or heart beating.

"It becomes hotter and hotter, brighter and brighter. You are aware only of red, orange, and heat . . . The fire extinguishes. The room becomes gray and cool. You are enveloped in a cool grayness."

STRONGER IMAGERY

The most common reaction to the *Mirrors Scene* concerns how vivid the fire seems. "The fire was absolutely blinding," said a young man in his late teens. "I've never seen such a brilliant orange or any color that bright in an image before. Astounding." Sarah, a 42-year-old physics teacher, had soaked through her slacks and blouse with perspiration by the time the image was over. "I'm so hot." She laughed, fanning herself. "My gosh, I'm wringing wet. Why did I get so warm? I never got this heat in my other images, not even the one of the hayloft where I was standing in the middle of the barbecue pit and ignited to become fire. What happened?"

What happened to Sarah is exactly what will happen to you when you begin cleaning up your sensory impressions. There will be less noise, distraction, in your sensory circuits, leaving you more room to process more information. A basic psychophysical principle is at work here: When you clarify your sensory world, whether it be your "real" or your imaginary one, that which remains is intensified.

The positive results of this principle will become even more apparent when you begin incorporating the negative hallucination into your imagery. When you remove an entire sense, not just noise and distraction, from your experiencing of an element, this leaves more room in your channels to process the *remaining* senses and your image is vastly enhanced.

You thus vivify one sense by eliminating another. The negative hallucination enables you to do this. It tunes out part of your sensorium so that that which remains can come to the fore. The negative hallucination therefore not only leaves more room in your sensory channels to process the "extra" senses we discussed in earlier sections of this book, it also expands your capacity to receive in those senses that are remaining.

The first time I gave Anne the *Mirrors Scene*, she said on coming out of the image, "I flashed on that image two days ago, when I was practicing the *Sound Stage Scene*. I saw a mirrored tunnel and door after mirrored door opening." Once again I found her precognition intriguing. Her seeing the *Egypt Scene* ahead of time could have been labeled telepathy as well as precognition, because I was there at the time and had the *Egypt Scene* on my mind. However, I couldn't see how this present incident could be attributed to telepathy. I was nowhere near when Anne practiced the *Sound Stage Scene* and I hadn't thought of the *Mirrors Scene* in weeks. As usual, my logic said it was coincidence. But that explanation was getting harder and harder for me to buy.

CHATEAU SCENE

Now that you've practiced the *Mirrors Scene* as a primer, removing competing stimuli in order to create a pure sensory impression of the element fire, you're ready to introduce your first negative hallucination. In this image you visually negatively hallucinate fire. You thus experience fire only through touch, vastly enhancing your tactile experience of this element.

CHATEAU SCENE:
"It's a beautiful summer day. You are drifting in a boat on a large lake. A massive French chateau stands by the lake. Graceful swans of iridescent white float in the water beside you. Brilliant bluebirds circle overhead. Vivid pink flamingos wade near shore. A silvery blue sky with fluffy, billowing clouds is above you. The boat drifts to the far shore.

"Get out of the boat. Walk barefoot along the sand in the cool, purple shade of giant oak trees. Suddenly feel a burning in your right foot. Withdraw it instantly. Hold your right hand over the footprint. It feels like lapping tongues of fire. There is no smell, no sound. Feel the heat in your hand. Sweat appears on your palm. Pick a dry rush. Hold it over the footprint. It turns black at the tip, burning to charcoal. There is no smoke.

"Night falls. Sit by the footprint, feeling its warmth. Look up at the night sky. It's clear, filled with stars. Sleep on the beach to the sound of waves rolling against the sand."

HEAT AND ENERGY

The heat you experience from imagining fire minus interference in the *Mirrors Scene* is further intensified in the *Chateau Scene* by your negatively hallucinating your visual experience of it, thus leaving more room to process fire tactilely. I often find that people's hands are sweating by the end of this image.

Concomitant with your growing ability to generate heat comes increased energy. Heat is energy and you cannot induce one without benefiting from the appearance of the other. With energy comes motivation and action. Work goes better and you get more done.

SHUTTING OUT UNDESIRED VISUAL STIMULI

The *Chateau Scene* is good practice and lays the groundwork for your learning to selectively tune out anything in your field of vision that you don't want to see. Vince, a 32-year-old actor, came to me with a bad case of stage fright. He was opening in a new play at a major theater in Los Angeles and was counting on a career break coming from it. "I've done lots of plays and never had this problem before," he said. "I guess it's because I've got so much riding on it. This drama could make or break me. If I don't get cast in a movie or TV or at least get a decent agent out of it, I'm throwing in the towel. I've been a starving actor too long."

I asked Vince to practice the *Chateau Scene* for a week, really concentrating on his experiencing of fire tactilely, shutting out his visual impression of it. Then I told him, "Just as you can shut out your visual experiencing of fire, you can shut out seeing an audience. Just as you saw the sand, the waves, and the footprint, but not the fire, in the *Chateau Scene*, you can see the actors, the set, and the stage, but not the audience, when you do your play. You do this by directing your total attention to that which remains exclusive of the audience." After he opened, I asked Vince how the audience had affected him. "What audience?" he asked. "I didn't pay any attention to them and they ceased to exist."

PLANTATION SCENE

This is the last image where you work with the element of fire. When you master your ability to positively and negatively hallucinate fire, water, earth, and air in all of your five senses, you have gained control over your five-sensory reality. You can experience anything in any of your five senses that you wish.

The *Plantation Scene* asks you to tactilely negatively hallucinate fire. You see fire in brilliant red, orange flames. Then you walk through it and feel nothing, no sense of warmth or heat.

PLANTATION SCENE:

"You are walking down a winding road in the deep South. The road is lined with honeysuckle bushes, jasmine, and red bougainvillea. The scent of honeysuckle and jasmine is heavy in the sultry air. Ancient, gnarled trees covered with hanging moss stand back from the hedge. Pass a pond of water lilies. Round a bend. Behold an enormous white plantation with tall, slender columns and an ambling veranda. Brightly colored peacocks graze on the deep green lawn that slopes down from the porch.

"Walk up to the veranda. Lie in a hammock. Swing back and

forth, to and fro, in the lazy southern afternoon. Beside you on a white wicker table is a mint julep with ice and a sprig of mint in it. Drink the julep. Taste its minty sweetness. Feel its coolness running down your throat, quenching your thirst.

"Leave the hammock. Go inside. A red carpeted spiral staircase leads to the upper level. Ascend the stairs. Enter a long hall. Follow it to the master bedroom. A sparkling chandelier hangs from the ceiling.

"Walk to the window. Look out over the lawn and cotton fields. Hear the cry of the peacocks below. Suddenly hear a crash behind you. Turn. See that the chandelier has fallen. The room is ablaze. Walk toward the fire. Feel so cool, so calm, so at peace. Lift two burning timbers to clear the doorway. Feel so cool.

"The hall is a mass of flames. Walk the hall of fire and down the staircase of spiraling tongues of flame. Feel no heat. Feel so cool. You are engulfed in red-orange light of pulsating brilliant intensity.

"Exit the building. Mount a horse. Ride like the wind. Your clothes are on fire, a flashing, flaming body on horseback. Feel so cool. Come to a bridge. Bring your horse to a halt. Jump off. Run into the river, dousing the flames from your clothes.

"Night overtakes you. Lie in the deep, dark water of the river. Gaze at the crimson sky where was once the plantation. You drift, you float, under the southern night sky."

MORE VIVID IMAGERY

People usually report how dazzlingly intense their visual component of fire appears in their imagery when that is the only sense in which they experience this element. "I can't believe how real the fire looked," or "That's the best color recall I've ever done," or "I thought my eyelids were on fire, the red was so bright," are typical comments, all illustrating what a remarkably effective tool the negative hallucination can be for helping to make your images seem more real. Again, the more real your images seem, the greater will be their positive effects on your reality.

PAIN

You can learn to shut out any undesired stimulus in any sense by first working on negative hallucinations in imagery. First determine what sense or senses you wish to tune out in reality. Then practice an image where you negatively hallucinate fire in this or these senses, as you did in the *Chateau* and *Plantation* scenes; and/or water, as you will be doing in the *Surf* and *Capri* scenes that follow. Next imagine a scene where you are negatively hallucinating the stimuli you wish not to respond to in reality.

There is probably no stimulus you wish to shut out more than pain. Joan, a 30-year-old health spa director and ex-body builder, suffered intense, constant pain under her left breast and down her left arm from damage done to her intercostal nerve during breast implantation surgery. "The pain was excrutiating," she said. "I haven't been able to exercise in over four years. I tried spinal blocks, nerve blocks, acupuncture, pain clinics. Nothing helped. I'm stressed out and in pain all the time. Now they want to cut into my spinal column but it'll cause muscle damage cutting to the nerve. The pain seems to center in my left elbow, the ulnar nerve."

I asked Joan to practice the *Plantation Scene* three times a day, focusing especially on the tactile negative hallucination of fire, until her next visit, which was two days later. "I did real well with that," she said. "It was fun." Then I told her, "If you can tactilely negatively hallucinate fire, you can certainly tactilely negatively hallucinate any other kind of pain." I asked her to practice the *Plantation Scene* again, only this time without the fire. She was to imagine walking down the spiral staircase, negatively hallucinating the pain from her surgery rather than the pain from the fire.

Joan was the kind of patient a therapist dreams of. In two days all her pain was completely gone. I was as surprised as she. I'd never seen such a refractory case clear up so rapidly. "I'm already doing twists and stretches," she said. "I'll be back to body building in no time."

POWER

I also often hear people say they get a wonderful sense of power from practicing the *Plantation Scene*. "I got such a sense of omnipotence," said Anne, as she lay on the couch, still feeling the image's effects. "I felt strong, all-powerful, from my ability to conceive of fire without heat." Once again I saw that strange, enigmatic smile illuminate her face and felt a silken, etheric texture to the air.

I suddenly had a strong impulse to have someone or something speak to Anne in an image and say, "You've been here before. You'll be here again. Don't you know who I am? Why did you take so long to come?" As you know, because you've read every image I'd given Anne to this point, there had never been anyone speaking to anybody in any of the images, and I didn't have any intention of adding this feature in the future images I had already planned. It seemed like an odd idea to me and I wondered why I had come up with it.

I heard Anne move on the couch and I was startled out of my reverie. She was looking straight at me, smiling. "I have a sense," she said, fixing me with her gaze, "that I've been traveling many places during many lives, looking, always searching. I think it's time to discover what I'm searching for."

Because the events that were about to unfold were so amazing to me, so irrevocably impressed me and changed the course of my life forever, I'm going to restrict the remainder of my case discussions to Anne—and the fruits of her search.

SURF SCENE

The capacity to experience matter in any of its properties to the exclusion of its other properties is not unheard of. Fire walkers, for example, can experience fire visually, but not tactilely, thereby walking on coals without burning. Christians thrown to the lions were said to sing while being eaten, tactilely negatively hallucinating their pain. Witches burned at the stake often laughed in ecstasy, tactilely negatively hallucinating fire as the flames enveloped them. Championship swimmers report being able to experience the wetness and buoyancy of cold water, tactilely negatively hallucinating its chill.

In the *Surf Scene* you continue to develop your powers to negatively hallucinate, selectively tuning out aspects of your five-sensory reality. You thus gain more room to process additional "reality" or data. This leads to the intensification of the sensations that remain, in addition to glimpsing what lies beyond traditional five-sensory reality.

This is your first image in which you focus on water, continuing your coverage of the Aristotelian elements: fire, water, earth, and air. In this scene you olfactorily negatively hallucinate water. You imagine removing smell from your experiencing of water. The remaining senses that you do experience water in—sight, sound, touch, and taste—are thus intensified. New knowledge and experience from a realm beyond five-sensory reality will also begin coming to you. Transcendence of the five-sensory world expands your perception immeasurably.

SURF SCENE:

"You are walking along the beach on a warm afternoon. The sky is a vivid blue, the sun a blazing yellow, the sand a dazzling, shimmering white in the sunlight. Feel the heat from the sun's rays against your skin; feel the warmth from the sun against your body.

"You are barefoot. Feel the wet, cold, firmly packed sand beneath your feet. Feel the cold water rushing over your feet. Hear the rhythmic crashing of the waves against the sand, back and forth, to and fro, of the sea against the shore. You can taste the salt in the air. There is a residue of salt deposited upon your lips from the ocean spray. You can taste it if you lick your lips. The air has no odor, the sea has no smell. You are eating a hot dog with relish, mustard, and catsup. Taste the spicy flavor.

"Bend down beside the water. Cup your hands. Scoop up the sea water. Bring it to your nostrils. Sniff. It has no smell. Drink. It tastes salty.

"A long, dark breakwater of brown rock extends out into the sea. A young man and woman come from this area. The woman comes closest you and speaks: 'You've been here before. You'll be here again. Don't you know who I am? Why did you take so long to come?' Then they leave, disappearing around the breakwater.

"Take off your clothes. Swim out to sea. Your eyes sting from the salt. Doing a crawl stroke, you suck water in and out of your mouth as you lift your head in and out of the water on each arm stroke. Taste the salt. Water is odorless. Surface dive. Swim underwater to a reef of bright salmon coral. The reef forms a lagoon where the water is still and protected from the waves. Lying there on the coral is a surfboard.

"Push off into the water with the board. Lie face down and paddle out away from the reef. Wait for a wave. Hear the roar of a massive wave behind you. Paddle rapidly with your hands, shooting through the water ahead of the wave. Now the wave overtakes you. Feel it swell underneath your body. Stand on the board. The wave surges underfoot, carrying you through the water. Your face tingles in the salt air. You can taste, but not smell the salt from the sea. The wave carries you to shore.

"Bask in the hot sun. Notice a raft wash up on shore. Go to it. Get in the raft and shove off, drifting out to sea. Float for miles and miles. The sun sets. Sky turns orange, then indigo blue. The constellations and the Big Dipper appear. The sea and sky become one. You are floating up into the universe in a sea of stars."

LOVE: PEOPLE IN AN IMAGE SPEAK TO ANNE

The day that I planned on giving Anne the *Surf Scene* she came to her session with a typewritten copy of a dream she had had the night before. "It was the most vivid dream I've ever had," she said, handing me the paper on which she'd typed it. "What do you think it means?"

I felt goose bumps on my arms when I looked at what she'd written. Her dream had the identical setting as the image I was about to give her that day, the *Surf Scene*. I'd created this image more than a month earlier. Once again Anne was evidencing the phenomenon of precognition. Seeing a component of an image beforehand, as she'd done with the *Egypt Scene* by jumping ahead to the locale, or the *Mirrors Scene* where she'd seen a tunnel of mirrors before being given the image, was easy enough to ascribe to coincidence, but typing out an *entire* image ahead of time?

There was only one difference between Anne's dream and the *Surf Scene* as I'd planned to give it to her that day. In her dream she observed from afar a man and woman playing together on the sand.

I told Anne how happy I was that her powers were growing, not letting on that I had no idea what was going on. It is true that I was delighted. She was charged with an energy I'd never seen in anyone before and I was eager to see where it would take her.

I asked her to lie down on the couch, and she quickly went into hypnosis. I had just finished setting the scene, describing the long, dark breakwater of brown rock, when I again found myself beset by an impulse. I suddenly felt like adding the man and woman of Anne's dream to her image. "Why not?" I asked myself. It would be interesting to see what effect it might have.

I suggested that Anne see a young man and woman approaching her from the breakwater. Then I was seized by another impulse, this time to have the woman ask Anne the questions that had come to me after her last session, after I'd given her the *Plantation Scene*. It seemed like a perfectly natural thing to do at the time, although in my entire working life I had never spontaneously altered an image before in the course of giving it.

I told Anne to imagine the young woman coming forward and saying to her, "You've been here before. You'll be here again. Don't you know who I am? Why did you take so long to come?" (Note that this is the same way I've asked you to practice this image.)

As long as I live I'll never forget Anne's reaction when I asked her, "Don't you know who I am?" Her body arched in spasm and she gasped loudly, raspingly drawing in a stream of air. Then she relaxed deeply, melting into the couch. A joyous smile radiated her face and tears streamed down her cheeks from her closed eyes.

"At first I didn't recognize the two people in the image," Anne said when the image was completed and she opened her eyes. "But as soon as the woman asked me if I knew who she was, I knew it was my grandmother. She died when I was thirteen. We'd always been so close. The man was my grandfather."

Anne slowly raised herself to a sitting position on the couch. The radiance of her face seemed to light the whole room. Tears of joy wet her cheeks. "I can feel my grandmother's love," she sobbed. "It's everywhere."

A moment later Anne gasped, "I've just experienced infinity."

I remained silent, transfixed by her experience, not wanting it to end.

"Do you see what I see?" Anne suddenly asked, her eyes wide with astonishment as they rapidly surveyed the room, appearing to be observing some great activity in the air. "There are flowers blooming, unfolding all over." She laughed in childish delight. "They're deep red."

PARADISE: PEOPLE OF THE IMAGE SPEAK TO ME

I didn't see flowers unfolding in the air as Anne had, but as I drove home from work that evening I couldn't get Anne's session out of my mind. Heading east on Santa Monica Boulevard that cold, clear March night of 1974, leaving Beverly Hills for the hills of Hollywood, I sensed an inchoate purpose press my mind.

"Something is going to happen," a voice in my head said as I turned north on Crescent Heights moving toward Laurel Canyon. I couldn't shake the premonition.

Quickening shadows clung to the canyon hillsides as I snaked my way through the gridlock of rush-hour traffic. Voices, urgent and charged with electricity, intruded upon my consciousness. Unsolicited thoughts. Flashes. Bits of information or messages. Messages *as if* they had come from Anne's grandmother and I was to relay them to Anne. I drew a deep breath. The people in Anne's image were talking to me. This is ridiculous. I'd let my thoughts get away from me. I remembered Dr. Kroger's wise admonition, "It's a wise hypnotist who knows who is hypnotizing whom." I'd been so eager to believe Anne was having a metaphysical experience that I'd fallen under her spell. It was time to get back to reality, get a grip on things.

I made a sharp left turn, climbing up the mud-stained incline of Lookout Mountain Drive. The voices grew more insistent. It was *as if* I was to be the intermediary, liaison, medium between Anne and her grandmother. It was imperative she get this information. By the time I pulled off Wonderland Park Avenue and reached my home, I knew I'd get no peace until I put the stirrings of my brain to paper.

The goldfish in the mirrored pond of my foyer swam up to greet me as I entered the house and I thought how lucky they were not to have the cosmic concerns that befuddled humanity.

I went straight to the cupboard beneath the stairwell and pulled out a fresh notebook. The thoughts filled two pages. They came to me *as if* they were messages given to me by Anne's grandmother that I was to give to Anne. I was an adamant disbeliever in spiritualism but I knew that a good technique for clearing a troubled mind was to write down your thoughts. It was certainly worth a try. The voices were giving me no letup. They were speaking of cosmic, universal truths of life and death. This is what I wrote:

"Direct your attention to the water.
You are over 80% water.

"Don't presuppose that death reveals the universal or ultimate truth . . . You've died before.
Don't blow it this time.

"Do not assume that our state is inferior or superior to yours.

"You are on the brink of a realization greater than we have ever experienced. We want you to reach it.

"Don't assume that all people are in the same state or level of awareness after death.

"The levels after and before your state are infinite.

"Death is but a change in levels, and not necessarily an enlightenment.

"You have been chosen. You have been selected. At this point in time you are special."

As soon as I finished writing the messages down I felt a great sense of relief. I was no longer bothered by the voices inside my head.

The things I'd written amazed me. That death did not necessarily lead to truth or greater knowledge was certainly news to me. I'd always thought that the great mysteries of existence would be revealed to me upon my death. Implied in these messages, however, was that knowledge came from life, not death. If we died in ignorance, we'd be as uninformed in the hereafter as we were before.

"Don't blow it this time," held a special immediacy for me. Did that mean that if Anne didn't reach a certain level of knowledge in this life, she'd have to start over again in this or another form? Was she "on the brink of a realization" which, if she realized, would save her from having to start again at the same or lower level of awareness than the one she attained at her death? Could this possibly be Anne's last incarnation? If she could gain the necessary knowledge she would no longer need to incarnate again. She would no longer have need of her body.

I stared entranced through the glass wall of my canyon home into the deep blues of the night shadows and twinkling lights on Mount Olympus. My musings took me ever further out of myself. The body was like training wheels on a bicycle, I thought. When you learned to travel without it, you threw it away. We kept incarnating, assuming bodily forms, coming back to this dimension, this plane of consciousness, until we learned to navigate without our bodies. Then we threw away our training wheels and went on to paradise. The realization that Anne was on the brink of learning how to navigate without her body!

UNIVERSAL ANSWERS AND UNIVERSAL QUESTIONS

By the time Anne's next session came around I'd returned to the senses of my five-sensory reality. The ideas of reincarnation and navigating without a body in the next dimension seemed preposterous. Even in the heart of my experience when I truly believed the messages I had written, I never thought the information had come from Anne's disincarnate grandmother, but rather from the ether, the interface between this dimension and the next, or possibly simply from a higher state of my own consciousness.

The morning of the day Anne was to come in I decided not to give her the messages. They seemed more a figment of my imagination than anything else and I didn't want to lead her on.

My first patient that day, a chronic smoker, suddenly revealed that he was seeing spirits in his apartment. "I see a head in the drawer almost every time I open it," he said. "I most often see them in the shower. Spirits always come near the water. My sister is really into spiritualism. She keeps vials of water all around the house." I couldn't help thinking of the fish pond in my foyer where I'd sat to write down Anne's messages.

My next patient was new, Hank, a 46-year-old marketing analyst who told me on the phone he needed to work on increasing his sex drive. "You see," he said when I asked him to tell me about it, "psychics are draining me sexually. They're very competitive and jealous of me. I'm an ordained spiritual medium and practicing exorcist. I was one of the eight psychics called in on the Manson murders. I came up with two of the people involved. I psychically made one of the murderers impotent so that he couldn't father any children, but this man's spirit came after me one night. He almost blew my car off the road." Hank stopped talking and looked me squarely in the eye. "I can feel you have great psychic powers," he said. "You are a medium."

I wanted to tell you about these two cases to illustrate what a bizarre period in my practice this was. In my eighteen years as a therapist this was the only time I had a client who saw spirits or was an exorcist and they both showed up right before the session I was supposed to give Anne the messages. Their strangeness only further validated my decision to say nothing to Anne of the voices I'd heard.

"I heard my grandmother's voice twice since our last session," Anne said, starting her hour. "Once when I was hurrying on my way to the washroom I heard her say, 'Now, now, little Anne. You don't need to do that. Slow down. You're better than you know, Anne. You're better.' Then last night she asked me to reevaluate my feelings about death, to listen to someone who would explain death to me. After she nagged me an hour to heed someone else's advice, I said out loud, as if to my grandmother, 'All right already, I'll do what's required! Then the nagging feeling left me."

I was compelled to give her the messages. I explained that I had felt *as if* her grandmother was talking with me, insisting I give Anne this information.

"That's amazing," Anne said after I read her the messages. "For years I've been preoccupied with the concept of the ultimate realization of truth in death. At one time I even thought about taking my life, not because I was depressed, but just to discover this truth. Now I see that knowledge comes from living, not dying." She paused a moment to reflect. "I had another past-life regression since our last session," she said. "I was doing the *Surf Scene* and I saw myself burned at the stake as a witch. I think it was in Salem. It's like I've had several lives where I'm getting close to this great metaphysical realization before death stops my progress; once as an Egyptian high priestess, once as a witch, who knows how many other times?

"Does my grandmother saying, 'Don't blow it this time, direct your attention to the water, you are over 80 percent water,' mean that through an understanding of the physical and chemical properties of water I'll gain an understanding of what constitutes me, of what is life, an answer to the questions: Where do I come from? What am I? Where am I going?"

CAPRI SCENE

Not only could I not answer Anne's questions, it was time to get on with her next image. Her hour was half gone and I hoped that maybe her further sojourn in the imagery progression would provide more pieces to the puzzle.

In the *Capri Scene*, your last image in this book, you gustatorily negatively hallucinate water. You experience water without taste. Your reception of water through your senses of sight, sound, touch, and smell is thus intensified. In addition, you partially clear one of your five-sensory channels to process a reality that lies above it. Step by step, image by image, the negative hallucination will provide you with a vehicle for transcending your five-sensory reality to reach the expanded truth and paradise that lies beyond.

CAPRI SCENE:

"You are walking along a beach on the Mediterranean Sea. The sky is intense blue, the sun vibrant yellow, the sand hot and shimmering white in the sunlight. High cliffs behind you are covered with cedar and cypress trees. Fishing boats are out on the sea. Hear the sound of water lapping against the shore. Smell the salt in the air. Bend down. Cup your hands, filling them with sea water. Bring the water to your nostrils. Sniff the salt in the water. Drink. The water is tasteless, cold, and clear.

"Take off your clothes. Swim out toward a fishing boat, taking water in and out of your mouth as you do a crawl stroke. There is no taste to the water. Climb a fishing net hanging over the boat's side to board.

"The boat begins to move, speeding toward an island in the warm Mediterranean sun. Smell the salt breeze. Feel the stinging wind blow your hair. Pink, yellow, and blue adobe buildings loom larger as you approach the island. Dive from the deck with a great splash. Swim to shore.

"Follow a long, dusty path lined with currant bushes to a vineyard of purple grapes, ripening in the sun. The path next leads you to a grove of cinnamon trees. The scent of sweet cinnamon permeates the dry air. Peel bark from one of the trees. Chew. Taste the sweet, tangy flavor.

"Move to a stone well in the middle of the grove. Pull up a wooden bucket. Drink the cold, pure well water. It has no taste.

Finish the water and lie down in the shade of the cinnamon trees. You drift . . . you float . . . you dream."

PREPARING FOR TAKEOFF

After receiving the *Capri Scene*, Anne said, "I feel very strange . . . All my body water has just been replaced by the water from the well. I feel like I have to hold myself down mentally . . . feels light . . . really spooky . . . I'm afraid to move . . . everything is tingling, absolutely everything. I really feel that peace. I'm immune to everything."

Having to hold herself down mentally meant that Anne could have had an out-of-body experience if she hadn't willed herself to remain earthbound. There was still a little fear keeping her from taking off. But her sense of peace and immunity showed she was nearly there. Everything tingling pointed to her rising energy, her increased vibratory rate before takeoff. It takes energy for you to scale a new dimension.

"Even though you mentioned the Mediterranean Sea," she continued, "it seemed to me like the Sea of Galilee. It's as vivid an image as I've ever had."

Then something struck me. "I forgot that I used my memory of a well by the Sea of Galilee from an old childhood Sunday School flier to construct the end of that image," I told her. "Your telepathy is even reaching into my subconscious."

CHRIST CONSCIOUSNESS

The next time I saw Anne she wept in joy recounting the intensity of a spiritual experience that happened to her upon leaving my office after doing the *Capri Scene*: "I was driving home the night after my last session with you," she said excitedly. "A John Denver tape was playing on my tape deck. He was singing, 'Lady, my sweet lady, do the tears belong to me? I'm as close as I can be. I swear our time has just begun.'

"Suddenly something snapped, something like a click. It was no longer John Denver singing." Anne stopped and looked at me uncertainly, afraid to go on. I smiled, nodding for her to continue. "It was Christ. And the words were no longer sung, but spoken. I began to cry.

"Then I saw in front of me, on the road, a huge head of Christ." Anne was crying with joy. "My mind blows up with the experience. I drove into his head. The car vanished and I saw myself in blue with dark hair, crying. Words of comfort came to me from Christ as if I were his mother.

"I was very frightened. I tried to deny it and said to myself, 'You're going to be Napoleon next.' It was like two realities coexisting, both equally real. I was always simultaneously aware of both the road and the Christ image."

I suddenly understood. Anne *was* the mother of Christ. She was the mother of all things. We are all the mother of all things. We all create our own realities, including our own selves. Her experience was an emotional understanding of the power of creation within her. She was to progress through many more images beyond the scope of this book in the development of that power.

"Then today," she went on, "driving to session, I had a sensation like butterflies in my stomach, like crackling energy that filled me with a greater joy than I've ever known. It moved out of my stomach and floated up to eye level. It was a white light like crackling electricity."

The sound of crackling energy and appearance of white light have often been reported in conjunction with experiences of enlightenment, cosmic consciousness, and accessing higher realities or paradise. The white light experience after raising the kundalini force, piercing the 33 compartments of the spinal column and awakening the 7 chakras, to raise Christ consciousness, the goal of kundalini yoga, is also similar, as are the after-death revelations of those who have medically died and been brought back.

Anne had made a major breakthrough. She experienced a higher reality, joy. A glimpse of paradise, if you will.

It is my greatest wish that this book will give you the ability to experience your own higher reality, joy, and glimpse of paradise, through the vehicle of the imagery progression I've given you within. Love be with you.

Index of

Specific Problems

If you want to focus on eliminating specific problems, here is a list of some of the most common areas I've covered, along with accounts of using the images most suited to working on them. I use the word "specific" below to denote imagery that is not a part of your natural sequence of images, i.e., special images pertaining only to particular problems. Please keep in mind that *all* the images I've given you in your imagery progression will reduce your stress and increase your peace, confidence, relaxation, concentration, energy, and motivation.

ENURESIS: Desert, 99–100, 181–82; Lake, 180–81; Volcano, 204

GASTROINTESTINAL DISORDERS: Hypnotic Induction, 20; Mountain Cabin II, 92; Space, 121–22

INSOMNIA: Mountain Cabin, 61, 74; Garden, 74; Farm, 131; Thundershower, 184; Autumn, 225

MEMORY: Space, 129; Farm, 131; Clock, 158

PAIN: Beach, 45, 49, 83, 85–86; Specific, 86–87; Mountain Cabin, 87; Garden, 81–83, 87; Mountain Cabin II, 89–93, 94–95, 159; Desert, 98–99; Space, 116–17, 159; Farm, 130, 159; Jungle, 139–40, 159; Jungle with Heat Transfer, 148–49; Clock, 159–60; Bluebird, 162; Autumn, 225; Chateau, 248; Plantation, 248–49; Surf, 248; Capri, 248

PHOBIAS: Hypnotic Induction, 20–22; Beach, 47–48; Space, 125–27; Jungle, 140–44, 159; Clock, 158; Bluebird, 102; Specific, 176; Hayloft, 210–12; Sand Pit, 214–15; Autumn, 225; Chateau, 245–46

RELATIONSHIPS: Autumn, 224; This Room, 226–27

SEXUAL DYSFUNCTION (FEMALE): Beach, 51–53, 64, 179, 207; Mountain Cabin, 64–65, 179, 207; Garden, 74, 179, 207; Space, 112–14, 179, 207; Farm, 136, 179, 207; Jungle, 138–39, 179–80, 207; Jungle with Heat Transfer, 150–51, 180, 207; Lake, 179–80, 207; Cantina, 206–7; Autumn, 225; Athens, 229

SEXUAL DYSFUNCTION (MALE): Beach, 53–54, 63, 139; Mountain Cabin, 63–64, 139; Garden, 74; Space, 114–16, 179; Farm, 130; Jungle, 139; Jungle with Heat Transfer, 151–53, 180; Cantina, 207–8; Autumn, 225; Athens, 229

SKIN: Beach, 49–50, 149, 181; Mountain Cabin, 63, 100, 149; Desert, 100, 149, 181; Farm, 130–31, 149, 181; Jungle, 143; Jungle with Heat Transfer, 149–50; Lake, 181; Thundershower, 183

SMOKING: Specific, 69; Desert, 100–101; Space, 117–19; Farm, 130; Clock, 160; Autumn, 225

STUTTERING AND RELATED SPEECH PROBLEMS: Beach, 50–51; Space, 122–23; Farm, 130; Autumn, 225

SWEATING SPELLS: Arctic, 174; Hayloft, 210–12

TELEPATHY: Desert, 104–5; Athens, 230–31

WEIGHT CONTROL: Garden, 69–71; Specific, 71–72; Mountain Cabin II, 92–93; Space, 119–20; Farm, 130; Jungle, 142–43; Autumn, 225

WORK EFFICIENCY: Specific, 77–78; Farm, 130; Clock, 158; Lake, 178; Sound Stage, 28

INDEX

acne, 31, 100, 131, 181
  heat recall and, 149–50, 183–84
  negative feelings and, 49–50
  pressure recall and, 183–84
affirmations, 22–26
  best place to give, 23
  in cancer and disease cure, 186
  as key to manifestation, 25–26
  Kroger's use of, 27–28
  more powerful if given in hypnotic
    state, 7–8, 22, 28
  in self-hypnosis technique, 14, 15,
    16, 18
  seven keys to making of, 23–25
afterimages, 75–76
age regression, 219–25
  Autumn Scene and, 221–25
  return to better level of functioning
    in, 225
  return to more positive outlook in,
    223–24
alcoholism, 240
  negative imagery and, 72, 194–95
  time concentration and, 164
  time expansion and, 120
amnesia, 7, 48
anesthesia, 28, 29, 31
  glove, 87–93, 167–68
  pressure recall in, 97–103
  in surgery, 88
anger, 74
anorexia nervosa:
  drive induction and, 130
  lightness in stomach and, 199
  and turning on to eating, 72–74,
    164, 192–93
anxiety, 3, 16, 46–47, 140
  blood circulation and, 147–48
  pain threshold lowered by, 48
  performance, 240, 241
  physical restrictions and, 126–27
  stuttering and, 122

time expansion and, 120–21
anxiety attacks, 147–48
apathy, dispelling, 101–2, 114, 130
appetite, improving, 72–74, 164,
  192–93
Arctic Scene, 172–75
  description of, 172–73
  reactions to, 173
  uses of, 174–75
Aristotle, 241
asthma, 61–62
Athens Scene, 227–31
  description of, 228–29
  heightened sensuality in, 229
Autumn Scene, 221–25
  description of, 222–23
  reactions to, 223
  return to better level of functioning
    in, 225
  return to more positive outlook in,
    223–24

Beach Scene, 43–54, 58, 74
  description of, 45–46
  drug addiction and, 54–55
  in pain control, 48–49
  phobias and, 47–48
  reactions to, 46
  relaxation and, 46–47
  sensory components of, 58
  sexual performance and, 51–54
  skin problems and, 49–50
  stuttering and, 50–51
bedwetting, 99–100, 180–81, 204
behavior modification, 2–3, 34, 69
  desensitization in, 28–29, 73–74,
    132
  see also covert sensitization
biofeedback, 38
bitterness (smell and taste), 57
bladder control, 99–100, 180–81,
  204